Master of the Age

The Institute of Ismaili Studies
Ismaili Texts and Translations Series, 9

Previously published titles:

1. Ibn al-Haytham. *The Advent of the Fatimids: A Contemporary Shiʿi Witness*. An Edition and English Translation of Ibn al-Haytham's *Kitāb al-Munāẓarāt*, by Wilferd Madelung and Paul E. Walker (2000).
2. al-Shahrastānī, Muḥammad b. ʿAbd al-Karīm. *Struggling with the Philosopher: A Refutation of Avicenna's Metaphysics*. A New Arabic Edition and English translation of al-Shahrastānī's *Kitāb al-Muṣāraʿa*, by Wilferd Madelung and Toby Mayer (2001).
3. Jaʿfar b. Manṣūr al-Yaman. *The Master and the Disciple: An Early Islamic Spiritual Dialogue*. Arabic Edition and English translation of Jaʿfar b. Manṣūr al-Yaman's *Kitāb al-ʿĀlim wa'l-ghulām*, by James W. Morris (2001).
4. Idrīs ʿImād al-Dīn. *The Fatimids and their Successors in Yaman: The History of an Islamic Community*. Arabic Edition and English Summary of Idrīs ʿImād al-Dīn's *ʿUyūn al-akhbār*, vol. 7, by Ayman Fuʾād Sayyid, in collaboration with Paul E. Walker and Maurice A. Pomerantz (2002).
5. Naṣīr al-Dīn Ṭūsī. *Paradise of Submission: A Medieval Treatise on Ismaili Thought*. A New Persian Edition and English Translation of Naṣīr al-Dīn Ṭūsī's *Rawḍa-yi taslīm*, by S. J. Badakhchani with an introduction by Hermann Landolt and a philosophical commentary by Christian Jambet (2005).
6. al-Qāḍī al-Nuʿmān. *Founding the Fatimid State: The Rise of an Early Islamic Empire*. An annotated English translation of al-Qāḍī al-Nuʿmān's *Iftitāḥ al-Daʿwa*, by Hamid Haji (2006).
7. Idrīs ʿImād al-Dīn b. al-Ḥasan. *ʿUyūn al-akhbār wa-funūn al-āthār*. Arabic critical edition in 7 (a–g) volumes by Ahmad Chleilat, Mahmoud Fakhoury, Yousef S. Fattoum, Maʾmoun al-Sagherji and Ayman Fuʾad Sayyid (2007).

Master of the Age:

An Islamic Treatise on the Necessity of the Imamate

A critical edition of the Arabic text and English translation of
Ḥamīd al-Dīn Aḥmad b. ʿAbd Allāh al-Kirmānī's
al-Maṣābīḥ fī ithbāt al-imāma

by

Paul E. Walker

I.B.Tauris *Publishers*
LONDON • NEW YORK
in association with
The Institute of Ismaili Studies
LONDON

Published in 2007 by I.B.Tauris & Co Ltd
6 Salem Rd, London W2 4BU
175 Fifth Avenue, New York NY 10010
www.ibtauris.com

in association with The Institute of Ismaili Studies
42–44 Grosvenor Gardens, London SW1W 0EB
www.iis.ac.uk

In the United States of America and in Canada distributed by
St Martin's Press, 175 Fifth Avenue, New York NY 10010

ISBN 978 1 84511 604 0

A full CIP record for this book is available from the British Library
A full CIP record for this book is available from the Library of Congress

Library of Congress catalog card: available

Typeset in Minion Tra for The Institute of Ismaili Studies
Printed and bound in Great Britain by TJ International Ltd, Padstow, Cornwall

The Institute of Ismaili Studies

The Institute of Ismaili Studies was established in 1977 with the object of promoting scholarship and learning on Islam, in the historical as well as contemporary contexts, and a better understanding of its relationship with other societies and faiths.

The Institute's programmes encourage a perspective which is not confined to the theological and religious heritage of Islam, but seeks to explore the relationship of religious ideas to broader dimensions of society and culture. The programmes thus encourage an interdisciplinary approach to the materials of Islamic history and thought. Particular attention is also given to issues of modernity that arise as Muslims seek to relate their heritage to the contemporary situation.

Within the Islamic tradition, the Institute's programmes promote research on those areas which have, to date, received relatively little attention from scholars. These include the intellectual and literary expressions of Shiʿism in general, and Ismailism in particular.

In the context of Islamic societies, the Institute's programmes are informed by the full range and diversity of cultures in which Islam is practised today, from the Middle East, South and Central Asia, and Africa to the industrialized societies of the West, thus taking into consideration the variety of contexts which shape the ideals, beliefs and practices of the faith.

These objectives are realized through concrete programmes and activities organised and implemented by various departments of the Institute. The Institute also collaborates periodically, on a programme-specific basis, with other institutions of learning in the United Kingdom and abroad.

The Institute's academic publications fall into a number of interrelated categories:

1. Occasional papers or essays addressing broad themes of the relationship between religion and society, with special reference to Islam.
2. Monographs exploring specific aspects of Islamic faith and culture, or the contributions of individual Muslim thinkers or writers.
3. Editions or translations of significant primary or secondary texts.
4. Translations of poetic or literary texts which illustrate the rich heritage of spiritual, devotional and symbolic expressions in Muslim history.
5. Works on Ismaili history and thought, and the relationship of the Ismailis to other traditions, communities and schools of thought in Islam.
6. Proceedings of conferences and seminars sponsored by the Institute.
7. Bibliographical works and catalogues which document manuscripts, printed texts and other source materials.

This book falls into category three listed above.

In facilitating these and other publications, the Institute's sole aim is to encourage original research and analysis of relevant issues. While every effort is made to ensure that the publications are of a high academic standard, there is naturally bound to be a diversity of views, ideas and interpretations. As such, the opinions expressed in these publications must be understood as belonging to their authors alone.

Table of Contents

Preface and Acknowledgements

The work presented here in a new critical edition of the Arabic text, with full translation and introduction, represents a major statement of the argument for the absolute necessity of the imam and the imamate as understood by the Ismaili *daʿwa* and its *dāʿīs* nearly a millennium ago. The author, Ḥamīd al-Dīn al-Kirmānī, was then generally acknowledged as the leading advocate and supporter of the Fatimid imam-caliph al-Ḥākim bi-amr Allāh for whom he appealed and to whom he was steadfastly loyal. Nevertheless an important aspect of this treatise is that it was composed not for that *daʿwa* but for an audience of non-Ismailis outside of the Fatimid domain, specifically to include the ruling elite of the Buyid east and its wazir in Baghdad, Fakhr al-Mulk. Many of this group, the wazir among them, were Shīʿī, although they were not adherents of the Fatimid dynasty or its line of imams. Al-Kirmānī's task combined thus a formidable challenge with a delicate, quite possibly dangerous, purpose. And he most certainly wrote it while he himself lived and worked in Iraq, the territory of these same Buyids and of the Abbasid caliphs, the sworn enemies of those he favoured.

Typically for the scholarly intellectual that he was, al-Kirmānī constructed his proof for the imamate from, in the first instance, a set of philosophically grounded premises, leading from them to the actual argument for the necessity of the Islamic imamate, and then of the particular historical circumstances that precluded various claimants to it and upheld a single line of transmission running from ʿAlī b. Abī Ṭālib to al-Ḥākim. The separate elements of his argument are especially interesting, both the philosophical doctrine and the historical facts, but it is ultimately the combination of them that raises this treatise above most others. Here we begin with Aristotle and end with the Ismaili imam, with an Islamic theory of government and authority as rational in its movement from premise to premise as it is religiously grounded in the revelation and the prophetic office.

It has been more than three decades since Muṣṭafā Ghālib published in Beirut an edition of this same work. Over the intervening period it has attracted the attention of a number of scholars. I was one of them, reading it carefully on several occasions for this or that research on Fatimid-era Ismaili thinkers, among whom al-Kirmānī was one of the masters. But all along the version offered by Ghālib, as has so often happened with the first printings of Ismaili texts, clearly needed revision in conjunction with a critical rechecking of the manuscript tradition that has preserved it. At the very least I decided to read his text against a reasonably sound manuscript—one that he had not used in preparing his edition. Innocently I asked The Institute of Ismaili Studies (IIS) if I could have a photocopy of the best of their manuscripts. To my surprise the reply came back asking if I would consider preparing a new edition of it and perhaps a translation also. Given that Ghālib's text did not appear insurmountably long and knowing that the Institute possessed a number of manuscripts, I agreed to do it without much thought about exactly how much time and effort would be involved. As it turned out, in contrast to many, if not most, Ismaili texts from the Fatimid period, this work of al-Kirmānī is represented by a great number of manuscripts. Because it was from the beginning a document for public use rather than one restricted to the Ismaili *da'wa* and its members, it has been copied more broadly and less guardedly among the Ṭayyibī Ismailis. Thus, where we are not infrequently faced with having but a single copy of another text, in this instance, copies abound. The Institute in London alone owns ten. In the end I gained access either directly or indirectly to eighteen or nineteen. The problem went from too little evidence for the text to too much, with the resulting burden of having to keep track of it all.

Fortunately, many friends and colleagues were willing to help. Here I must thank a number of them by name beginning with Nader El-Bizri, Research Associate at The Institute of Ismaili Studies, who first suggested this project and who facilitated access to manuscripts as well as offering advice on aspects of the work. Alnoor Merchant, Senior Librarian at the Institute kindly arranged the photocopying of manuscripts as well as support during my visit there in March of 2004 to examine the same manuscripts in person, as well as to review additional copies that I had not seen already in photocopies.

Even before receiving copies from the Institute, I asked Abbas Hamdani, Professor of Islamic History at the University of Wisconsin, Milwaukee, if he could let me have a photocopy of one of his. He readily provided this and later also a copy of a second from his family collection. Professor Hamdani has done a great deal to promote Ismaili studies over the years and I have often been the direct beneficiary of his generosity, knowledge and scholarly advice. Luckily, in addition, I was able to consult Ismail K. Poonawala, Professor of Arabic at UCLA, like Abbas Hamdani an old friend who is also an expert in the subject. He most kindly offered me a photocopy of a manuscript from his family's collection. At a later stage he looked over a section of the preliminary version of my edition with the master's eye for the highest standards of Arabic text editing. His is a most enviable model of an exacting thoroughness few can match and is rarely upheld, especially for Ismaili texts. The rest of us, myself included, can only hope to learn from his example.

At both an early and later stage, Wilferd Madelung kindly read the Arabic text, and a number of readings in it are the result of his queries and suggestions. He also contributed to the material in the introduction and the translation.

Tahera Qutbuddin, Professor of Arabic at the University of Chicago, both answered my numerous questions and provided initial contact for me with her sister Sayfiyah Qutbuddin. Both of them are not only scholars of Ismaili history and literature but have unique access to the manuscript holdings of the Ṭayyibī *daʿwa*. Besides responding to my queries, they kindly checked the reading of several passages of this text in the manuscripts available to them. Others who provided information and advice include David King and Farhad Daftary.

As with several other works by al-Kirmānī, this one contains quotations from the Hebrew and Syriac Bibles in Arabic transliteration and in translation. Already over seventy years ago the orientalist

Paul Kraus drew notice to them and to some of the problems involved in ascertaining precisely what al-Kirmānī knew of his source for either language. Lacking competence in these languages, I resolved to follow the reconstruction provided by Kraus. Still, it was necessary to consult colleagues about them, most particularly about an appropriate transliteration of them into Latin script. For the Syriac passage I had the help of Stuart Cresson who teaches that language in the Department of Near Eastern Languages and Civilization at the University of Chicago. He and several others at the University of Chicago aided me with the Hebrew. I must thank in particular Robert Dankoff and Joel Kraemer. Along the way I had a chance to discuss aspects of the problem with David Hollenberg, Camilla Adang and Sidney Griffith.

Paul E. Walker

Introduction

The Imamate in Islamic Thought

In the doctrine of classical Islam, the imamate, here denoting the supreme leadership of the Muslim community, held major importance for all legal and theological schools and the various sectarian positions.[1] Each vigorously supported the continuing need for, in nearly all cases, a single, properly chosen successor to the Prophet Muḥammad, who could maintain among them the governing functions, religious as well as political, that he had formerly performed. Despite many differences of detail and specifics, this general requirement is equally a necessity in Sunnī theory as it is for the Shīʿa. Likewise it retains its centrality among the Muʿtazila, the Khawārij and the rest.

Broadly speaking the range of opinion broke into two camps. One believed that it was the duty of the community itself to select its supreme imam—the caliph—and that, when and where possible, that person should be the most excellent, the man most eminent in those virtues of righteousness and true faith that belonged to the Prophet. In practice their choice had already fallen on, first, the 'Rightly Guided Caliphs'—the four immediate successors of the Prophet—and then later, on whomever the electors of the community had seen fit to recognize. Needless to say, sharp disagreements arose concerning many of the particular points, either in the theory or in the historical meaning of actual events surrounding the transition from one caliph to the next, or one dynasty (the Umayyads) to another (the Abbasids). The majority tended to favour the idea that the individual merit of

1. For a succinct but comprehensive survey of the full range of Islamic doctrine, see Wilferd Madelung, 'Imāma' in *EI2*.

the first four caliphs agreed with their chronological rank: Abū Bakr thus representing the highest excellence, followed by ʿUmar, ʿUthmān and ʿAlī in that order. Later caliphs never attained such a level and many were distinctly inferior, some even so unrighteous as to deserve repudiation. But the doctrine that eventually dominated declared that active opposition to an unjust imam, once he had been elected, would not be permitted, in part as a result of the ongoing development of a concept of rule by the less excellent in those circumstances that required it to preserve proper public order. That exigency became commonplace and the theory supporting it ever more flexible.

The other group denied the validity of communal choice. For them the matter had been settled by the Prophet's designation of ʿAlī as his successor, an action that bore the force of divine sanction. ʿAlī was thus chosen by God. When the Prophet announced his appointment of ʿAlī at the pool of Ghadīr Khumm and took the assent of the Muslims to it, that act was final. Not to accept or uphold that decision or to deny it in some way was to reject and thereby rebel against the wishes of both the Prophet and God. The matter was, and is not, ambiguous or subject to doubt. This is the position of the Twelver and Ismaili Shīʿa. The main group of the Zaydīs, though themselves a part of the Shīʿa, consider the issue to be less clear. But for the mainstream of the Shīʿa, the imamate is, because it functions as the divinely ordained continuation of prophetic government in every respect save that of the revelation of the law and scripture, not the responsibility of the community but that of God alone, whose choice for the role of successor to the Prophet began with ʿAlī and continues imam by imam in lineal order through ʿAlī's sons Ḥasan[2] and Ḥusayn and then the latter's offspring, all explicitly designated one after the other, father to son.[3]

The Shīʿī imamate is an office closely related to that of prophecy, less in degree and importance but only barely so. The imams are

2. It should be noted that many Ismailis no longer count Ḥasan as an imam. In the period of the Fatimid dynasty, however, texts such as this work of al-Kirmānī included him in the list of previous imams.

3. For the Zaydīs, by contrast, any descendant of Ḥasan or Ḥusayn who fulfils the requirement of learning can become the legitimate imam by putting forward his claim (*daʿwa*) to it.

infallible and incapable of sinful actions; their knowledge is more perfect than that of any other person in their time. They alone determine what religion is and what it consists of, a rank so exalted, perhaps impossibly so, it stands in stark contrast to the authority accorded to Sunnī caliphs by those who recognize them. Sunnī and Shīʿī theories of the imamate are thus quite at odds.

As with the range of doctrinal opinions about the imamate, so too the variety in writings on the subject. These vary from al-Māwardī's 5th/11th century *al-Aḥkām al-sulṭāniyya*, on the side of the Sunnīs, to the section of al-Kulaynī's *al-Uṣūl min al-kāfī*, the 'kitāb al-ḥujja', which represents the Twelver Imāmī position, and many, many others, both individual treatises and major chapters, devoted to this issue.

Ismaili Writings on the Imamate

For the Ismailis the work presented in this volume is a remarkably clear and comprehensive example, unusually so, of the subject. Given that its purpose is to defend the Shīʿī position in general and that of the Fatimid line of imams in particular, it deserves a status comparable to the best of those composed by advocates of the other schools. But it is unique as well in several ways. For one its author, al-Kirmānī, intends in his treatise to prove demonstrably that the imamate, as understood in the Shīʿī sense, is absolutely essential and he attempts to do exactly that on the basis of rational, that is, scientific, reasoning in accord with the rules of formal logic. For another, as a work on the proof of the imamate, as opposed to its conditions and historical circumstances, or its meaning and implications for law and religion, it is among the very few of its kind in the literature of the Ismailis. Earlier Ismaili writing on the general subject does exist, notably in the works of al-Qāḍī al-Nuʿmān. His *Kitāb al-himma fī ādāb atbāʿ al-aʾimma*,[4] on the proper comportment of the followers in respect to the imams, is one example. Others include his *Sharḥ al-akhbār*[5] on the history of the imams, the *Kitāb al-majālis waʾl-musāyarāt*,[6] which

4. Ed. Muḥammad Kāmil Ḥusayn (Cairo, 1948).

5. 3 vols. (Beirut, 1994).

6. Ed. al-Ḥabīb al-Faqī, Ibrāhīm Shabbūḥ and Muḥammad al-Yaʿlāwī (Tunis, 1978).

illustrates the imams in action, and portions of his *Asās al-ta'wīl*.[7] Ismaili writing did not lack material on the imamate, but the subgenre devoted to proving it rationally is less well represented. Only one treatise has come to light for the period prior to al-Kirmānī. That is the *Kitāb tathbīt al-imāma*, or *Tathbīt imāmat Amīr al-mu'minīn ʿAlī*, by the imam-caliph al-Manṣūr himself (ruled 334/946 to 341/953). It has yet to be published.[8]

For reasons as yet uncertain the next major examples all come from the era of al-Ḥākim, which saw three works on the imamate, two of which, moreover, fall into the category of those that attempt to 'prove' it. The third constitutes a set of answers provided by a *dāʿī* of the time, Abu'l-Fawāris Aḥmad b. Yaʿqūb, to questions about the imamate put to him by some of his subordinates in the *daʿwa*. Although it now bears the tentative title *al-Risāla fi'l-imāma*,[9] that it ever existed as a separate treatise or actually carried such a title is hard to determine. It has been preserved only as part of a later Yemeni collection, the *Majmūʿ al-tarbiya*, from the immediate post-Fatimid period.[10] While it offers an interesting view of official or semi-official doctrine about the imamate, it neither seeks to prove it rationally nor was it likely circulated outside of the *daʿwa*.[11]

The other two, by contrast, appear to have been public and, whether they actually did or not, were intended for wider circulation. Significantly, both claim to prove the absolute necessity of the imamate with arguments and demonstrations designed to win over a broad spectrum of the Muslim community, not simply to

---

7. Ed. ʿĀrif Tāmir (Beirut, 1960).

8. For an analysis of its contents and importance, see the study of it by Wilferd Madelung, 'A Treatise on the Imamate of the Fatimid Caliph al-Manṣūr Bi-Allāh', in Chase F. Robinson, ed., *Texts, Documents and Artefacts: Islamic Studies in Honour of D. S. Richards* (Leiden, 2003), pp. 69–77.

9. Edited and published with an English translation by Sami Nasib Makarem as *The Political Doctrine of the Ismāʿīlīs (The Imamate)* (Delmar, NY, 1977).

10. On this work and its author, Muḥammad b. Ṭāhir al-Ḥārithī, see Ismail K. Poonawala, *Biobibliography of Ismāʿīlī Literature* (Malibu, CA, 1977), pp. 143–148.

11. On this treatise see also the remarks by W. Ivanow, *Ismaili Tradition Concerning the Rise of the Fatimids* (London, etc., 1942), pp. 145–146.

reinforce the appeal of the Ismaili *daʿwa* for its own adherents. One is the work of al-Kirmānī, here presented in its entirety. The other is Aḥmad b. Ibrāhīm al-Naysābūrī's *Ithbāt al-imāma*.[12] He was an important figure in the *daʿwa* during the reigns of al-ʿAzīz and al-Ḥākim, although, as so often is the case, little is known about him other than the evidence of his writings, three of which survive, this one included.[13]

What is curious in addition is that both of these works on the proof of the imamate come from the final phase (if that is the right word for the last seven years) of al-Ḥākim's rule, a period which, according to several contemporary or near-contemporary sources, saw several changes in the imam's public actions and the way he presented himself to his followers. The most easily seen example of the latter was his decision to ride in public exclusively on a donkey and never a horse. But there are other examples as well.

A major purpose of both these treatises is to validate the imamate of al-Ḥākim in as explicit a manner as possible, thereby not merely to prove the obligation of the Muslim community to recognize that the imamate is an essential institution of Islamic governance, but that specifically of the Fatimid imam-caliph who held it at the time of writing. Thus, the reign of al-Ḥākim is a critical factor in both. And, in that sense, both are political works with a clear agenda to establish the right of the Fatimid dynasty to universal allegiance against all other claimants, Abbasids, Umayyads, Zaydīs and the rest.[14]

---

12. Muṣṭafā Ghālib published an edition of this work in 1984 in Beirut. A new edition with a complete English translation has been prepared by Arzina Lalani and will appear shortly. I must again note here my gratitude to her for sharing her text and notes with me prior to undertaking this project.

13. Al-Naysābūrī's two remaining treatises are the *Istitār al-imām* (ed. W. Ivanow in the *Majallat Kulliyyat al-Ādāb al-Jāmiʿa al-Miṣriyya*, *Bulletin of the Faculty of Arts, University of Egypt*, vol. 4, part 2 (1936), pp. 93–107) with an English trans. in Ivanow's *Ismaili Tradition Concerning the Rise of the Fatimids* (London, etc., 1942), and the *Risāla al-mūjaza al-kāfiya fī ādāb al-duʿāt*.

14. For a list of those who, according to al-Kirmānī, claimed the supreme leadership of the Muslims at this time, see the fifth demonstration of the seventh light of the present treatise.

Al-Ḥākim and his Times

The reign of al-Ḥākim was a watershed event in the progress of Fatimid rule. He more than any of its caliphs confronted prevailing social and political conditions directly and attempted to change them in conformity with his understanding of Islam—him, after all, having precedence in all matters as the most eminent living representative of the Prophet, the one occupying his place and fulfilling his functions in all ways save that of conveying revelation. Each of the Fatimid imam-caliphs, however, performed that role, at least in theory. With al-Ḥākim, nonetheless, the intensity of his personal involvement in the directions of affairs was remarkable. His orders and edicts on a wide array of issues, which were, and to an extent still are, a matter of controversy elicited then and now both approval by his supporters and condemnation by his detractors. But for the most part they are not to be denied as they are confirmed in many details by too many sources, including eyewitnesses, among them the authors of the Druze epistles and both al-Naysābūrī and al-Kirmānī, not to mention the Christian and non-Ismaili Muslim chroniclers of the time.

Al-Kirmānī thus alludes, in several of his writings, to the policies and actions of his imam, al-Ḥākim. In the present treatise he outlines a series of traits or qualities of the ideal ruler-imam and shows that, of his generation, only al-Ḥākim has them. And these characteristics are proven by his actions, which al-Kirmānī reviews, either in specific detail or in pointed allusions that would not have been missed by a contemporary reader. One prime example is the destruction of churches and synagogues, the most famous case of which was the Church of the Holy Sepulchre in Jerusalem. Because of an unacceptable religious fraud practised in it, the caliph ordered it destroyed in the year 400/1009.[15] Other churches and some synagogues were

---

15. On this event see the classical study of it by Marius Canard, 'La Destruction de l'Église de la Résurrection par le calife Ḥākim et l'histoire de la descente du feu sacré', *Byzantion* 35 (1965), pp. 16–43, reprinted in his *Byzance et les Musulmans du Proche Orient* (London, 1973), article XX; and the more recent re-examination by J. Van Reeth, '*Al-Qumāma* et le *Qā'im* de 400 H: le trucage de la lampe sur le tombeau du Christ', in U. Vermeulen and D. De Smet, ed., *Egypt and Syria in the Fatimid, Ayyubid and Mamluk Eras*, II (Louvain, 1998), pp. 171–190.

likewise ransacked and torn down near that time. Although over the final years of his reign al-Ḥākim allowed many to be rebuilt, even, it is said, contributing funds for that purpose, Europe remembered only the Church of the Holy Sepulchre, perhaps because Christians there knew nothing of the rest and were not interested in them. Condemnation of that act remained alive well through the era of the Crusades.[16] Muslims, by direct contrast, at least in the popular imagination of the time, saw the policies of the Fatimid ruler as appropriate and necessary, a sign, in fact, that a Muslim ruler was actively doing what he was supposed to do.[17]

But it is wrong to focus narrowly on this one area. Al-Ḥākim's policies covered many other problems, including the consumption of intoxicating beverages, forms of gambling and illicit public movements of women, some of which appear now, to modern sensibilities, hard to accept. In any case they were not all prohibitions; he was responsible for others as well, all falling, in Islamic terms, under the concept of 'commanding the good and forbidding the bad'. The point is that he was, during much of his reign, extremely active in this fashion personally, a point not lost on Muslims everywhere. His reputation spread accordingly. Like no other Fatimid, he gained a following beyond his immediate political domain. Naturally, there were many who objected as well. The Shīʿī imamate was anathema to the Sunnīs in any case. Still, among the Shīʿa and others, in the eastern territories of the Abbasids, he gained acceptance. Street demonstrations in Baghdad had crowds crying out his name, 'O Ḥākim! O Manṣūr!',[18] even though presumably most of these Shīʿa

16. See, for example, the remarks of the medieval Latin crusader historian William of Tyre at the beginning of his *A History of Deeds Done beyond the Sea*, trans. by E. A. Babcock and A. C. Krey, 2 vols. (New York, 1943), vol. 1, pp. 65–67.

17. Note here al-Kirmānī's allusion to the role of the Islamic prophet in this regard; see the seventh demonstration of the fifth light.

18. Manṣūr is the personal, given name of al-Ḥākim. It also has here an apocalyptic significance. One such event is the Sunnī-Shīʿa riot of 398/1007–1008. Ibn al-Jawzī, *al-Muntaẓam* (Hyderabad, 1939), vol. 7, p. 238; John J. Donahue, *The Buwayhid Dynasty in Iraq* (Leiden, 2003), p. 284; Heinz Halm, *Die Kaliefen von Kairo. Die Fatimiden in Ägypten 973–1074* (Munich, 2003), p. 264. Another example

were Twelvers and thus not normally thought to support the imamate of the Fatimids.

One quite striking piece of evidence is the declaration in the year 401/1010 by the ʿUqaylid ruler of northern Mesopotamia, Qirwāsh b. Muqallad, that he would henceforth recognize the Fatimid caliph as imam of the Muslim community.[19] His commitment, made public in the Friday *khuṭba* in towns and cities of his realm, meant that a significant portion of Abbasid territory had seceded from their rule and been won over to the Fatimids.[20] Abbasid reaction was swift, indicating both the seriousness of this threat to their dominance and the disquiet of the caliph al-Qādir. The latter, however, well understood that his powers in the situation were limited. He had been elevated to the caliphate by the Buyid amir, Bahā' al-Dawla, following the latter's deposition of the previous caliph. He had therefore, in one sense, been appointed to his office by a mere amir. He owed his position to the Buyids and they were themselves, moreover, partial to the Shīʿī cause, if not outrightly Shīʿa in all other respects. Al-Qādir had no army; he could not himself reassert his right by force. Instead he chose the famous Malikī-Ashʿarī jurist and theologian, Abū Bakr al-Bāqillānī, to act for him. Al-Bāqillānī succeeded and the revolt of Qirwāsh disappeared quickly.

The general threat posed by al-Ḥākim and the Ismailis did not, however, go away as easily. Al-Qādir next summoned the leading

---

of the same or similar expression of this sentiment occurred in 394/1003–1004 in response to the controversy over differing versions of the Qur'ān, that of Ibn Masʿūd and that of ʿUthmān, again in Baghdad. See Ibn al-Dawādārī, *Kanz al-durar*, vol. 6, ed. Ṣ. al-Munajjid (Cairo, 1961), p. 272.

19. This event occurred in Muḥarram 401/August 1010. See Ibn al-Athīr, *al-Kāmil fi'l-ta'rīkh*, ed. C. J. Tornberg (Leiden, 1864, Beirut reprint), vol. 9, p. 223; al-Maqrīzī, *Ittiʿāẓ al-ḥunafā' bi-akhbār al-a'imma al-Fāṭimiyyīn al-khulafā'*, vol. 1, ed. J. al-Shayyāl (Cairo, 1967), vols. 2 and 3, ed. M. H. M. Aḥmad (Cairo, 1971 and 1973), 2, p. 88; Ibn al-Jawzī, *al-Muntaẓam*, (Hyderabad, 1939), vol. 7, pp. 249–251, the latter source gives a verbatim transcription of the quite interesting *khuṭba* pronounced for the Fatimids on this occasion. Also Ibn Taghrībirdī, *al-Nujūm al-zāhira fī mulūk Miṣr wa'l-Qāhira* (Cairo, 1348–1391/1929–1972), vol. 4, pp. 224–227.

20. There is also a declaration in favour of al-Ḥākim by ʿAlī b. al-Asadī of the Banū Asad in Ḥilla, on which see Farhad Daftary, *The Ismāʿīlīs: Their History and Doctrines* (Cambridge, 1990), p. 193.

scholars and religious authorities resident in Baghdad and had them sign in 402 a manifesto attesting that the genealogy of the Fatimids was bogus. He also commissioned another theologian, the Muʿtazilī ʿAlī b. Saʿīd al-Iṣṭakhrī, to write for him a refutation and condemnation of Fatimid doctrine.[21]

Over the same period or slightly earlier, several other scholars composed denunciations of Ismaili and Fatimid doctrine, among them al-Bāqillānī himself[22] and the Zaydīs Abu'l-Qāsim al-Bustī and his imam Abu'l-Ḥasan al-Mu'ayyad bi-llāh Aḥmad b. Ḥusayn b. Hārūn, who resided in the Caspian region. Neither al-Bāqillānī's work, which was called *Kashf al-asrār wa hatk al-astār*, nor that of al-Iṣṭakhrī appears to have survived, but major portions of al-Bustī's *Kashf al-asrār wa-naqd al-afkār* are available.[23] The Zaydī imam's treatise against the Fatimids was answered by al-Kirmānī in a work he called *al-Risāla al-kāfiya fi'l-radd ʿalā'l-Hārūnī al-Ḥusaynī* and that we have, though not what it responded to.[24]

Al-Kirmānī: His Life and Works

In all of this agitation for and against the Fatimids, al-Kirmānī was an important participant. So much is clear from his writings. But typically for an Ismaili *dāʿī* of that period, there exists no information about him in any of the contemporary chronicles and other records. All we know of his life and career depend on a series of references scattered

21. Al-Iṣṭakhrī died in 404/1013–1014 and, therefore, his anti-Fatimid work likely dates to the period 402–404. Ibn al-Jawzī, *al-Muntaẓam*, vol. 7, p. 268; Ibn al-Athīr, *al-Kāmil,* vol. 9, p. 246; Ibn Kathīr, *Bidāya wa'l-nihāya fī ta'rīkh* (Cairo, 1932–), vol. 11, p. 352.

22. Al-Bāqillānī's refutation of the Ismailis had the title *Kashf al-asrār wa hatk al-astār*. On it see Ibn Kathīr, *al-Bidāya wa'l-nihāya fī ta'rīkh* (Cairo, 1932–), vol. 11, p. 346; the editor's introduction to al-Bāqillānī's *Tamḥīd*, (Cairo, 1947) p. 259, note 3; and Ibn Khaldūn, *Muqaddima*, tr. F. Rosenthal (New York, 1958), vol. 1, pp. 43–44, esp. note 122.

23. Ed. ʿAdil Sālim al-ʿAbd al-Jādir in his *al-Ismāʿīliyyūn* (no. 2) (Kuwait, 2002).

24. Ed. by Muṣṭafā Ghālib as part of his *Majmūʿat rasā'il al-Kirmānī* (Beirut, 1983).

here and there in his written works.[25] Even the later Ṭayyibī Ismailis of the Yemen, who came to regard him with special reverence as the head of the *daʿwa* (the *bāb*) under al-Ḥākim, could not find material about al-Kirmānī that had not been extracted directly from his books and treatises.

Still the evidence of his own words has proved useful. We can thus verify his involvement in the Fatimid *daʿwa* of what was then called the 'Two Iraqs': Iraq of the Arabs and Iraq of the Persians. His *nisba* indicates that he came originally from the Iranian province of Kirman. The title of one work suggests that he was active, most likely as a senior member of the Ismaili *daʿwa*, in both Baghdad and Basra. Near the end of 405/1015, he left Iraq for Egypt, where he taught under the leadership of the *dāʿī*-in-chief (*dāʿī al-duʿāt*) Khatkīn al-Ḍayf and wrote a number of pamphlets and other works, before finally, at an imprecise date but later than 408/1017, returning to Iraq once again. Thereafter he disappears and evidence of his writings ends (along with the meagre information about him contained in them). In all likelihood he died in 411 or a short time later, the year 411/1020 being when he finished revising his *magnum opus*, the *Rāḥat al-ʿaql* (*Comfort of Reason*), almost certainly the last of his works.

By that time he had composed a substantial body of writings. The 15th-century Yemeni authority Idrīs ʿImād al-Dīn knew of 29 titles, of which he had located copies of some 18, the rest having never reached the Yemen. Given that it is exactly the same 18 that now exist either in printed editions or in known manuscript sources, it is likely that none of the others survive. All appear to date to a period between 399/1008 and 411/1020 and all are dedicated to the imam of that time, al-Ḥākim.

Al-Kirmānī's missionary activities and his writings in support of them were an important part of an attempt by the Fatimids to overthrow and replace the Abbasids. To carry out that task in Baghdad or anywhere else in Iraq must have been extremely dangerous and risky. Yet it also may indicate that he found some protection and assistance there, perhaps sympathetic partisans of the Shīʿī cause. Nonetheless,

---

25. For a full accounting of this evidence and what it means, see Walker, *Ḥamīd al-Dīn al-Kirmānī: Ismaili Thought in the Age of al-Ḥākim* (London, 1999).

for him to disappear from view after returning to Iraq suggests that he met an untimely fate once there. It is thus truly fortunate and perhaps fortuitous that well over half of his books and treatises survive. Though some were written in Egypt, the rest must have either come with him and copies of them remained there, or copies of many of those from the east later managed to find a way to Cairo.

In addition to the *Maṣābīḥ fī ithbāt al-imāma*, the subject of the present volume, there are six major works: the *Rāḥat al-ʿaql*,[26] a grand summation of his theological and philosophical doctrines; the *Kitāb al-riyāḍ*, on his solution to some disagreements among Ismaili *dāʿī*s prior to his time; *al-Aqwāl al-dhahabiyya*, a refutation of *al-Ṭibb al-rūḥānī* (*The Spiritual Physick*) by the physician-philosopher Abū Bakr al-Rāzī; *al-Waḍīʾa fī maʿālim al-dīn wa-uṣūlihi*, on the details of worship by knowledge and practice; *Tanbīh al-hādī waʾl-mustahdī*, a kind of heresiography of sects and opinions he found unacceptable; and *Maʿāṣim al-hudā waʾl-iṣāba fī tafḍīl ʿAlī ʿalā al-ṣaḥāba*, on the superior excellence of ʿAlī b. Abī Ṭālib in comparison with the other Companions of the Prophet. Of these the first four have been published; the latter two are available only in manuscripts, the last having survived without its first part, which was apparently lost long ago.

The shorter treatises and pamphlets are on the whole less important but nevertheless often contain interesting information especially for details about the occasion of their composition. His *Mabāsim al-bishārāt*, which describes his reaction to the state of affairs when he first arrived in Egypt, is particularly valuable for that reason. Another, the *Risāla al-durriyya fī maʿnā al-tawḥīd waʾl-muwaḥḥid waʾl-muwaḥḥad*, expresses approval of the recently appointed *dāʿī*-in-chief whom al-Kirmānī says is the *bāb* to al-Ḥākim and whose new honorific title is al-Ṣādiq al-Maʾmūn. It must therefore date to 406. Yet one more, the *Risāla al-wāʿiẓa*, from the middle of the year 408/1017, consists of a refutation of the doctrines advocated by a rebel or dissident *dāʿī*, a man named al-Akhram, which tended to deify the imam (or possibly to claim it outright)—a position subsequently held by the Druze.

26. For more information about al-Kirmānī's individual works and their editions, see the general bibliography at the end of this volume, and Walker, *Ḥamīd al-Dīn al-Kirmānī*.

Al-Kirmānī's thought is quite complex and difficult to describe, most particularly in regard to its philosophical content.[27] He was a master of several traditions, the best elements of which he attempted to combine in a single coherent doctrine—a task not easily accomplished. What we now possess of his writings, moreover, do not adequately explain the system he proposed. Possibly, even if we had all that he wrote, he had never managed to complete it or to reveal it in sufficient detail. But another answer is that the synthesis he wanted could not be achieved due to inherent conflicts among the various strands of the earlier thought he inherited.

He obviously began with a basic Islamic approach, most likely in part related to that of the Muʿtazila. Many of the Shīʿī theologians of his time had adopted the doctrine of that school. His background in the Ismaili *daʿwa* and its teachings from a period before his were clearly also paramount. But in each case he modified, often profoundly, what he received from either. Two prior elements of Ismaili thought feature, on one side, a kind of gnostic cosmology and, on another, philosophical Neoplatonism. Both tended to disappear in his hands, Neoplatonism less so than the elements of the gnostic myth. As a philosopher he espoused a set of doctrines closely related to those put forth by Abū Naṣr al-Fārābī and which derive principally from Aristotle or from later interpreters of Aristotle. In that respect al-Kirmānī is much like his contemporary, Ibn Sīnā. Yet the older ideas—those of his predecessors in the *daʿwa*, such as Abū Ḥātim al-Rāzī and Abū Yaʿqūb al-Sijistānī—do not recede altogether but continue to loom in the background of his thought.

Aside from the philosophical component, al-Kirmānī upheld a range of Shīʿī doctrines, particularly as interpreted by the Ismailis. For him the imamate was a living institution with a visible imam. It was of paramount importance in religion and all aspects of life that required the constant attention of its supreme leader. The imam was (and is) the repository of knowledge and truth. He is the heir of the

27. For a more complete introduction to his thought, see Walker, *Ḥamīd al-Dīn al-Kirmānī* (chapters four to six) and D. De Smet, *La Quiétude de l'Intellect: Néoplatonisme et gnose ismaélienne dans l'oeuvre de Ḥamîd ad-Dîn al-Kirmânî (Xe/XIe s.)* (Louvain, 1995). There is a good but brief outline by M. T. P. de Bruijn in *EI2*.

Prophet, the one who assumes the Prophet's place, and who functions as the Prophet had in his time in leading the human community. Al-Kirmānī's imam was al-Ḥākim, who had, in his view, inherited his sacred position from his ancestors running in a line from him through ʿAlī to the Prophet Muḥammad. He had been designated and appointed by them and he performed the same functions as they. He was in fact the surety in the present of the validity in the past of their sanctity. He confirmed them just as they had designated him.

Although he names only al-Ḥākim, al-Kirmānī's adherence to the Fatimid imams covered the entire dynasty and its *daʿwa*. Against attempts to deify al-Ḥākim or to make of him the last and ultimate imam, or to claim that the imam's interpretation of the law in any way served to nullify the requirement of observing its particular obligations and of performing the duties it lay down, he resolutely maintained a doctrine he characterized as the 'double worship' (*ʿibādatayn*) and of the continuing necessity of a lineal succession of imams. The imamate must exist, and must continue, to ensure the proper observance of the worship of God, which is the principal duty of humankind and its path to salvation and paradise. That path consists of parallel means: one, the acquisition of knowledge and the other, the performance of works. The latter are the rites and rituals of Islam; the former is its meaning in rational terms. Both are essential; one has little value without the other.

The present treatise is a clear affirmation of his position concerning the imamate, including the doctrine of the requirement of the double worship, a two-fold observance of the necessity of acquiring knowledge and performing works. It has, by contrast, little to say about philosophical issues except for the section on the soul, which contains a series of demonstrations designed to establish, first that the human soul exists and second what it is. The third chapter of the first part, which is thus devoted to the topic of the soul serves as an entry point into a larger realm of his thought. What he says there offers an Aristotelian view of the soul entirely in line with his statements elsewhere. But the context also supposes his doctrine of the heavenly intellects and their providential interest in terrestrial affairs, most particularly the salvation of humankind. The influence of the angelic intellects provides the most perfect of human intellects, namely the prophets and their heirs the imams, with the means to induce others of their species to move toward that salvation. Born devoid of knowledge and lacking a sure way to understand what is required for learning it and, subsequently, of acting in accord with the law incumbent upon them, individual humans must accept the guidance and instruction of the imam in order to achieve in the end a place in paradise.

Historical Circumstances that Prompted the *Maṣābīḥ*

For al-Kirmānī not to have dwelt at length on philosophical matters in this treatise is understandable. His aim was less abstract. On this occasion his purpose was to prove the absolute necessity of the imamate and to indicate what it is as precisely as he could, all the while affirming the Fatimid position and that of his imam, al-Ḥākim. Had he written it for the Ismaili *daʿwa*, as was the case with the work of Abu'l-Fawāris, his contemporary, he might have proceeded differently. The same is partially true of al-Naysābūrī's *Ithbāt al-imāma*, although the latter treatise was likely composed for public consumption as well. Both of these *dāʿī*s lived and wrote in the shadow of the Fatimids, in Egypt or Syria, safe from the hostility of anti-Fatimid reactions. By contrast, al-Kirmānī was at the time of writing almost certainly in Iraq, perhaps in Baghdad itself.

Al-Kirmānī himself suggests the circumstances surrounding its composition. To begin with, he notes in his introduction that he was compelled to write this work as a way to convince the Buyid wazir Fakhr al-Mulk[28] to support the Fatimids. Al-Kirmānī obviously knew that the wazir was loyal to the Shīʿī cause and was devoted in some manner to the family of the Prophet. The Buyid amirs were Shīʿī in general, though not necessarily overtly so. They did not abolish the Abbasid caliphate nor did they suppress Sunnī institutions or persecute Sunnī authorities. Instead they tended to maintain close relationships with the major Zaydī and Twelver Imāmī figures, among them the two brothers, the Sharīfs al-Raḍī and al-Murtaḍā,[29] both

28. For historical sources on the life and career of Fakhr al-Mulk, see Ibn Khallikān, *Wafayāt al-aʿyān*, tr. de Slane, vol. 3, pp. 278–280; Ibn al-Jawzī, *al-Muntaẓam*, vol. 7: index; Ibn al-Athīr, *al-Kāmil*, index.

29. Al-Murtaḍā, for example, said the eulogy for Fakhr al-Mulk.

contemporaries of al-Kirmānī, who were the leaders of the Shīʿa in Baghdad at that time. Significantly, al-Kirmānī complains that there appears to be no one at the wazir's court to uphold the Fatimid position or answer charges made against it.

It is especially noteworthy that he appeals to this wazir and to his court, not to the Abbasid caliph al-Qādir whom he goes out of his way to disparage as being blatantly unqualified for the imamate. The immediate impression is that al-Kirmānī sensed an opportunity with the wazir, whose evident Shīʿīsm and fond regard for the family of the Prophet made him a suitable subject for the proof of the imamate he intended to offer.

Al-Qādir, the Abbasid caliph throughout the period, was the appointee in 381/991 of the amir Bahāʾ al-Dawla, who had simply deposed his Abbasid predecessor because he wanted someone more amenable in that office. Al-Kirmānī takes explicit note of that act, claiming that because al-Qādir had been elevated by Bahāʾ al-Dawla, his appointment to universal Islamic leadership—the imamate—is not valid. Al-Qādir had not been designated by anyone with the authority to do so. Nonetheless, al-Kirmānī added to his mention of Bahāʾ al-Dawla the pious wish 'may God's mercy be upon him' (*raḥmat Allāh ʿalayhi*). For him to have done so indicates both that, at the time of writing, Bahāʾ al-Dawla was fairly recently deceased and that al-Kirmānī wanted to honour his memory.[30] But why, exactly? One connection is that it was Bahāʾ al-Dawla who had appointed Fakhr al-Mulk wazir. The Buyid amir was also certainly in some sense Shīʿī. At death both men, the wazir and the amir, were transported to the Shīʿī holy city and interred at the shrine of the imam [ʿAlī].[31] Could al-Kirmānī have had a much earlier association with either one?

Fakhr al-Mulk became wazir in 401; his duties in that office made him the Buyid governor of Baghdad and thus technically in charge of relations with al-Qādir. What al-Kirmānī says about Fakhr al-Mulk is generally favourable, even laudatory. Yet there is as well a tone of disappointment, as if he expected, or had reason to expect, that the

30. It is worth noting that al-Basāsīrī, who was to conquer Baghdad on behalf of the Fatimids, had been a *mamlūk* of Bahāʾ al-Dawla: al-Maqrīzī, *Ittiʿāẓ*, vol. 2, p. 232.

31. Ibn al-Athīr, *al-Kāmil*, vol. 9, pp. 241, 260.

wazir would have followed a more pro-Fatimid policy. Did he have a valid expectation and, if so, based on what? Curiously, Fakhr al-Mulk's son much later moved to Egypt and there served, albeit briefly, as wazir to the Fatimid imam-caliph al-Mustanṣir.[32]

But the immediate question is: what caused al-Kirmānī to write this particular proof of the imamate and defence of al-Ḥākim, especially under the circumstances in Iraq at that time, and aim it at the Buyid wazir? Fakhr al-Mulk held the wazirate from 401 until his arrest and execution at the beginning of 407. Al-Kirmānī's *Maṣābīḥ*, which carries no specific date for itself, must fall between those two dates. The year 401 saw also the declaration by Qirwāsh of his loyalty to the Fatimids and the reversal of it as engineered by the Sunnī theologian-jurist al-Bāqillānī at the urging of al-Qādir. Al-Bāqillānī died in Dhu'l-Qaʿda 403/1013. Al-Iṣṭakhrī, the other (Muʿtazilī) theologian al-Qādir employed to write against the Fatimids, also died in the same year. Yet al-Kirmānī cites by name only al-Bāqillānī as the prime example of the kind of Sunnī scholar al-Qādir relied on, presumably for a matter he could not take care of himself. Is he alluding to al-Bāqillānī's role in suppressing the pro-Fatimid revolt of Qirwāsh? It appears quite possible. Thus, al-Kirmānī's complaint is not a matter of simply al-Bāqillānī having written an anti-Ismaili work; that had been done by several scholars and al-Bāqillānī was only one among them.

But what of the so-called Baghdad Manifesto of 402[33] for which al-Qādir rounded up many local authorities, particularly the leaders of the Ashrāf ʿAlid nobility, al-Raḍī[34] and al-Murtaḍā included, to

32. *Ittiʿāẓ*, vol. 2, pp. 271f, 313, 333.

33. On the Baghdad manifesto, see Daftary, *The Ismāʿīlīs*, p. 604, n. 93, for citations. The manifesto was issued on Rabīʿ II 402/November 1011. Sources for it include: Ibn Khaldūn, *Muqaddima*, tr. Rosenthal vol. 1, pp. 45–47 esp. n. 129; Ibn al-Jawzī, *al-Muntaẓam*, vol. 7, pp. 255–256; Ibn al-Athīr, *al-Kāmil*, vol. 9, pp. 236; Juwaynī, *Ta'rīkh*, vol. 3, pp. 174–177, tr. Boyle vol. 2, pp. 558–600; al-Maqrīzī, *Ittiʿāẓ*, vol. 1, pp. 43–44. Manifesto signatories are listed in Ibn al-Jawzī, *al-Muntaẓam*, vol. 7, pp. 255–256, giving 16 names: 6 of the ʿAlids, 3 judges, 6 *faqīh*s, and 1 of the *shuhadā'*. Al-Murtaḍā and al-Raḍī are both on the list.

34. On al-Raḍī, who died on the 6th of Muḥarram 406/1016—Fakhr al-Mulk conducted the prayers for him—see the entry on him by Moktar Djebli 'al-Sharīf al-Raḍī' in the *EI2*. Al-Raḍī had been close to Bahā' al-Dawla but not to al-Qādir. However, the rumour that he was actually pro-Fatimid rests on misinformation

sign a denunciation of the Fatimid genealogy? On that subject al-Kirmānī seems to say nothing. In truth the manifesto itself made so improbable a claim it was hardly credible. Those who signed could also insist that they were coerced. It was in al-Kirmānī's interest not to make a point of it, especially as many leading Shīʿī authorities such as al-Raḍī and al-Murtaḍā were involved.

Where were Fakhr al-Mulk and Bahāʾ al-Dawla when these events transpired and to what degree did either participate? What role Fakhr al-Mulk played is uncertain but Bahāʾ al-Dawla is said to have supported the mission of al-Bāqillānī to Qirwāsh. The amir died in Jumādā II 403/December 1012 and was succeed by his son Sulṭān al-Dawla, who confirmed Fakhr al-Mulk in office. Al-Kirmānī is thus writing after that. But even so he does not appear to blame the dead amir. Nevertheless, could these events and Fakhr al-Mulk's failure to control them be the immediate cause for al-Kirmānī's treatise? Had our author, for example, been a direct participant in the affair of Qirwāsh in 401?

These considerations help determine the earliest date for the treatise: late 403, perhaps the beginning of 404. Various comments al-Kirmānī makes about al-Ḥākim, particularly his riding nearly alone in public without fear of assassination, although many in the military and others had sworn to kill him, suggests a date of 404 or 405. In 405 al-Kirmānī left Iraq for Egypt. The tenure and the content of this work indicate that he composed it in Iraq, not Egypt. Thus, it precedes his arrival in Cairo. His writing afterwards, notably the *Mabāsim al-bishārāt*, but also the *Risāla al-durriyya* and the individual treatises that follow it, focused on the problems of the *daʿwa* in Egypt as if, once there, al-Kirmānī quickly turned his attention away from what he had left behind.

The Relationship of the *Maṣābīḥ* to the Rest of al-Kirmānī's Works

Although the *Maṣābīḥ* mentions only one other of al-Kirmānī's various writings, it appears itself in as many as nine of the others, including most prominently the *Rāḥat al-ʿaql* which cites it in four separate places (Cairo edition, pp. 20, 22, 300, and 359). The one the

---

from Ibn al-Jawzī, *al-Muntaẓam*, vol. 7, p. 282.

Maṣābīḥ cites is this very *Rāḥat al-ʿaql*, a work that the author most certainly composed over a period of years. He quite possibly completed a version early in his career which he subsequently revised and issued in a final form once he had returned to Iraq in the year 411, a fact revealed in the introduction to the work itself as we have it now. Thus, for al-Kirmānī to refer to his *Rāḥat al-ʿaql* in the *Maṣābīḥ* and to the *Maṣābīḥ* in the *Rāḥat al-ʿaql*, means that the ultimate text of the latter comes from a date later than the composition of the former.

The pattern of the citations of the *Maṣābīḥ* in all nine of these cases is, however, indicative, quite likely, of the order of composition, it predating all of these others. Nonetheless, with al-Kirmānī's works, which not infrequently refer to each other, that is not a sure conclusion, but the additional evidence in the manner of these citations and the specificity of most, strongly suggest that all the others come later. The *Maʿāṣim al-hudā* (f.45b, ms. no. 724 in the library of The Institute of Ismaili Studies) notes rather pointedly 'as it is mentioned in the Torah', followed by words in Hebrew that begin the quotation from Genesis 17: 20: *ûleyišmāʿēʾl šemaʿtîka*—on the full meaning of which see the comments below on the Hebrew and fifth light, seventh demonstration, of the *Maṣābīḥ* itself—but in this instance al-Kirmānī does not continue with the whole of the passage and instead simply says, 'to the ending of his statement with *mēʿōdmā* who is Muḥammad, may the blessing of God be upon him, in accord with what we explained in the book *Maṣābīḥ fiʾl-imāma*'. Thus, rather than repeating the complete phrase, he merely alludes to what he had already said in the earlier work. In his *al-Waḍīʾa fī maʿālim al-dīn* (f. 47b = p. 123 of the edition), as another example, he states even more directly: 'Our arguments in support of the necessity of the interpretation (*taʾwīl*) that have appeared previously in our book known as the *Kitāb al-maṣābīḥ fīʾl-imāma* and in our epistle *al-Kāfiya* are sufficient.'

Most of the remaining references to the *Maṣābīḥ* consist likewise of specific citations of a subject or an issue dealt with previously. They refer to individual sections or arguments in the older treatise.[35]

35. In the notes to the translation I have indicated the details. The complete list of such citations is as follows: *Kitāb al-riyāḍ*, pp. 138, 190; *al-Waḍīʾa fī maʿālim al-dīn*, f. 20b (= p. 82 of the edition), f. 47b (= p. 123 of the edition); *Maʿāṣim al-hudā*, f. 45b (ms. 724, Institute of Ismaili Studies); *Tanbīh al-hādī*, p. 228 and 232 (ms. 723,

Almost certainly, therefore, the *Maṣābīḥ* predates any of the works al-Kirmānī wrote in Egypt and quite possibly even several he composed in Iraq. Significantly, it comes before the *Mabāsim al-bishārāt*, which describes the conditions he found when he first arrived in Cairo and which likely dates itself to the end of 405.[36]

A Comparison with al-Naysābūrī's *Proof of the Imamate*

It is interesting at this point to compare al-Kirmānī's proof of the imamate with that of al-Naysābūrī. The latter treatise likewise carries no specific date but it does name, among those on whom it wishes a benediction, the 'Walī ʿahd al-Muslimīn' (Guardian of the Covenant of the Muslims) who is also the 'Khalīfat Amīr al-Muʾminīn' (Successor of the Commander of the Believers). That exact formulation belongs at the time of al-Ḥākim to the caliph's cousin ʿAbd al-Raḥīm b. Ilyās, who was appointed heir apparent in Rabīʿ II 404/ September 1013 with the express proviso that his name appear with this formula thereafter on all public documents including coins, textiles (*ṭirāz*), flags (*bunūd*), and works written for public consumption. That provision remained in effect until the end of al-Ḥākim's reign in 411/1021. Near the end of the work al-Naysābūrī also mentions those who regard the imam's actions 'with the exaggerator's eye to claim thereby divinity for him'. From a variety of evidence, including al-Kirmānī's pamphlet directed against such people from 408, as well as dated Druze epistles, we know that those who proclaimed the divinity of al-Ḥākim went public with it starting in that year. It is possible that such a doctrine was taught less openly earlier but al-Naysābūrī would have been reluctant to admit it—especially in a work for general use—before that time. Given these facts it appears that his treatise was written two or three years after that of al-Kirmānī and it addresses an audience in Egypt, perhaps in answer to damage done by those he accuses of exaggeration (*ghuluww*).

IIS); *al-Risāla al-muḍīʾa*, p. 53; *al-Risāla al-kāfiya*, p. 151; *al-Aqwāl al-dhahabiyya*, p. 94; *Mabāsim al-bishārāt*, p. 118; and *Rāḥat al-ʿaql*, pp. 20, 22, 300 and 359.

36. The *Mabāsim al-bishārāt* specifically credits the *Maṣābīḥ* as having made the argument for the imamate of al-Ḥākim, (pp. 117–118).

But his treatise is not simply that. Early in it he states his purpose:

> Many works on the proof of the imamate by the masters in the *da'wa* employ inferences from and quotations of the Qur'ānic verses that are well accepted as having been revealed in the matter of imamate and the imams. Reports have also been related concerning it from the Prophet. Those who came before have left nothing in this regard for those who come later and there is not much benefit in simply repeating the same concepts using different words. Our intention is rather to compose a treatise on the proof of the imamate based on adducing evidence and drawing inferences from the natural world and social and political regulations, and as well on the basis of intellect, necessity, innate disposition and character, from the consensus of the adherents of each of the religious communities, and from the philosophers and mathematicians.

Al-Naysābūrī surely is referring, when he cites earlier works on the proof of the imamate, to, among others, the writings of al-Kirmānī on the same subject. Obviously there were yet others that we do not have. Still, despite his stated intention, the approach of the two that survive indicates a difference as to what constitutes a proof. Al-Naysābūrī depends on argumentation based on the inference of analogy. All things exist in a structured, hierarchical relationship, some better than others, the superior ruling over the inferior by nature. Such differential disparity means that in every species and genus there is one kind or one individual better than all the rest. The best of humankind is the imam.

A similar point with some of the same evidence was made by al-Naysābūrī's famous predecessor in the *da'wa*, al-Sijistānī, in his proof of prophecy, the *Ithbāt al-nubuwwāt*.[37] Al-Sijistānī, at least in extant works, is quite ambiguous about the imamate. He says little about it and although he did recognize the Fatimids he cites no imams by name. For him the differential disparity of all things and their hierarchical ranking proves prophecy, a subject he treats at great length. Much of the same material reappears in al-Naysābūrī's depiction of the imamate.

---

37. An edition, for the most part unreliable, of this work was published by 'Ārif Tāmir in Beirut in 1966.

In contrast, al-Kirmānī employs a series of demonstrations, each following the rules of syllogistic reasoning, to prove point after point, from establishing that the world has a Maker to the absolutely undeniable validity of the imamate of al-Ḥākim. The whole presents a single coherent argument, divided into two parts, one on the necessity of the imamate in general and the other one establishing and verifying the exact historical conditions for it.

Al-Kirmānī makes his case for an audience that is not already Ismaili, though presumably Shīʿī. Al-Naysābūrī, who wrote within the safety and security of the Fatimid empire, proves the imamate to those who are, in some fashion, already its loyal adherents. His treatise has the air of celebrating existing fact; it is replete with comparisons that are rhetorically evocative rather than statements of an argument. According to his treatise, the imam is the best of creatures and the ultimate end of the created world; he is the best of human beings, God's shadow on earth, the sun, gold, the brain and head of the world. His position is that of the universal intellect (*al-ʿaql al-kullī*) in its realm; the imam is the universal intellect of this world. He is the speaking-prophet (*nāṭiq*) and the messiah of his time. To ascribe many of these attributes to the imam requires careful qualification for it would have been easy to slip into heresy; in any case it would have been folly to do so without the protection of the Fatimid caliphate. Significantly, al-Sijistānī claimed some of these attributes, if not all, for prophecy but not for the imamate. His reserve in that regard kept him and what he wrote on that subject safely orthodox. Al-Kirmānī, however, from what we can discern in his less public writings, might have accepted many of these same characterizations of the imam. But he did not do so in the treatise at hand and that is important, for what he wrote differed considerably from the work of al-Naysābūrī.

Major Themes in the *Maṣābīḥ*

Quite apart from its intention to prove rationally the necessity of the imamate, this work can also serve as a statement, surely official, of Fatimid doctrine in that regard from its time, if not from other periods as well. It contains a number of separate themes and issues, each of which comprise a major component of the Ismaili position. In Part

One, in addition to proving the existence of the Maker and the soul, al-Kirmānī takes up a subject he refers to as the divine regime (*al-siyāsa al-rabbāniyya*), which is here God's requital in the afterlife for good and bad behaviour in the here and now. That leads to a definition of what the believer must do and must think, consisting thus of acts and knowledge, both works and faith. To convey his message the prophet must express it in words using symbols and allusions, parables and similes. His charge is to teach humankind what it owes to its Maker.

All of the first part conforms both to al-Kirmānī's own doctrine and to Ismaili Shīʿism with little notice of partisanship. In the second part he moves on to the imamate and its necessity. The themes in this section are the requirement that the imams have infallibility and that they have been explicitly designated by, first, God and His Prophet, and then those who precede as imams. Designation is crucial. The community cannot validly elect an imam; its choice determines nothing in that regard and, if expressed, has no meaning. ʿAlī b. Abī Ṭālib was so designated by the Prophet, a point al-Kirmānī attempts to prove, before he traces the line of imams from him to Jaʿfar al-Ṣādiq and to the latter's son Ismāʿīl. From there it must, he says, continue in Ismāʿīl's progeny. Ultimately, it reaches the Fatimid imam-caliphs and specifically al-Ḥākim, the sixth of them. His argument at this point is one of the most historically interesting in the work. Ismāʿīl's imamate was valid because he produced offspring who continued the imamate; it is an essential aspect of their authenticity that a descendant of his perform in the present the required functions of the office. If there were no imam now, there could not have been one in the past; if the duties of the imam are not currently fulfilled by a properly designated descendant, the ancestor cannot have been the imam.

Al-Kirmānī provides a list of what an imam must do and what virtues he must display. Moreover, he names all those in his time who claim the imamate but who either are not qualified for it or fail to perform the actions it requires or fulfil the duties incumbent on them as true imams. His roster of 'false' imams has special interest. They are Aḥmad b. Isḥāq (al-Qādir), the Abbasid caliph in Baghdad; al-Hārūnī (al-Mu'ayyad bi-llāh), the Zaydī imam in Hawsam in Jīlān; ʿUmar al-Nazwānī, the Ibāḍī imam in ʿUmān; the Umayyad ruler in Spain and the Maghrib; and the leaders of the Qarmaṭī remnant in al-Aḥsā'. His references cite quite specific individuals of a fairly limited time and set of places. He also mentions the expected imam of the Twelver Shīʿa.

Much of the information, especially of details, in these final sections is provided in a set of tables rather than in the body of the text. Tables, diagrams and various kinds of charts were important to al-Kirmānī, and he used them in many of his works. Here he makes a special point of how a table presents evidence in such a way as to prove at a glance the principle in question. His paradigm is the definition of the *utrūj* (the etrog or citron) and how a table of its true characteristics readily separates it from something, in this case a quince, that shares some of these characteristics but not all of them.

The other tables cover first the virtues, traits and characteristics of the Prophet, given in the seventh demonstration of the fifth light, which constitute a prelude to the real theme of that chapter as a whole: the imamate of ʿAlī b. Abī Ṭālib. Al-Kirmānī intends to show graphically that a list of the sixteen virtues of the Prophet has no parallel in any of his prominent companions except for ʿAlī who, by contrast, shares with him all but one, that being the recipient of revelation. There are thus two tables (the second is repeated in the form of a circular graph): one for the character traits of the Prophet and another for those of the companions. At the end of the fifth demonstration of the sixth light, which is on the succession to the imamate after Jaʿfar al-Ṣādiq, he inserts a small table to illustrate his point about the citron and then a larger one to establish the falseness of the claims put forth by the other candidates at the time of Jaʿfar. He thus proves that the imamate belonged to Jaʿfar and then to his son Ismāʿīl. Two more tables, at the end of the fifth and the seventh demonstrations of the seventh light, both closely related, reveal the invalidity of the imamate of all the others who claim it in the era of al-Ḥākim and, conversely, the authenticity of the Fatimid imam whose imamate is the only true and valid one.

Quotations from the Hebrew and Syriac Bibles

Curiously, in the very first of these tables, in the second category of traits considered (the first was to have received revelation), that of having been properly designated—an issue of crucial importance for the imamate commencing with ʿAlī—al-Kirmānī makes a case for the designation of Muḥammad by God and by the earlier prophets on His behalf. 'He was designated', says al-Kirmānī, 'in the tongues of His messengers ... in the fifth book of the Torah with words that indicate him; Moses said... '. Here the author quotes in Hebrew (in Arabic script) the passage from Deuteronomy 33:2 about God coming from Sinai and dawning from Se'ir upon them. Al-Kirmānī also provides in the same place an interlineal Arabic translation of the same. All of this material belongs in a single block of the table as one out of sixteen characteristics of the Prophet.

Having opened the subject, however, al-Kirmānī continues with it at the conclusion of the table itself. There he explains how the words of Deuteronomy foretell the advent of Muḥammad and thus constitute a 'designation' of him by Moses (and by God). Not content with that, he adds to it Genesis 17:20, God's answer to the prayer of Abraham concerning Ishmael (Ismāʿīl), ending with 'I will make of him a great nation', again pointing to Muḥammad, the descendant of Ishmael. Two more Biblical quotations follow: Isaiah 21: 6–9 about the riders and the watcher on the watchtower who sees them coming, one on a donkey and the other on a camel; and a second passage, this time from the Syriac New Testament about the Paraclete from the Gospel of John. The latter al-Kirmānī gives in Syriac (again in Arabic script), the tongue presumably of Jesus, who is here the prophet designating Muḥammad. He also, as before, provides an Arabic translation.

There is more to this portion of the treatise which, in its citation of Biblical and other proof texts, hardly fits the tenor of the rest of the work which depends, by contrast, on rational proof and argumentation. Though interesting and notable, it is surely a digression. However, these citations of Biblical passages by a Muslim author elicited special attention from modern scholars long ago.

As early as 1931 the orientalist Paul Kraus,[38] then still in his twenties, published a pioneering study of those passages from this very treatise, as well as others that appear elsewhere in al-Kirmānī's writings.[39] Kraus knew of this material from notes gathered by his friend and colleague Husain Hamdani, who had access to important holdings of Ismaili manuscripts, those of his own family and possibly others.

That al-Kirmānī could and did quote such material either in Hebrew or in Syriac raises the question of whether or not he knew these languages. (It also seriously complicates the task of preparing an edition of this work; but on that see the comments below about the edition.) For a Muslim author merely to cite a Biblical passage by providing a translation of it is, however, not rare.[40] Many medieval authors did it and al-Kirmānī's predecessors in the Ismaili *daʿwa* did so fairly frequently.[41] What seems to distinguish al-Kirmānī is his ability to quote in Hebrew or Syriac, but even that is not unheard of among Muslim writers prior to his time.[42] In fact, it occurred

38. On Kraus see now the important study of him by Joel L. Kraemer, 'The Death of an Orientalist: Paul Kraus from Prague to Cairo' in Martin Kramer, ed. *The Jewish Discovery of Islam* (Tel Aviv, 1999), pp. 181–223.

39. Paul Kraus, 'Hebräische und syrische Zitate in ismāʿīlitischen Schriften', *Der Islam,* 19 (1931), pp. 243–263. See also A. Baumstark, 'Zu den Schriftzitaten al-Kirmānīs', *Der Islam* 20 (1932), pp. 308–313; and D. De Smet and J. M. F. Van Reeth, 'Les citations bibliques dans l'oeuvre du *dāʿī* ismaélien Ḥamīd ad-Dīn al-Kirmānī', in U. Vermeulen and J. M. F. Van Reeth, ed., *Law, Christianity and Modernism in Islamic Society.* Proceedings of the Eighteenth Congress of the Union Européenne des Arabistants et Islamisants, 1996 (Louvain, 1998), pp. 147–160.

40. On the general question of quotations from the Hebrew bible in Muslim literature, see Camilla Adang, *Muslim Writers on Judaism and the Hebrew Bible: From Ibn Rabban to Ibn Hazm* (Leiden, 1996) and Hava Lazarus-Yafeh, *Intertwined Worlds: Medieval Islam and Bible Criticism* (Princeton, 1992).

41. Two notable examples are Abū Ḥātim al-Rāzī in his *Aʿlām al-nubuwwa* and al-Qāḍī al-Nuʿmān in his *Asās al-taʾwīl*; for specific references see below.

42. See, as one major and particularly interesting example, the quotations given by Muṭahhar b. Ṭāhir al-Maqdīsī using Hebrew script, Arabic transliterations of it and an Arabic translation in the *Kitāb al-badʾ waʾl-taʾrīkh* ascribed to him *(Le livre de la création et de l'histoire de Motahhar ben Tahir el-Maqdisi),* ed. M. Cl. Huart, (6 vols. Paris, 1899–1916), vol. 5, Arabic pp. 28–33, French trans. pp. 31–35. His examples, all to prove a similar point to those made by al-Kirmānī, in fact include

commonly enough that it is possible he picked up such material, not from the Hebrew or Syriac versions of the Bible, but from secondary use of such quotations in works by Muslim apologists.

But assuming the Hebrew and Syriac we have for the four passages in the present treatise are accurate, it is nevertheless odd that our author's Arabic translations do not match those provided by, for example, Qāḍī al-Nuʿmān, for the same citations. Al-Nuʿmān's are better, conforming, in contrast to those of al-Kirmānī, quite closely to the standard version of the original text. But that might suggest that al-Kirmānī preferred to make his own translations.[43]

The Manuscript Tradition behind the *Maṣābīḥ*

The preservation of such passages that are in a language most likely quite foreign to any of the later copyists is a problem in and of itself. That a semblance of the original survived over the intervening centuries is a testimony to the tradition of the study and copying of this and similar texts by the Ṭayyibī *daʿwa* first in the Yemen and later in both the Yemen and India. Although the Ismaili mission reached the Yemen much earlier, its flowering depended on a rebirth in the middle of the fifth/eleventh century under ʿAlī b. Muḥammad al-Ṣulayḥī and the Ṣulayḥid dynasty. Subsequently, it grew in importance, eventually becoming strong enough to endure as an independent entity following the demise of the Fatimids in Egypt. Its literary tradition likewise goes back to the same period. Ṭayyibī historians credit the embassy of the scholar-jurist Lamak b. Malik to Cairo for it. Lamak lived and studied with the chief *dāʿī* al-Muʾayyad fiʾl-Dīn al-Shīrāzī for five years, 454–459, and it is then, according to these reports, that the transfer of Fatimid Ismaili writings to the Yemen began.

---

the reference to the Paraclete from John and versions of both *Gen.* 17: 20 and *Deut.* 33: 2. This work was written about 355/966 and thus predates al-Kirmānī by half a century. Nonetheless, these Arabic translations appear not to have influenced the author of the *Maṣābīḥ* who, therefore, may not have known of them.

43. Or, possibly, that he had not read al-Qāḍī al-Nuʿmān's *Asās al-taʾwīl*, where these passages occur, at the time he composed the present work, it having not circulated in Iraq and the east, or at least not yet.

The final line of the *Maṣābīḥ* in nearly all known manuscripts[44] cites, as the imam of the time, al-Mustanṣir, whose reign commenced in 427, even though the sure date of the work's composition has to have been prior to 407, long before. Al-Kirmānī clearly specifies that the imam of his time is al-Ḥākim; this imam is in fact the principal subject of the treatise itself. There is, moreover, no evidence that al-Kirmānī remained active or even alive into the era of al-Mustanṣir. The best explanation for the recognition of al-Mustanṣir in this fashion (note that the text mentions only al-Mustanṣir and not his predecessor al-Ẓāhir or any later imam) is that it indicates the period during which the oldest copy to reach the Yemen was made. If Lamak himself had copied the text, he might well have credited al-Mustanṣir under whom he worked, and his high status as a major figure at the very beginning of the Yemeni *daʿwa* would lend his own copy special respect. According to this theory, all later Ṭayyibī copies, and thus all known examples of the text, depend on it.

In keeping with the work's original public appeal for support of al-Ḥākim's imamate generally and the absence in it of any specific trace of esoteric doctrine, the Ṭayyibīs have always considered it as not belonging to the *ḥaqāʾiq*, those writings that contain material so sensitive that access to them is restricted. To be allowed to read and copy these essentially secret texts, special permission is needed. Other works of al-Kirmānī do fall into this category, but not the *Maṣābīḥ*, which means that students and potential copyists have encountered it at a fairly early stage in their education. That fact likely explains the relatively large number of copies available. The Institute of Ismaili Studies in London, for example, has acquired 10 and there are a number of others elsewhere.

The easy proliferation of copies and their accessibility is both good and bad for the recovery of al-Kirmānī's original words. The Ṭayyibī manuscript tradition in this case has preserved the text through an intense and continuing interest in it and what it says. Copying it again and again over eight or nine centuries has kept the work alive. But it has

44. It appears in 10 out of the 13 manuscripts surveyed. I have heard from a scholar in Bombay with access to yet other copies (five of them) that this line appears in all of them as well.

put some limitations on what can be done with the textual evidence. Significantly, none of the 13 manuscripts examined directly for the present edition indicate the exact source in front of the copyist. And, though some show signs of collation with additional manuscripts, they are not specified. Moreover, there are no obvious families of variations in the copies. Above all, the existing manuscripts are not old, having been produced in the 19th or 20th century. The very earliest that I have heard a report of—some I have not seen—are from the 18th century.

Given that a relatively small and isolated community preserved the work under circumstances that fostered both repeated copying and internal self-correction over the generations, to expect a true stemma for the manuscript tradition is unrealistic. The oldest copies have been replaced by newer ones and we are at the end of that process. But, although there are limitations, the situation in this case is not unenviable in comparison to other examples of the preservation of Islamic manuscripts, both non-Ismaili and those Ismaili texts not well represented even by modern copies.

The Present Edition of the Arabic Text

This edition is based in the first instance on the careful detailed collation of the following five manuscripts:

1. A copy from the Collection of Mulla Kurban Husain Godhrawala, now in the possession of Ismail K. Poonawala, Professor of Arabic at the University of California, Los Angeles.[45] It is dated Dhu'l-Ḥijja 1341/1923 and has been carefully executed with signs of collation. Most of the tables in it are reasonably complete. It consists of about 58 folios[46] with 16 lines per page. Variants from this manuscript appear in the apparatus marked by the letter پ (*pā'*).
2. One of two copies in the Hamdani Family Collection, now in the possession of Abbas Hamdani, Professor of Middle East history

45. I must here reiterate my gratitude to Professor Poonawala for supplying me a photocopy of this manuscript (as well as for his advice here and elsewhere).

46. Pages are not numbered but the first word of the following page is indicated at the bottom of the previous one.

at the University of Wisconsin, Milwaukee.[47] This manuscript is undated though it is likely to be from the 19th century. It is not as well done as the previous one, only some tables have been completed, and at some time the pages were bound out of order. Nevertheless, it does supply useful readings in a number of places. It contains approximately 98 folios of 11 lines per page. This copy is marked in the apparatus with the letter ه (*hāʾ*).

3. A copy from the collection of the noted Ismaili scholar Zahid Ali, now in library of The Institute of Ismaili Studies. Dated 26 Rajab 1272/1 April 1856, it is exceptionally well executed in a fine elegant hand with some annotations and with complete tables throughout.[48] It is referred to in the apparatus by the letter ز (*zāʾ*).
4. The oldest of the ten manuscript copies held by the Institute, ms. no. 130 (Ar.). It was copied in Dhu'l-Ḥijja of the year 1248/1833.[49] Despite its non-formal hand, it contains a sound version of the text and all of the tables in complete form. I have noted readings from it in the apparatus by the Arabic number ٤٨ (48).
5. A second relatively early manuscript held by the Institute, ms. no. 131 (Ar.), which dates to Jumādā II 1274/1858.[50] Though, like the previous manuscript, it was written in an informal hand, it has been checked and corrections added; the tables are also reasonably complete. In the apparatus I have noted its variants by the number ٧٤ (74).

After finishing the preparation of a preliminary edition of the text, Abbas Hamdani, at my request, kindly forwarded a photocopy of a second manuscript of the work from his family collection. That

47. Professor Hamdani deserves special thanks for providing copies of this manuscript and the second from his family collection. I have thanked him so many times for so much of his help in the past but it is necessary again in this case.

48. For a full description of this manuscript, see Delia Cortese, *Arabic Ismaili Manuscripts: The Zāhid ʿAlī Collection in the Library of The Institute of Ismaili Studies* (London, 2003), pp. 77–78.

49. It is described along with six others in Adam Gacek's *Catalogue of Arabic Manuscripts in the Library of The Institute of Ismaili Studies*, vol. 1 (London, 1984), pp. 46–47.

50. Described by Gacek in the preceding catalogue.

one carries the date Ṣafar 1275/1858. It has proven useful in regard to a number of issues. One other source of information about the text was Muṣṭafā Ghālib's 1969 Beirut edition of the work, though without access to his manuscripts, I hesitated to rely on it. Still later, however, I visited London to examine in person all ten of the manuscripts kept at the Institute. The seven among these not already considered in detail in the edition, are relatively late and of varying quality, some quite poor.[51] One, dated 1329/1911, which carries the Institute's number 982, proved to be the principal source for Muṣṭafā Ghālib's edition from 1969. It has his stamp of ownership and otherwise matches generally that printing of the text. Tables not included there, for example, are not in that manuscript.

A check for variants in these seven manuscripts tended to confirm the readings and the variations present in those already cited in the apparatus.

With all of this evidence for the text, however, several problems remain. They are for the most part due to the predilections of the copyists and various peculiarities of their work. The goal here is to ascertain the original version of al-Kirmānī and not to document the vagaries of copying. Thus in the following areas there appears to be no benefit in carefully recording variations and they have not all been entered in the apparatus.

1. The insertion of standard pious wishes and benedictions after a reference to God, to the Prophet, or to the imams. Many are given only in abbreviated form and their use varies considerably from manuscript to manuscript, indicating in all likelihood that they represent the inclination of the copyist and not necessarily that of the author. Some, however, surely do, those that are not common, for example. And the original likely expressed them generally where the author felt them appropriate. Thus, while

51. They are numbers C549 (dated 1310), D 2644 (dated 1314), E 265 (dated 1328) and F 266 (mid-14th century) from Gacek's *Catalogue of Arabic Manuscripts*, vol. 1 (London, 1984), and numbers 57/982 (dated 1329), 58/907 (date 1336) and 59/980 (dated 1356) from Cortese's *Ismaili and Other Arabic Manuscripts: A Descriptive Catalogue of Manuscripts in the Library of The Institute of Ismaili Studies* (London, 2000).

some certainly belong to the original, in most cases the evidence from these modern copies offers no sure way to establish exactly which do. For the present edition I have preserved those that appear in ms. no. 130, from 1248/1833, the oldest available to me.

2. Use of the phrase *fa-iʿrifhu* (in one instance *fa-iʿlamhu*) as a concluding interjection at the end of a paragraph varies greatly, suggesting again that it may not belong to the original and is, perhaps, a sign of an oral reading of the text, possibly in dictating it to a copyist. Accordingly I have not noted all variants of its appearance but keep only those in ms. no. 130 from 1248/1833.
3. Problems of word order involved, ranged from the reversal of two terms in a list of items where the variation makes no difference in the meaning, to the more serious dropping and adding of a whole phrase. Al-Kirmānī's arguments frequently hinge on the repetition of conditional clauses: if such and such, then x follows, and given that such and such and x is the result, then y must be true. He tends to repeat the whole of each conditional and that makes the task of the inattentive copyist difficult, leading to the leaving out of a line of text here and there as the eye moves from the source to the copy and back, often alighting on the same words a line or two below. Again, noting such variations in all cases would merely prove that it happened and would not necessarily help to establish the exact words of the author.
4. The tables and the text contained therein represent a special challenge. With a few notable exceptions, most of the copyists, if they intended to include the tables, appear to have drawn the necessary grid (or diagram), hoping to return and fill in the blank spaces later. Often they did not allow sufficient space for longer entries and subsequently needed to shorten what they wrote in order to have it fit. Some entries are quite abbreviated in comparison with what appears for that same item in a more complete manuscript. Just as often a given copyist never completed the task, leaving whole tables empty. Of the thirteen manuscripts surveyed, only six have reasonably complete versions of all of the tables. Only two of them—not including the manuscript in the Zāhid ʿAlī collection, which is otherwise the most carefully produced among them—have the final two tables correctly located at the end of

the fifth and seventh demonstrations respectively of the seventh chapter.[52]

One extra problem is that several of the tables depend on the alignment of vertical columns and horizontal rows, the meaning of the next succeeding space follows that of the one before. Thus for the virtues (or lack thereof) for ʿUmar, the author simply put the words *tilka sabīluhu* ('it was the same with him') which refers to the entry immediately above for Abū Bakr. There, for example, it says of Abū Bakr that he was not chaste because of having drunk wine in the period of Jāhiliyya. We must therefore understand that the same was true of ʿUmār. However, as the copyist continues the table for the other Companions, these entries become blank spaces, which now presumably indicate the lack of that virtue in the person. In a poorly drawn table the alignment tends to break down for the rows and columns in the middle, leaving us with great difficulty in determining which virtues belong or do not belong to which of the Companions. The listings for Salmān, Abū Dharr, Miqdād and ʿAbdallāh b. ʿAbbās, for example, are quite uncertain for this reason.

Because of these problems in determining the exact wording of the text and also the difficulty of reproducing an acceptable version of the tables either in the Arabic edition or in the English translation, I have opted to illustrate them here by including examples from the best of the manuscripts.

5. One casualty of the lack of space is the entry in the first table for Muḥammad's trait of having been designated by God. Commonly the copyist simply could not fit the Hebrew passage into the box he had allotted for it. But the question of what the manuscripts say about these Hebrew quotations is only further complicated by such omissions. The evidence for either the Hebrew or the Syriac is not good in any case.[53] It is quite likely that none of the copyists

52. The two mss. that have these final tables correctly at the end of 7.5 and 7.7 respectively are IIS mss. nos. 549 and 907. Additional copies in Bombay are reported likewise to have these tables where they belong.

53. This is also true of the Arabic translation in some cases. For example, in ms. 74, even the Arabic of that passage in the table of the Prophet's virtues is quite garbled and incomplete.

knew either language. They simply tried to put down a facsimile of what they saw in their source, not knowing any more about it except that it came from the Torah or, in the latter case, from the Gospels. Whether or not the manuscripts can reliably offer evidence to establish with any accuracy the wording of either the Hebrew or the Syriac is doubtful.[54] I have therefore opted to follow Kraus's reconstruction of both, which in any case adheres to the standard Biblical text where possible, even though we cannot be certain that that is exactly what al-Kirmānī knew and tried to represent in Arabic characters. His translation, as noted earlier, does not match that given by other Muslim writers, even in the case of al-Qāḍī al-Nuʿmān and Abū Ḥātim al-Rāzī,[55] his own Ismaili predecessors. The quotation from Syriac, moreover, does not reflect any single instance of several in the Gospel of John that mention the Paraclete and must, therefore, be some conflation of parts of two of them. Kraus, accordingly, artificially combined the Syriac phrases that might match al-Kirmānī's translation, although there is no such passage in John exactly like it. For the words of Deuteronomy there is a similar problem. That passage as it appears in the manuscript tradition leaves out the reference to God's right hand holding a fire and follows with an uncertain phrase *shibh lahum* (*shubbiha lahum*?). Al-Qāḍī al-Nuʿmān says here,[56] *fī yamīnihi nārun, hiya sharīʿatun lahu* ('in his right hand a fire which is his law'). Surely al-Kirmānī intended something quite similar, the phrase 'in his right hand' having dropped out

54. However, some of the mss. come much closer than others. Even so it is fair to ask if modern scholars could have identified these passages if al-Kirmānī had not indicated what they were supposed to be through his Arabic translation of them. Daniel De Smet and J. Van Reeth have announced a forthcoming study of all the Hebrew and Syriac quotations that appear in various works of al-Kirmānī; other scholars have indicated similar research into the use of such material by other Ismaili writers. They may be able to answer this question as well as determine more precisely the most likely version of al-Kirmānī's Hebrew and Syriac.

55. Specifically for al-Rāzī in his *al-Aʿlām al-nubuwwa*, ed. Ṣalāḥ al-Ṣāwī and G. R. Aʿwānī (Tehran 1977), pp. 195–197.

56. *Asās al-taʾwīl*, ed. Tāmir, pp. 320–321, with corrections based on mss. of the same work held by The Institute of Ismaili Studies.

in the process of transmission of the text, and the words *sharīʿa lahu* having been misread as *shibh lahum* (*shubbiha lahum*). Still, all the manuscripts that have the passage agree on the latter reading. Is the mistake therefore that of the copyist or of al-Kirmānī himself?

A Note on the Title

At the beginning of the treatise al-Kirmānī explains the word *maṣābīḥ* in his title as, in the first instance, a reference to the Qurʾānic passage 'And We have adorned the earthly sky with lights (*maṣābīḥ*) and made them things to throw at satans' (67: 5), a concept of the term clearly related to another passage, which is partially identical, Qurʾān 41: 12, 'And We adorned the earthly sky with lights . . .'. Al-Kirmānī says the proofs he will offer to establish the necessity of the imamate 'resemble the lights that are "like the things to throw at satans"' (*ka'l-rujūm li'l-shayāṭīn*). But exactly what that phrase means is not clear, either in the Qurʾān or for al-Kirmānī's treatise. Even so his introduction also contains two important instances of the term *maṣābīḥ* both of which refer to the imams, one at the end of the very first paragraph invoking God's 'saints who are lights in the darkness', and the other a paragraph further on where he speaks of 'the imams of guidance' who are again 'the lights in the darkness'.

Ḥamīd al-Dīn Aḥmad b. ʿAbd Allāh al-Kirmānī

al-Maṣābīḥ fī ithbāt al-imāma

Praise God who originated existence and what it includes, and created eternity and what it excludes. Gleaming flashes of sacred light in the essences of minds that approve testify that, in the absence of both existence and non-existence, He existed; and everlasting [heavenly] influences on pure souls declare that, without a thing having come into being or already existing, He existed. The unfolding of both the existent and the eternal depends on Him, as with the first to come into being at the very beginning whom the ignorant take as an object of worship and associate with God, supposing that it makes Him absolutely one if there is no other god but Him. Nor are there innovated beings in any other way that He has not fashioned. But, by virtue of His having innovated all that, He is powerful beyond any comparison, immeasurable, surpassing all limitation in the greatest of His achievement, exalted high indeed above what the iniquitous say. I praise Him with those glorious names of His that have been indicated to us and I worship Him on account of His saints, who are the lights in the darkness. I furthermore testify that, among what falls under innovation or is confined by the characteristic of existence and creation, there is no god but He, a God hallowed above attributes, too glorious for depictions, too powerful to be characterized, transcending any and all description.

I further affirm that Muḥammad is His servant and apostle, who was chosen, selected, and favoured by Him. God thus inspired him with the elements of blessings that sanctify and extended to him the emanation of spiritual felicity. Muḥammad then instituted the holy law and decreed its rules, spreading wisdom, revealing wonders, bringing tranquility by the hoisting of flags, and admonishing the community to follow the imam, upon whom may there be God's blessings, a blessing ever increasing with the succession of night upon day and the day upon the night. And may the most excellent benediction and salutations fall upon the righteous members of his family, the imams of guidance, the lights in the darkness through whom God illuminates the black courtyards of the night, and repels the false representations of devils.

Now then: I observed that the Lord of the Mighty and the Ornament of the leading and honourable ministers, Commander of the noble armies, Fakhr al-Mulk,[1] the wazir of all wazirs—may God prolong his life—had been endowed by God with particular intelligence and understanding, granted knowledge and perception, crowned with the nobility of prophetic guardianship, made infallible through 'Alid[2] infallibility, and had professed devotion through the love of the pure family—the family of Ṭāhā and Yaṣīn. But I imagined further that one of the satans who intimate in the hearts of the people, one of those abominable devils, had assumed a lofty station in his council and reported to him some notions that produced in him an obstacle to the way of God, [creating in him] an insolence toward God, a breaking-away from obedience to God, and a denial of God's signs. And, in addition, nobody in his service cares to make known what he has attained of the substance of the blessings emanating from the Saints of Felicity, the Lords of the Community, those to whom God enjoins obedience—may God keep them, past and present—and, in particular, the one of them ruling among us, the Guardian. Deep concern for the faith and the truth of fully convinced devotion, a judgment regarding what, in the matter of God, I ascribe to as being true belief, and the determination of what *jihād* God has imposed on me in order to follow His way, has provoked me to establish firmly

---

1. Wazir and governor of Baghdad from 401/1011 to 407/1016, first on behalf of the Buyid ruler Bahā' al-Dawla and then the latter's son Sulṭān al-Dawla. His full name was Abū Ghālib Muḥammad b. 'Alī b. Khalaf. Born 354/965, he was executed by the Buyid amir on the 27th of Rabī' I, 407/3rd September 1016. On him and his son Abū Shujā' al-Ashraf, who much later twice served as wazir to the Fatimid caliph al-Mustanṣir, see 'Ibn Khalaf' by Abdel Hamid Saleh in the *EI2 Supplement*, as well as Walker, *Ḥamīd al-Dīn al-Kirmānī*, pp. 11–14.

2. Meaning of or pertaining to the family of 'Alī, hence the imams.

the necessity of the imamate, and to demonstrate truthfully its being located among the imams—may God grant them benediction and peace—in the family of Ṭāhā and Yaṣīn, and most especially the correctness of the imamate of the one among them who occupies it in our own time, our master, the Commander of the Faithful, the Servant of God and His friend, al-Manṣūr Abū ʿAlī al-Ḥākim bi-amr Allāh—may God keep him and all the imams. The obligation to obey and adhere to him is a consequence of the slight measure of their radiance that has been communicated to me. Accordingly, I will produce brilliant proofs for it that defy refutation, based on evidence that withstands subversion. All this I now put into a book in order to make him [Fakhr al-Mulk] understand and apprehend through it the correctness of that most noble doctrine and belief, so that there be conceived in him an inclination in favour of the people of obedience to the extent that the bounty of God provides them support. I have done exactly that and called it the *Book of Lights to Illuminate the Proof of the Imamate*—the imamate that belongs to the Master of the Age, on whom be peace. The proofs in it resemble the lights that are like 'the things to throw at satans'.[3] I have arranged it in two parts, one of them proving the premises required for the proof of the imamate, and the second on the imamate itself. I seek the aid of God and His guardian, upon whom be peace, in order to complete this task, and I hope to derive support from Him and from the goodness of His guardian's favour. I ask of Him immunity from error, and success so as to relate things exactly as they have come to me from the Saints of Blessing, on whom be peace.

The two parts incorporate fourteen individual 'Lights', comprising in all a hundred and five separate demonstrations.

3. The reference here is to Qur'ān 67: 5 which reads 'We have adorned the earthly sky with lights and made them things to throw (*rujūm*) at satans'. The exact meaning of the phrase *rujūman lil-shayāṭīn* is not clear and it has been translated variously as 'missiles (projectiles, shooting stars) against (or to drive away) the devils', 'things to stone satans'.

The First Part: In Proof of the Premises, comprising Seven 'Lights'

The First Light:[4] The introduction to the book with an explanation as to the reason that calls for setting out the premises at the beginning and how they are to be ordered, all in a single proof.

The Second Light: In proof of the Maker, comprising seven demonstrations.

The Third Light: In proof of the soul and that it is an everlasting, living substance without knowledge at the beginning of its existence, comprising ten demonstrations.

The Fourth Light: In proof of the form of the divine regime, which is the recompense, and that its abode is not this world, comprising ten demonstrations.

The Fifth Light: In proof of the necessity of the laws and regulations, which consist of actions, comprising seven demonstrations.

The Sixth Light: In proof of the necessity of interpretation, which consists of knowledge, comprising seven demonstrations.

The Seventh Light: In proof of the prophetic office and its necessity.

The Second Part: In Proof of the Imamate and its Necessity, comprising Seven 'Lights'

The First Light: In proof of the imamate and its necessity, comprising fourteen demonstrations.

The Second Light: In proof of the necessity of the imam's infallibility, comprising seven demonstrations.

The Third Light: In proof that it is not valid for the community to elect the imam, comprising seven demonstrations.

The Fourth Light: In proof that the true imamate exists by the designation of God, the Most High, and by the choice of the Apostle, comprising seven demonstrations.

The Fifth Light: That, following the Prophet, may God bless him and his family, the imamate went to the Commander of the Faithful, 'Alī

4. It should be noted that the wording of several chapter titles listed here do not match exactly the titles that appear at the head of these chapters later in the text.

b. Abī Ṭālib, rather than anyone else, comprising seven demonstrations.

The Sixth Light: That, after the designation had progressed to Jaʿfar b. Muḥammad al-Ṣādiq, on whom be peace, the imamate went to Ismāʿīl and to his progeny, on whom be peace, to the exclusion of his brothers, comprising seven demonstrations.

The Seventh Light: In proof of the necessity of the imamate of the Master of the Age, the Imam al-Ḥākim bi-amr Allāh, Commander of the Faithful, may God keep him, and that obedience to him is incumbent on any and all factions, comprising seven demonstrations.

Here then is the start of the First Part.

PART ONE

The Proof of the Premises

The First Light

The introduction to the book with an explanation as to the reason that calls for setting out the premises at the beginning and ordering them as done here, all in a single proof.

The first demonstration: We note that all things have foundations to which they revert for their affirmation, causes that precede them which validate their essences, and principles to which one can refer in confirming them. When such principles are out of order and those causes undetermined or the foundations not well established, a statement about things derived therefrom will be incomprehensible and unintelligible. Because the principles behind it are dubious, someone hearing of it will quickly turn aside and reject it. But, if the foundations are well established and the causes soundly determined, what derives from it is a necessary consequence of it, from which there is no escape. An example is fire which is the cause of burning and heating. When it is present, that it burns and heats follows as a necessary consequence that cannot be disputed. [Another example is] a lantern which is the cause for light in darkness. When it is present, that light is an undeniable consequence of it. Or it is like the recompense which, if proven to exist, working [for it] is an obligatory consequence of that fact. The imamate of the imam and his caliphate have validity on the basis of the validity of the Messenger's existence and his message, and yet also the impossibility of his permanent existence. There is no message of the Messenger unless the sender of the message and those to whom the message is sent both validly exist and, despite having the capacity to receive the message and act in accord with it, the recipient of it is unable actually to link up with the sender. The necessity of recompense for acts of obedience and disobedience is due to the impossibility that this deputy appoint, as a deputy, a deputy who is also permanent, and the coincident unacceptability of assuming him to be in occultation. It is likewise impossible that the sender's sending a messenger is required if there is no one to whom he is sent, or that the one sent to is not able and has neither the capability nor the capacity to accept the message and act in accord with it, or that the one sent to might find a way to the sender without an intermediary, or that the falsity of the recompense is based on the message's acceptance by the one it is sent to and his either obeying it or rejecting it. Every one of these stipulations verify the message which is itself the reason for the imamate. Each of these stipulations is a cause for something else and is connected with that other thing. Each is thus like a foundation that, in order to provide us a means to our ultimate goal, requires us, as a starting point, to speak about it first.

Given that our aim is to confirm the imamate and prove its validity, it behoves us to put in first position the argument that proves the Maker, who is the Sender, on whose existence depends the existence of all and without whom there would be no such thing as existence.

Next is proof of the souls in humans because, in requiring the message in the first place, something must exist to which it is sent, and it has to be a noble, living, capable substance, not knowledgeable in the beginning of its existence but receptive to the effects of knowledge and choice, and imperishable following the extinction of its individual [bodily] identity.

Next is proof of the form of the divine regime, which is the recompense, because given that the souls are free and able to do either good or evil, wisdom requires a way to distinguish master from servant.

Next is proof of the laws and of the required acts because, in order for the souls to deserve the recompense, the essential features of noble actions must be set out in such a way that they conform with the world of Soul. Next is proof of the interpretation which is knowledge. Souls need a way to learn about their reward, their punishment and their eternal return, by means of what they can see and perceive through the senses. They thus come to understand, thereby, the rule and import of what comes to them from their Creator. It is a message that conveys the essential features of these actions but in the form of sensate indications of something they cannot see in actuality.

Next is proof of the prophetic office, which is the last of the preliminaries. Wisdom requires the coming into existence of essential features of those actions, the performing of which makes the recompense deserved. Due to the impossibility of the souls coming to understand the eternal return in any other way, the creation of representations of them is a necessary consequence of that fact. Were the setting up of such a medium not obligatory for that purpose because God the Highest cannot be seen, there would be no need for the messenger who fashions those representations, prescribes those actions and serves as the medium.

Subsequently, we move on to the discourse about the imamate which is the goal of this book. Given the impossibility of the messenger remaining forever in this world, the imamate is required so that, in totality, it all becomes a chain, some parts of which are linked to others. That we have done and thus made the lights that illuminate a combination of what is specific to each as needed. And God is the One who directs to what is right.

The Second Light

In proof of the Maker.

The first demonstration: We say that the method of knowing what one wants to understand has three avenues: from sensation in accord with the subdivisions of it, which are hearing, sight, smell, taste and feel, and which apply primarily to the understanding of the essences of things. Or it comes from intellect in conformity with what its provisions and its subdivisions dictate through the medium of sensation. Or it derives from demonstration and deduction that arise out of a combination of sensation and intellection. Because the Maker has no quality that renders Him perceptible to sensation, nor does He have a trait that allows Him to be apprehended by the intellect, the way to prove Him follows the setting up of demonstrations consisting of both sensation and intellection as applied to the product of His making, which is itself 'the greatest evidence' [Qurʾān 6: 19]. That being so, we should desire to explain the world and to establish that it has come into being; its having come into being requires that which brought it into being, a Maker, in the same way that someone who has been beaten, if evidence of that fact is to be taken, requires for it both a beating and someone who administered the beating (the beater). We maintain that the cause of a thing having existence is not in that thing in and of itself.[5] We see clearly, for example, that the cause that makes a millstone move is not the millstone. The cause for the motion in an individual living being is not the individual in and of itself since, if its mere being in and of itself were what caused its motion, it would always be in motion by and of its essential being. And, in that case, this would not be a cause [acting on it] but rather the thing in and of itself. However, since we see that it itself remains after having been in motion but not then in motion, it is true that the cause for the existence of something is not its own essential self. And, if it is true that the cause for the existence of something is not its own self, and that the world with all that it contains constitutes a single thing in the sense that, in so far as it is bodily, it is one thing, and that portions of it are in motion and portions at rest, it follows necessarily that the motion of what is in motion and the being-at-rest of what is at rest are not due to its own essential self. If it were due to its own essence, the parts would all be in motion or all at rest. Given that the essential selves are one essence only, and having established that the motion of the thing in motion and the rest of the thing at rest are not due to its own essence, it follows necessarily that there is a mover or quieter who maintains the order of the whole and its regulation, and that that is other than it. The mover and quieter is the maker and, therefore, the Maker is proven.

The second demonstration: The world in its entirety is a body that has various parts and components, limited in number and of different shapes and forms. We observe, for example, that the form of the spheres and planets, which are components of the world, are other than the form of water or the form of fire, and their shape is not the form of earth or air. The form of the individual members of the

5. Al-Kirmānī reports in his treatise entitled *al-Muḍī'a* (p. 53) that he had already explained in the Second Light of the book *al-Maṣābīḥ* that the cause of a thing is other than that thing.

kingdoms [animal, vegetable and mineral] is not the form of air or of the spheres. All of them have forms that differ in a consistent order. Some are linked in association with others, as in the case of a gate that consists entirely of wood yet it also has parts and various components, and the form of certain of its parts, such as the boards, differ with respect to form from other parts, such as the posts or something else. All of it differs in forms that are nevertheless linked together and the parts mutually interrelated in a consistent manner. It is well known that each thing that shares with another thing has itself that [shared] aspect, even though each one of them is particular in other respects to those of similar kind and shape. Since we find an aspect that separates the parts, and yet an ordering that is common to the world and the gate, and that the parts of the gate would not have been joined together were it not for the agency of an agent, the world itself, in that its parts would not be combined other than by the agency of an agent, is like the gate. Thus, the world has been made and brought into existence, and what has been brought into existence requires what brought it into existence, namely a maker. The Maker is thus proven.

The third demonstration: Of what is visible, the realm of languages with its various kinds, such as Arabic, Persian, Hebrew, Syriac, Nabatean, Greek, Zanjī,[6] Turkish and others, are composed of known and limited parts, as, for example, the simple letters, which are *alif*, *bā'*, *tā'*, *thā'*, by means of which an expression in speech can be formed for what exists in the soul as forms of things sensed and intellected. These letters do not compose themselves but rather are composed by a composer who arranges them such to have one precede and another follow. An example is our saying the word 'silver' (*fiḍḍa*). Having the letter *fā'* precede the *ḍād*, although it, in the original order of the letters [i.e. in the alphabetic order], follows the *ḍād*, happens because someone puts it forward or moves the other backward. The world is a realm of body that is similar to the realm of language and of speech in that its parts are determined, yet differ in and of themselves and have different forms. From this fact comes the knowledge that the arranging of its

6. Zanjī is presumably the language spoken by the black inhabitants of the Indian Ocean littoral of Africa. See 'Al-Zandj' by G. S. P. Freeman-Grenville in *EI2*.

parts in a composition—since we know that it does not have the capacity to move and is neither living nor knowing—cannot be assumed to have been the result of a composing of themselves by themselves, nor have components of it combined with other components on their own. Were that possible, even though its parts, which have remained themselves mutually distinct and incongruous, have been arranged in a composition, [it] cannot have happened without the agency of an agent and the combining of a combiner. If its being composed cannot happen without the agency of an agent and the agent is the maker, the Maker is proven.

The fourth demonstration: A characteristic of what does not transform from what its elements are, or change, and is not susceptible to an action, is that it is not an effect, and the characteristic of what is susceptible to an action on the basis of which it undergoes transformation from one state into another and changes overtake it, is that it is an effect. The world in its spheres, stars and kingdoms does not appear in a single state but such that its planets are eternally rising or setting, or such that it is always either day or night, or that what exists in the natural kingdoms could remain forever in its present condition. The transformation from the state of coming to be, rising and daylight into a state of corruption, setting and night-time exist in it. For that reason, we know that it is the kind of thing that is receptive to an act that transforms and changes it. If it is of the sort that submits to such an act, it is an effect. If it is an effect, that requires an agent and the agent is the maker. Thus the Maker is proven.

The fifth demonstration: Given that the world is an object of sensation and perception, everything in it is subject to its five divisions: namely, something seen—that is, perceived by sight; heard—that is, perceived by hearing; smelled—that is, perceived by smell; tasted—that is, perceived by taste; or felt—that is, perceived by feel. Were the world with such divisions as these properly classed as eternal, that which perceives it, namely its perceiver is more certainly eternal, since one of the dictates of reason is that what perceives is more sublime than what it perceives, and that what contains is greater than what it contains. The power by which it perceives the world, which are the five sensations, has come into being. Accordingly, the world, which is perceived, has with even greater certainty come into being. If the world has come into being and what has come into being requires that which brings it into being, and that is the maker, the Maker is thereby proven.

The sixth demonstration: Since a thing cannot perceive except what is of its own elements and it cannot perceive what is more exalted than it but only what is lower, and [since] what has come into being is not of the same sort as the eternal nor is it more exalted, from that we judge that the world, if it were eternal, would be imperceptible and not the object of sensing by the senses that have come into being.

Because it is perceptible and an object of sensation—it is felt, seen and tasted—by senses that have come into being, it is an effect the senses have caused through their perception of it. Because there is no other physical world, for that reason we know that it has also come into being. What has come into being requires that which brings it into being. Thus, there is a maker of the world and the Maker is thus proven.

The seventh demonstration: Given that the world has parts and components and that each component is particular to an aspect that does not exist in another component—such as brightness, fineness, heaviness, transparency, lightness, darkness—if the world were eternal, the Maker would not have precedence over His product and its rank in the way that He does. That would mean that the sun's body having the particular distinction of shining is not more certain for it than for the body of the earth, nor would the special feature of water be that it is moist and flowing any more than fire, nor the particularity of air be that it is light any more than earth, nor the particularity of earth be that it is dense and heavy any more than air and fire. Because these particularities are present in its components, it follows necessarily that there is a cause that makes such a particularity in one category but which is also non-existent in another. And the result of such a cause is that it requires that it have an agent to bring it about. If there were not an agent and its causing the particularity by which each component is particular, with the non-existence of the agent, the particularity of each thing to its category rather than to another would not be necessary. Then the components altogether would be one thing only, dense or light, radiant or dark. Thus, the world has a maker and the Maker is proven.

The Third Light

In proof of the soul[7] and that it is a living substance with capability, despite not having knowledge at the commencement of its existence, though everlasting following the corruption of the physical body by means of which it acquires knowledge and acts.

The first demonstration: Given that the motion of every movable thing comes to it either from inside or from outside, and that for which the motion is external is either drawn into it by some draw or pushed away from it by a push, and since it is false that the motion [or animation[8]] of the human person takes place by pull or push, it is established that its motion is internal to it. That to which the motion comes from inside is either its by nature or due to a voluntary mover. For that for which the motion is its by nature, it does not rest at all, as in the motion of fire. For that for which the motion comes from a voluntary mover, it is at times in motion and at times at rest. Because it is untrue that the motion [or animation] of the person is natural and never at rest, it is established that its motion derives from a voluntary mover. That voluntary mover we call the soul and hence the soul is proven.

---

7. Al-Kirmānī refers to this chapter in at least three of his other works. In his *Kitāb al-riyāḍ* (p. 138), in asserting that soul is not body nor mixed in body and is not apprehended by the senses as if it were subject to the nine accidents, he comments, 'and our book known as *al-Maṣābīḥ fī'l-imāma* contains enough on that score'. In his *al-Aqwāl al-dhahabiyya* (p. 94) he says, 'The moving other for its body is what we call soul, as we have made clear in our book called *al-Maṣābīḥ* and the book *Rāḥat al-ʿaql*'. He also cites it in the *Rāḥat al-ʿaql* (Cairo edition, p. 300): as for the 'indication of the existence of the soul … we have explained that sufficiently in our treatise called *al-Maṣābīḥ fī ithbāt al-imāma*'. As well this general subject may have formed a major part of his now lost *Naqd wa'l-ilzām* which was his refutation of the famous Muʿtazilī theologian ʿAbd al-Jabbār; see Walker, *Ḥamīd al-Dīn al-Kirmānī*, p. 36.

8. To understand al-Kirmānī's arguments about motion (the Arabic word is *ḥaraka*) in this section, it helps to think of it as 'animation', that is, having been made alive and thus moving. Humans as living beings are animated, that is, they have movement. The author, following Aristotle, says that what animates the individual is its soul and that such soul possesses will. It causes both the movement and the resting of the body in which it is.

The second demonstration: The human person has power, anger and resents things, as, for example, what is done to a corpse, such as washing, embalming, shrouding and blocking its orifices, and yet, in the dead state, it does not get angry or refuse when those things are done to it. Its anger and being able to refuse is denied it, yet without rendering it non-existent or eliminating any of its extremities. From that fact we know that its anger does not come from its existence, nor does its power, because if it were from its very existence, it would be, by the very essence of its existence, angry, preventive and resentful. Given that it is not from its existence, it is from something else. That something else is what we call soul. Thus, the soul is proven.

The third demonstration: The rest of anything that begins to rest comes to it either by nature or by coercion. Anything whose rest is by nature, for its being-at-rest to cease, requires the movement of a mover, such as is the case of the millstone, which, when what moves it stops, it reverts to a state of rest. What is moved by coercion does not come to rest except when restrained by a restrainer, such as is the case with the agitation of a reed in flowing water, which is not stilled except by the restraint of a restrainer. If the restraining force goes away, it resumes its movement. The rest of the human person at death is due neither to the coercion of a coercive force nor to the restraint of it by a restraining force. Therefore, it is proven that its rest is natural, and if its rest is by nature, the cessation of its rest, when it was in motion, must be due to movement imparted to it by a mover, and its rest, when it comes to rest, must be due to the mover having stopped moving it. Given that it is necessary that the cessation of its rest be due to a mover's moving it, and its coming to rest be due to the mover's ceasing to move it, it follows necessarily that, in its state of motion, it has a mover, since it would not move if that stopped. The mover is what we refer to as soul. Therefore, soul is proven.

The fourth demonstration: Any thing that is in agreement with the definition of something is identical to or the like of it. Since the definition of substance is that it accepts contraries without undergoing a transformation in its essence, and since the soul that moves the human person is receptive to contraries, such as knowledge and ignorance, bravery and cowardice, generosity and miserliness, without a transformation of its essence, and since everything that accepts contraries without undergoing a transformation in its essence is a substance, the soul is a substance. Because it is a substance, it is everlasting in and of itself. Hence, the soul is a substance that lasts forever.

The fifth demonstration: It is the nature of substance that it is a subject, and the nature of an accident that it is a predicate; substance accepts and the accident is accepted; substance is a locus and the accident is localized. The soul is something that carries, not what is carried; it receives and is not what is received; and [it is] what determines place, not what is put in place. From this fact it is necessary that it be classed in the category of substance. If it is classed in the category of substance by virtue of its being a substance and not a predicate, accepting and not what is accepted, a place and not what is put in a place, it is itself a substance. Therefore, the soul is a substance. If it is a substance, it endures eternally and will not perish.

The sixth demonstration: Knowledge is the form of a thing in accord with what it is—as to the state of its being in existence, its quality, quantity, manner and purpose—and the knower is what gives form to such understandings. Were the souls of humans, in the beginning of their active life, to refrain from learning such understandings of things one by one over the course of time, they would not rise above the beasts nor understand anything by which to distinguish themselves from the beasts. We observe this condition in children and others in their lack of knowledge of what their body brings them closest to comprehending, let alone what in their souls is distant, since the capacity they have for such perception is solely by means of a proof and guidance and of a teacher. From that we know that the soul is itself devoid of the forms of things and of the learning of them and is thus empty of the understanding of such things. If it were not empty and devoid, it would understand things and know about them by virtue of the fact that it exists. It would have no need for acquisition and education, and it would deserve a designation for erudition. In a similar way, if life were in the existence of a thing itself, it would not be without life and would deserve the term for being alive. It would not need to acquire that which brings it life because of its being already alive. If likewise it were capable and active by virtue of its very existence, which consists of motion and the activity derived from it, it would not be incapable and inactive, and would merit the term for ability and activity. It would not need to acquire that by which it becomes capable and active because of its being already capable and active. Since the soul is in its essence devoid of knowledge and is empty, it is established that it is not knowledgeable. If it is proven that it is not knowledgeable and yet that it is a repository for understandings by virtue of its being a substance, it is established that it is in need of knowledge in order to perfect itself. Therefore, the soul in the beginning of its existence lacks knowledge and is need of instruction.

The seventh demonstration: Death is the soul's ceasing to use and to move the members that together constitute the person, such as the hand, leg, eye, ear, nose, tongue and other than these that are found in the chest and bowels. The person merits the term for being alive because of the soul's use of those members. Thus, the soul, because of which the rest are alive, is more certain to be itself alive in its very essence. Hence, the soul is life. If it is life, it is everlasting and does not perish.

The eighth demonstration: The corruption of anything comes from what is opposite to it, either by virtue of being next to it or by mixing with it. Of anything that is above being next to or mixed with something, corruption cannot be imagined in it. The soul is not something with parts that have been put together so that another thing might enter it and mix with it, nor does it possess limits and dimensions in itself so that some other thing might adjoin it. Thus, the soul is not something that is next to or mixed with something else. If it is not something adjoining or mixed with something, corruption in it is unimaginable. Hence, the soul is everlasting and does not perish.

The ninth demonstration: Eternity and endless duration belong to the world of unity, and the eternity of what has eternity is extended to it by emanation from this world—that is, the world of unity. That which has extended to it the emanation of this world—namely, the world of unity—among those whose reception of it is based on knowledge and preference, its end is eternity. For those whose acceptance of that emanation is without knowledge and preference, its end is to be separated from it and [fall under] corruption. For souls that accept such emanation that comes by instruction with knowledge and preference, it is necessary that their end be one of either reward or punishment in eternity. It and the matter extended to it, which is the understanding of the world of unity, have become the same thing. If it has become the same thing, its end is eternal. Since its end is eternal, its corruption is unthinkable. Therefore, the soul is everlasting and will not perish.

The tenth demonstration: Everything comes into existence for something and it moves toward that thing. We observe this plainly in the progress of the three kingdoms, which are animals, plants and minerals, into that from which they have come into existence, which are the four mother elements.[9] The soul's coming into existence and its education from the beginning of its being lies in knowledge, which is not of the world of nature but rather of the world of the sacred, which is the realm of the eternal. The progress of the soul in accord with what it acquires of knowledge, whether bad or noble, is toward eternity. If its progress is to eternity, it is everlasting and will not perish. Hence, the soul is everlasting and will not perish. Understand that!

The Fourth Light

In proof of the form of the divine regime,[10] which is the recompense, and its existence and that its abode is not the abode of this world,[11] which is the world of nature, comprising ten demonstrations.

The first demonstration: God has made the substance of soul a living thing, capable of doing either good or evil and obeying or disobeying. Were its obeying and disobeying and doing good or evil the same thing with no difference between them, and were there no governing principle on the basis of which there was a way to distinguish the good,

9. The four *ummahāt* (mother elements) are air, fire, water and earth.

10. *Siyāsa rabbāniyya*. On the concept of *siyāsa* in this context, see Abū Ḥātim al-Rāzī, *Aʿlām al-nubuwwa*, ed. Ṣalāḥ al-Ṣāwī and G. R. Aʿwānī (Tehran, 1977), pp. 7–9; *Rāḥat al-ʿaql* (Cairo edition), index; and Walker, *Early Philosophical Shiism: The Ismaili Neoplatonism of Abū Yaʿqūb al-Sijistānī* (Cambridge, 1993), index.

11. In his *Rāḥat al-ʿaql* the author refers back to this chapter (p. 359). There in the thirteenth *mashraʿ* (pathway) of the seventh *sūr* (rampart) which has as its subject the human soul, he comments: 'We would say firstly in regard to the recompense being necessary that, in the book *al-Maṣābīḥ*, with respect to the necessity of the recompense and that its abode is not this world, we have already explained what we want here simply to reaffirm.'

obedient soul from the disobedient, wicked soul and to make manifest the commander from the commanded, the bestower of blessings from those on whom they are bestowed, the preceder from the one preceded, nor to distinguish the lord from the servant, the worshipper from what is worshipped, [then] the nobility of the creating force or the splendour of the divine would remain unmanifest—even though the soul is, in so far as it is alive, capable, knowledgeable, purposeful and able to perceive what is in the horizon of the divine world and what there is in wisdom, and from it to preserve the effects of that divinity. It is necessary for there to be maintained a form of government to which the splendour of divinity attaches and which functions as the separating distinction between lord and servant. That is the recompense and thus, the recompense is proven.

The second demonstration: The human species is legally capacitated, and falls under command and prohibition. But it does not fall on the particular individual body in isolation to perform the acts that deserve praise or condemnation, but rather the soul that employs it. Of the two, the individual body and the soul, it is more correct to ascribe the act to the soul because it uses the individual to do it. The individual personal body the soul uses in performing acts that contravene the prophetic regime are amputated as requital for such acts, as is the case in the amputation of the hand and foot for theft, or in hanging for murder. The hand is a part of the individual person but not a part of the soul. Thus, the soul most certainly is what receives the requital on its own self for what it has done in the way of good or of evil. Therefore, the recompense is proven.

The third demonstration: The justice of God, the Exalted, is perfect and what He creates by the way of the human species is distinctive over against the other species in having discrimination. The species is made up of individuals and the individuals possess souls. It is these souls that, instead of the pleasures of worldly sensations, are influenced by the pleasures of enduring spiritual intelligibles. Accordingly, they are prevented from pursuing the former by [instead] relying on obtaining these other influences on it, even though they be deferred. Those among them influenced by the pleasures of worldly sensation in place of enduring spiritual intelligibles search for it, steering away from doubting about what is deferred, and trusting the here and now. It would be to assume there is a defect in the justice of God, the Exalted, if there were no reward for those souls that migrate out of obedience to God for themselves and seek what He offers, and no punishment for the souls that embark upon the search for the worldly and shirk the command of God, the Exalted, despite His having sent messengers to warn them of the dangers in worldly vanities. But the justice of God is too sublime to suppose that there is a defect in it. For that reason it is necessary that the souls have a recompense. Hence, the recompense is necessary and is proven.

The fourth demonstration: The mercy of God, the Exalted, is perfect and God has sent messengers to keep His servants away from destructive worldly pleasures and desires. If what is better than the pleasures of worldly sensations did not exist, there would be a defect in keeping them away from these pleasures because of something that has no real connection to His mercy. The mercy of God is too exalted to suppose a defect in it. From this fact we know that, for the souls, in avoiding those pleasures of the here and now forbidden to them, and in those ordered to do so in doing what is best for them, there is a reward for avoiding the one and doing the other. Thus the reward is both necessary and proven.

The fifth demonstration: God, the Exalted, created the world of Intellect and Soul and made it an abode from which emanate the blessings of the word of God to what is lower as an emanation. It conveys to souls the munificence of the oneness of God as a present. In accepting what radiates in their essences in accord with what they acquire in the way of knowledge and deeds, the substances of souls are like mirrors being prepared and, in their being of the same kind as the world of Intellect and Soul, their movement is toward it in so far as the soul is receptive to it. The world of Intellect and Soul is an abode that emanates so that, in its [the soul's] progress, following the acquisition of knowledge and deeds, it receives the emanation of the world of Intellect and Soul. If it was radiant and good, it is received as that in which it delights and which makes it happy, such as health. If it was a depraved evil, its acceptance, by contrast, accords with what is painful for it and makes it sad, such as sickness. If it accepts, its acceptance is the recompense for previous knowledge and actions. Hence, the reward is necessary and is proven. Understand that well!

The sixth demonstration: Given that what God, the Exalted, has not originated has no form within existence as its origin, nor is there the possibility of its coming to exist, nor is its happening possible, and, given that the world of Intellect and Soul precede in the originating process the world of sensation, which is the here and now—in accord with the proof of it I presented in the book *The Comfort of Reason*[12]—it follows necessarily that the form of things in their entirety exist in the world of sensation in a manner commensurate with wisdom, and that that form is what God originates in the world of Soul. If that follows necessarily, and in the world there are existents that are the forms for regimes and for the censure of the criminal for his crime and punishment for his offence, it is established that, in the world of Soul, there is a recompense. Hence, the recompense is necessary and proven.

The seventh demonstration: Demonstrations have carefully established the truthfulness of the prophetic office of the prophets, upon whom be peace, and they, to the very last of them, informed their communities that its members would have a resurrection, an ingathering, a restoration to life, a requital and a reckoning for good and evil. The lord of the prophets and seal of them all, Muḥammad, the Chosen, may God bless him and keep him, reported the same on behalf of God in his statement: 'that He may requite those who do evil according to what they have done and those who do good with the best' [53: 31], and His words: 'thus, whosoever has done an atom's weight of good will see it and whosoever has done an atom's weight of evil shall see that' [99: 7–8], and again in His saying: 'Indeed, today I have requited them for their patience; they are the ones to triumph' [23: 111]. Accordingly, it is necessary that there be a recompense for souls and thus the recompense is both necessary and proven.

The eighth demonstration: Since justice requires that there be a recompense after having been deserved, whether for good or for evil, and, since merit applies only to deeds, it is necessary for deeds to take place prior to the recompense. If it is necessary for deeds to have occurred prior to the recompense, and given that in the here

12. His *Rāḥat al-ʿaql*.

and now the human being is responsible for deeds, from that fact we know that this world is the abode of deeds. If this world is the abode of deeds, it is not the abode of the recompense. Therefore, this world is not the abode of the recompense. Learn that well!

The ninth demonstration: Because the recompense covers previous achievements only and these achievements are the result of either deeds or thoughts, there is no means for the soul to have acquired deeds other than through the individual person and its bodily members, or to acquire thoughts and beliefs, except through instruction in the subject matter appropriate to it. The individual person and the instruction exist only in this world. From that fact we know that this world is the abode of acquisition and, if it is the abode of acquisition, it is not the abode of the recompense. Therefore, this world is not the abode of the recompense. Understand that!

The tenth demonstration: Human souls are an existing, proven essence. In their being a repository for intelligible forms, they are prepared to accept what radiates in their essence of the forms of existing things. Being a substance that receives, despite having this attribute, they are not free in the existence of their essence from one of two conditions: either they were an existing essence before the individual person, which prepared them for their activity and which was called a soul, or they did not exist as an essence before the individual person. If the existent essence was prior to the individual person and yet was called soul, it must be one of two: either it was in the world of Soul or in the world of body because of its being one of those things whose existence covers these two worlds. If it was in the world of Soul, the world of Soul possesses forms containing the comprehension of beings that had preceded and will follow, and a succession of distinct and multiple intelligible emanations. The soul's preparation for the reception requires that these comprehensions, which are the distinct forms and multiple emanations, have enlightened its essence so that it became thus a bearer of what exists in it. It is, thereby, knowing. Yet, because of its inability to recall events that have happened or that will occur, we observe that it is devoid of that capacity, even though it is able to remember forms of existing things and beings that come to it through instruction. We find it remembering and knowing only what it acquires from the teaching of a teacher. Since it is empty and needs the acquisition of learning, it is false that it existed [previously] in the world of Soul. If it was in thc world of body, its being there has one of two conditions: either it existed in and of itself or it existed through something other than itself. If it existed in and of itself, nothing that is not an everlasting substance can exist on its own, and there is no everlasting substance that has not received the word of God, the Exalted, which is the understanding of science. The word is the cause of the substantiality of substance in respect to its self-subsistence and eternity. By virtue of its being devoid of science and understanding so that it might be a substance, it is false that it has received the word of God, which constitutes the understanding of science. If it is not a substance, it is false that it exists in and of itself. If it does not exist in and of itself, this condition is precluded. If it exists through another, its existing through that other is because it is either adjoining or mixed or encompassed. But these three conditions are proven false in its not being what adjoins or is adjoined, nor what mixes or is mixed with, nor what has dimensions such as to encompass or be encompassed in its being, nor what is constituted of parts that would permit mixing, nor what has dimensions that would permit something to be next to it, nor what has action[13] so that it is confined to bodies, or is a body so that it encompasses body or that body [encompasses] it. Given the falsity of these three conditions, it is false that it is in the world of body. If its being in either one of these two worlds is false, it is established that it is an existent in of itself which is called soul. If it is proven that it is not an existent of and by itself that is called soul prior to the individual person, it is established that its existence depends on the existence of the individual that prepares it for training and acquisition. If it is proven that its existence depends on the existence of the individual, it is established that it does not acquire knowledge or deeds before that. If it does not acquire that knowledge before, it is impossible that this world be for it the abode of recompense. Hence, this world is not the abode of the recompense.

13. Reading *ʿamal* for *ʿilm*.

The Fifth Light

In proof of the law and the importance of works and their necessity, comprising seven demonstrations.

The first demonstration: God, the Exalted, created the human species and singled it out from the rest of His creation by an excellence. His justice required confirming the reward and that the deserving of the reward depends on works. Thus, it is essential that humans be the source of noble acts befitting the worship of God, the Exalted, in order that, for those acts, they merit the reward. Thus, works are proven to be necessary.

The second demonstration: Virtuous character is to souls as forms are to sensations, whether commendable or reprehensible, and the excellence of souls lies in those that are commendable, which consist of being just, merciful, controlling anger, being brave, worshipful, truthful, abstinent, pious, pure and devout, not in those that are reprehensible, which include injustice, lack of mercy, swiftness to anger, the cowardice of seeking to remain in this world, disdain for worship, lying, treachery, miserliness, committing venal sins, greed and failing to take proper note of God. In a youthful state, the souls of humans acquire moral traits that are worldly and natural, and the continuation of its habitual course causes it to acquire vile habits. These habits, which become its works, cause the consolidation of the forms of moral traits in the souls, be they commendable or reprehensible. With respect to the necessity of seeking the excellent, how impossible is the acquisition by the souls of the virtues, and its shedding what bad habits it acquired in its youthful state. But, it should be a consequence of devotions that are in themselves the acts by which the souls acquire the excellences of those moral traits that exist among humans. As a result, and in consequence thereof, souls gain the nobility of perfection because these devotions, which are its works, are essential for the training of the souls. And the works are the law with its stipulations and norms.

The third demonstration: God has decreed nothing so much as the building of the next life and the tearing down of this world, as the Messenger of God has indicated. Constructing the next life pertains to the souls of humans that devote themselves completely to acts of worship. The continuation of individual persons belonging to the human species and such devotion to acts of worship in this world depend on the prevalence of peace, refraining from the shedding of blood, and safeguarding sexual relations and property. All that in its entirety cannot happen except as in so far as it is based on regulations impressed among them in such a manner that they follow its programme and adopt its edicts. Were there no regulations, statutes and edicts, no one would have the woman that is in his own house any more than another, and the same would apply to property. No treasure would be his rather than another's. The fires of sedition would ignite with murder, the shedding of blood, the enslavement of progeny, sexual licence, and the powerful becoming the masters of the others. Because of being distracted by having to defend one's womenfolk and property, that would lead to ruin, destruction and the obstruction of the entry to houses for the worship of God. Accordingly, the path of reason requires that, in fulfilment of the wisdom of God among what He made and created in order to populate the next world, humans should have regulations and judgments that function in accord with its stipulations, in order to keep the gates of sedition shut.[14] Hence, the regulations, which are the law, and the works are necessary.

The fourth demonstration: The human species has no disposition that allows for the reception of all wisdom in one fell swoop, and yet it is impossible for the messenger of God to remain among them in order to instruct them day after day about the wisdom that God reveals to him. Nor does the person who takes over the role of the messenger and assumes his place as the provider of instruction have the ability to know it without a law to which he refers as he himself imparts wisdom. Hence, it is necessary that there be a law in the community, issued in accord with that wisdom and which serves as the source to which the person who occupies the place of the messenger

14. In his *Kitāb al-riyāḍ* (p. 190), al-Kirmānī defends the necessity of having the *sharīʿa*, the law, with a reference to this demonstration: 'We have explained in our book known as the *Lights to Illuminate the Imamate* that the most accessible reason in this case is the need of people from the start for a restraining institution to protect some from others, prevent bloodshed, and safeguard sexual relationships and property.'

refers in his own instruction. The law consists of books, ordinances, regulations and statutes. Hence, the regulations, which are the laws, are essential.

The fifth demonstration: Given that the emanation from the world of Soul falls specifically upon those who are inspired and is a spiritual thing, humans have no ability to obtain it other than from that one person whose soul is prepared for such reception and who obtains it by virtue of the nobility of his ancestry. Such wisdom and understanding as that which comes from the emanation of the sacred world and which shines in the inspired person's soul is converted into the objects of sensation and what is appropriate thereto, such as letters and edicts; humans might have no access to it. Such is the case in God's making the fineness of His work in originating abstract spiritual and pleasurable nourishment, which is too subtle to be grasped other than through objects that sensing bodies recognize. But by being set forth in this latter manner, the human being actually attains thereby those things; otherwise wisdom would seem false because of there being no way to take advantage of it. Thus, it is necessary that the emanation, which is the wisdom and understanding that reaches the souls of those among the messengers who are inspired by revelation, be a repository of regulations that are highly valued and precepts that are considered most correct, in order for humans to have a way to take advantage of them. Those regulations and precepts that come from the messengers are the laws and the scriptures. Hence, the laws are necessary.

The sixth demonstration: Every thing that exists must be either set in its actuality, as with the human being whose form exists in his rationality and action; or as it is with the source of blood whose form exists in the animal; or like the date palm whose form is in its trunk, fronds and date clusters; or like fire whose form is in its burning and heating; or is a potential as it is for sperm, which is potentially a human being; or the plants, which are potentially the blood in the animal, or the date pit, which is potentially a date palm, or the spark, which is potentially fire. What exists potentially is baser and more of this world in comparison with what exists in actuality. The elements of it achieve no nobility except by proceeding to actuality, and its proceeding to the state of actuality cannot happen without a transformation from the state it had in being potential. The transformation, by means of which it departs [from] the condition of its being potential, happens only because of the actual. The souls of humans exist as potentially knowing, understanding, rational, discriminating, and other than these that are there potentially, not actually, in accord with what is present in their condition as youngsters and children. From that we know that the souls, which do not have nobility, have not themselves proceeded to actuality. But, for what has in its potentiality the possibility of nobility upon becoming actual, to leave it as it was in its state of potentiality is not wise. Rather, making it proceed to actuality through action is the wise course. Thus, it is essential, with respect to the obligation of the wise course, for the All-wise to cause it to proceed to actuality through action. That action is work and the best of works are those that perform the worship of God, the Exalted. Thus, works are the sanctioned rules of the prophets and they are the exercises of the soul. Its proceeding to the state of actuality is necessary.

The seventh demonstration: Of that which it cannot see or sense, all that the soul does not have an example of that it can sense by means of sensation, it cannot perceive. An example is the order of the celestial spheres and their composition, about which there is no way for the soul to form a picture, except on the basis of geometrical models that are visible and which are thus representations of it in sensual form. The abode of the afterlife, which is the world of Soul, is not subject to the senses nor is it seen. It is the abode of the eternal return, and humans are summoned to it and spoken to about it. Thus, because humans are charged with the pursuit of it and understanding it, it is necessary for there to be representations of it that summon them to it, yet which can be sensed so they can comprehend it. This is as if understanding the configuration of the celestial spheres and their order were an obligation and as if humans were called upon to have a picture of it. Given the impossibility of their understanding it other than by means of visible, geometrical models, representations of it that are such geometrical models must exist among all of them. These representations are the laws and its positive regulations. Thus, the regulations and the laws, which are these representations to the soul in sensate form, are necessary for the world of Soul.

The Sixth Light

In proof of the interpretation[15] *of the revelation and the law that comes from the messengers, which is knowledge, comprising seven demonstrations.*

The first demonstration: Intellects and souls have no way to comprehend the Return or what is absent from the senses except through sensed representations that the messengers depict for them and by means of their decrees and instruction. The lord of the prophets and their seal, Muḥammad, the Chosen, put to use sensed representations which are extremely wise. Hence, it is necessary that this wisdom have a sure place in the horizon so that it is accepted, and that its stipulations be appropriate so that they are adhered to and its lights so fecund they cannot be cast off. However, what Muḥammad brought as the Qur'ān and the law differs in its exterior from the judgments of reason. An example is the statement of God: 'And when your Lord asked the tribe of Adam from those of their loins, their descendants, to have them testify concerning themselves, "Am I not your Lord?" they said, "yes"' [7: 172]. It is absurd to bring forth the progeny as if they were atoms, as put forth in the commentaries by those who adhere to the obvious meaning, and to ask them to confirm that God is their Lord despite what exists in the wisdom of God about not accepting the statement of the young, let alone little children, or the statement of little children, let alone atoms, because they are not under the obligation of the law nor under oath. It is also like the statement of the Prophet: 'Between my grave and my *minbar* is one of the gardens of paradise.' The absurdity of this statement, along with the place obviously lacking what is described in it as a garden, requires, in that the Messenger is a wise man to whom the attribute of ignorance is foreign, that it has a meaning that rational minds would accept and agree to, and on the basis of which the revelation's being true and comprised of wisdom is valid. Those meanings are what we

15. In his *al-Risāla al-waḍī'a fī ma'ālim al-dīn* (f. 47b = p. 82 of the edition), al-Kirmānī reports: 'We note that our statement given earlier concerning the necessity of interpretation (*ta'wīl*) in our book known as *al-Maṣābīḥ fī'l-imāma* and in our treatise *al-Kāfiya* is quite sufficient in regard to this subject.'

call interpretation, the inner sense, the explanation and the elucidation. Hence, the interpretation is necessary.

The second demonstration: We hold that the Prophet summoned to God by means of wisdom, just as he was commanded to do in God's statement: 'Summon to the way of your Lord with wisdom and fine preaching' [16: 125]. Anyone who imagines other than this on the part of the Messenger is a heretic. Because it is impermissible to suppose anything other than that; and yet one finds in the outward sense that the Prophet summoned to God and to the worship of Him by certain acts that, if a man were not to perform them in the place he was commanded to do, it would be said that he is mad, playing the jester, or forgetful. The actions of the pilgrimage and its wondrous rites are an example. The external features of these acts, such as addressing the stone, running on the tips of the feet, which is to advance in haste, holding off trimming the nails, cutting the hair of the head and the throwing of pebbles, are not associated with wisdom. Thus, for the Prophet to be summoning by means of wisdom, requires that that to which he summons by these actions has a meaning that is consistent with wisdom and by the understanding of which rational minds are shown what in them is for its salvation and which of them impregnate it with the light of sanctity. These meanings we call interpretation, inner sense, elucidation, significance and explanation. Therefore, the interpretation is necessary.

The third demonstration: In the justice of God, no one is punished for the crime of someone else. He has said: 'No one bears the burden of another', [6: 164]. Yet it is a prescription of the Messenger and of his law to punish the uncle for the crime of his nephew if he kills in error. That is contrary to the justice of God and what He ordered. But it is unthinkable for the Messenger to do what is contrary to His justice and mercy, or that he ordered what would contravene the command of God. Hence, it is necessary that, that and what is like it, have a meaning and a wisdom which, with regard to rational minds, brings it into conformity with the justice of God and His mercy. Those meanings which, with regard to rational minds brings it into conformity with the justice of God and His mercy, are the interpretation that we call the inner sense, the elucidation and the explanation. Therefore, the interpretation is essential.

The fourth demonstration: Those humans that are wise and intelligent appreciate the absurdity of addressing an order to the dead who lack life, have no reward or punishment, no instrument for accepting the commandment to do good and avoid evil, or to respond, let alone to He who is Most High and hallowed, the Lord of the heavens and the earth. Yet the Messenger related of God that He spoke to the heaven and the earth in His statement: 'Then He lifted Himself up to the celestial heaven when it was smoke; He said to it and to the earth, "Come willingly or unwillingly". They replied, "We come willingly"' [41: 11]. God is All-knowing and All-wise, and the heaven and the earth are inanimate, lacking a mind and having no tool for speech. Hence, in view of the absurdity of any wise person addressing the inanimate, it is necessary that there is, to His commanding the heavens and the earth and their answering Him, a meaning that makes the statement of God true and which is rationally acceptable as wisdom. That meaning is what we call the interpretation. Hence, the interpretation is necessary.

The fifth demonstration: God has said: 'When He was causing slumber to overcome you as a security from Him and He sent down to you from the skies water with which to purify you, to carry away from you the defilement of satan, and to strengthen your hearts and firm up your footsteps...' [8: 11]. It is known that the defilement of satan is unbelief, doubt, uncertainty, hypocrisy, ignorance and error and whatever else occurs in the heart, minds and spirits that functions as these do. Given that the defilement of satan is in hearts and minds, it cannot be supposed that water, which comes down from the sky and is felt and drunk, can purify them, because it is impossible that the matter is like this. And if the water that is mentioned here is natural water, everyone becomes pure, both the believer and the unbeliever. Hence, it is necessary that for this water there is a meaning which, if not for it, an absurdity would have come from God in His saying something that is contrary to it. That meaning we call an interpretation, an explanation, elucidation and an inner sense. Therefore, the interpretation for that and what is like it is necessary.

The sixth demonstration: God made the interpretation of what the Messenger brought obligatory by His saying: 'He it is who revealed to you the Book; of it parts are firmly fixed and they are the mother of the book, but others are ambiguous; those in whose hearts there is deviousness follow what is ambiguous, hoping thereby to spread sedition and the desire for its interpretation, but no one knows its interpretation except God and those firmly grounded in knowledge who say, "We believe in it, all is from our Lord", yet none remember except those with minds' [3: 7]. The protest of those who protest is to say that the interpretation is known only to God and that 'those who are firmly grounded in knowledge' is a subject and not predicated of what went before in the statement as a whole. That is false due to the existence of what invalidates their objection in the speech of the Arabs when being brief and concise, as in saying to someone else: 'No one will salute you except so-and-so who will excuse himself; no one knows medicine except so-and-so who argues about it; no one knows grammar except so-and-so who is absorbed in it; no one will come to you except so-and-so who will be riding.' The meaning is that each of the two will offer salutations and one of them will excuse himself; each of them knows medicine but one of the two argues about it; each of them knows grammar and one of the two is absorbed in it; each of them will come and one will be riding. Hence, it is essential that the interpretation be obligatory and that those firmly grounded in knowledge know it. Therefore, the interpretation is essential.

The seventh demonstration: There is no way to comprehend what is unseen and not subject to sensation other than by means of an expression for it, that is, something that can be seen and sensed. The Messenger reported about what cannot be seen or sensed, such as God, paradise and its felicity, hell and its torments. From this fact it follows that, in his reporting and his expression of what he reported about, he gave an account of what cannot be seen and sensed using what can be seen and sensed. Thus, for example, he reported about paradise, which is the abode of the afterlife and which is neither seen nor subject to sensation, by referring to gardens and streams and trees and fruit and flowing water, and in regard to the manner of being of those in it, [he referred to them] as newborns, cups, pitchers, dark-eyed women, well-kept pearls and all sort of physical benefits that are in their entirety seen and sensed. Another example is his report about hell and its torments, which are neither seen nor sensed, by reference to fire and burning and boiling water and burning thirst and iron chains and fetters and all manner of physical pains that are entirely seen and sensed. If that is a necessary consequence, what he said and did and summoned to in regard to the afterlife, follows the rule of similitudes in forming likenesses. Similitudes require the things that are represented by them and the things that are represented are designated by interpretation. Thus, for what the Messenger brought and summoned to in the revelation and law, there is an interpretation. Hence, the interpretation is necessary.

The Seventh Light

In proof of the prophetic office and its necessity.

The first demonstration: God created creatures but He did not make the human species, in so far as its understanding of what it needs, like the beasts and the birds and other species of animals who understand what is good for them. Their understanding of that is a natural self-instinct, as, for example, a goose in being able to swim or a young chicken in pecking and snatching in the search for the stones of jaundice when it sees in the young hen a yellow colour. Instead, God made the human such as to need instruction, as we readily see in regard to the young who, if their parents and teachers did not teach them, they would not know anything and would not surpass the beasts. The souls which are lacking on their own are debased by being devoid of understanding, and yet they are prepared to receive what emanates to it and to have their element ennobled. Its being relegated to that state despite being prepared for that reception is not the wise course. Hence, in that the wise action is an obligation on the wise man though it remains unseen, the emanation falls on the one of them most prepared to receive it and on the nearest of them to such a reception in terms of substance. The receiver by his reception of that emanation becomes the one who stands, in regard to instruction and guidance, in the place of the All-wise who emanates it. The emanating of the emanation is the sending of messengers and the receiver of the emanation is the messenger. Hence, the prophetic office is essential.

The second demonstration: Because beings that exist and have come into existence have a Creator, and humans among them all are particular in having discretion and a reward and punishment, reason dictates that the human should be a person who looks for a way to understand his Creator and his advantages. Since reason requires of the human an understanding of his Creator but there is no way for him to know whether his Creator is a sensed object and, therefore, to seek Him out accordingly, or an intelligible and so to do research about Him intellectually, that dilemma leads him into confusion and error. Accordingly, the perfection of mercy requires that because He cannot be seen, God appoint on behalf of Himself a guardian among humans to guide them to the understanding of Himself, an intermediary between Him and them, who directs them and makes them understand their creator. The intermediary is the person appointed to convey that understanding. It is the prophetic office. Thus, the prophetic office is essential.

The third demonstration: The souls at the commencement of their activity are essentially ignorant but brought forth for that afterlife which is the abode of the requital. That abode with its sublime glory, containing what no eye has seen nor ear heard nor entered the heart of a man,[16] is not an object of sight so as to see it and to prefer it. Hence, given the perfect mercy of God, the Exalted, it is necessary that there be an inducement for the soul which makes it known that that abode is better, thereby to create the desire for its treasures. It is essential to express them in terms of sensible objects so that they are closer to the comprehension of those who try to picture them. The one who provides that inducement is the inspired messenger. Thus, the prophetic office is essential.

The fourth demonstration: Each thing that does not join in the definition of another thing is distinct from that thing and separate from it. What participates in the definition of something else is within its horizon and is a part of its totality and its form. The progression of souls is toward the spiritual world by means of obedience to God and to His Messenger. There is no way for them, however, to participate in the definition of that other on their own and to assume its forms so that they might be in that horizon. If they separate from the world

16. The phrase 'containing what no eye has seen nor ear heard nor entered the heart of man' comes from a well-known *ḥadīth* that depicts paradise in this fashion.

of individual persons, they adhere to that of which they participate by its definition. Accordingly, wisdom and perfect mercy require that there be a preceptor for it who provides them with the features of the spiritual world so that they come to participate in the definition of the latter. The one who instills these features of the spiritual world is the inspired person and the inspired person is the messenger. Thus, the prophetic office is essential.

The fifth demonstration: God singled out humans among animals by replacing the weapons they have, such as claws, beaks, fangs, hooves and others, with discretion, good management, prowess and excellence of choice. It is thus in his nature to seek rulership and to hold on to it to the exclusion of others, and to love gaining ascendancy and subjugating others. With what they have been given in the form of excellence in knowledge, trickery and prowess, none of them are safe from the oppression of some by others and attempts to spread evil throughout the earth. Hence, in accord with wisdom, it is necessary to create a mediator on behalf of God who will command them and prohibit them and preserve the proper order among them to prevent the ruin of some at the hands of others. That mediator who commands and prohibits on the authority of God is the messenger. Thus, the prophetic office is essential.

The sixth demonstration: To achieve the immortality of the human being, there is an urgent need for regulations that are credible and ordinances that have extensive sway so that humans will act in accord with these ordinances and its programme, thereby to hold secure their blood, property and sexual relationships. Otherwise nothing one person possessed of money, treasure and womenfolk would be any more his than another's. These regulations, since they cover acts, are not created on their own. An action must derived from an agent. Hence, there must be an agent who fashions these regulations and issues them, who commands and prohibits, and deals with humans in accord with its stipulations. That agent is the one inspired by God, the Exalted, the One obeyed. The inspired person is the messenger, and thus, the prophetic office is necessary.

The seventh demonstration: Each species that falls within a genus ends, in the specifics of its species, at what is more noble than all the rest of that same species. It is the foremost of them all and their leader because God singled it out with a superior excellence. Examples include the following: for the various kinds of minerals, the ultimates are, for those that melt and can be forged, gold, and for those that are stone that neither melt nor are forged, the ruby. Among the various species of plants, the ultimates are, for edible grains, wheat, and for those that produce fruit, the date palm. The human being is a species of animal and it is likewise necessary that they, too, have an end, ultimately, in what is nobler than the rest and more knowledgeable than all of them. He is their chief because of God's singling him out with superior excellence, just as is the case with every other species. That person, who is the ultimate, is he whom God inspires with what He reveals to him and the inspired person is the messenger. Thus, the prophetic office is essential.

PART TWO

The Proof of the Imamate

The First Light

In proof of the imamate and of its necessity.

The first demonstration: The Messenger set forth on behalf of God wisdom that is far-reaching and it was incumbent upon him to convey it to those of the human species to whom he was sent, both those in existence in his time and those humans who would come into existence through procreation after him up to the Day of Judgement. The humans who lived in his time were not able to accept that wisdom in one fell swoop, nor was it feasible for the humans who were to come into existence up to the Day of Judgment to exist all together. Yet it was impossible that the Messenger himself remain in this world until the protection of God would cover all the nations to whom it was to be conveyed. As a result it was necessary to appoint someone to occupy his place in conveying that protection and to set up the perpetual designation of another when the time of his passing approached. The person appointed for that purpose is the imam. Hence, the imamate is essential.

The second demonstration: What the Prophet brought in the way of the Holy Book, the authoritative law, obligatory practice, religious regulations and well respected precepts can be added to or subtracted from, and it is possible to alter his regulations and pronouncements and to introduce deviation in them. But, given the possibility of adding to or subtracting from them and the feasibility of altering his regulations and pronouncements, and if addition, subtraction or alteration should occur, that would lead to tyranny, injustice, oppression, the hands of the unjust reaching for forbidden things and its becoming the cause for the appearance of errors, the spread of fear and the absence of security, the course of wisdom [therefore] requires that there be a person put in charge of them who guards over them in this respect and prevents additions, subtractions or alternations in them. The community will thus follow his practice and the commandments of God will be ever fresh, His word exalted and evil eradicated. The person so charged is the imam chosen on behalf of God. Therefore, the imamate is necessary.

The third demonstration: The revelation and law brought by the Prophet came in the Arabic language and that language sustains a variety of meanings since a single phrase in the speech of the Arabs conveys a wide range of interpretation because of metaphors that allow for variations of meaning and symbolic expressions that point to a variety of objects. It is thus possible to interpret each verse and each report in accord with what the interpreter wants. In various situations we observe among the community that often happens in each sect's setting itself apart in regard to a verse of the Qur'ān or one of the reports and using it to verify their own particular doctrine based on a meaning, which is not the meaning another sect adduces for the same verse, to validate its doctrine. An example is the statement of God: 'What prevents you from bowing down to what I created with my own hand (*bi-yadī*)?' [38: 75]. The Muʿtazila hold a view, in regard to this verse, which confirms their doctrine by claiming that the intended meaning in God's saying 'by my own hand' is strength and power. The view of another group is that it indicates benefit and benevolence. Yet another group—and they are the Predestinarians (al-Mujbira) of various types—maintain, in confirmation of their doctrine, that it means simply the hand that is a part of the body and is one of its limbs. Each of their doctrinal statements is undeniably correct because our saying 'hand' denotes a meaning which is that adduced by each sect within the community and advocated by them. In its being open to whatever interpretation accords with the intention of the interpreter, it is parallel to a piece of cloth that can be cut for whatever purpose a person who cuts it desires. A person wants to cut from it a shirt because he needs one and that is quite possible. Another wants to cut from it pants because that is what he needs. Yet another hopes to cut from it a vest and stockings and a collar, because that is what he requires and that is also possible. This is also like fire. One person has a lamp and wick to ignite in it, another a candle to light, yet another firewood to set ablaze. This situation has three stipulations: either all the meanings that are adduced from the outward sense of what the Prophet brought are reasonable and must be apprehended in the right manner; or what is intended in the large number of meanings that can be adduced for one phrase is one or two meanings only and the rest are erroneous, and that one must be grasped in order to avoid the others; or all of the meanings that the outward sense of the phrase entails are entirely erroneous and the intention in the phrase is something other than what its outward sense indicates. Thus the phrase performs in that case the function of a simile and a metaphor, and it is necessary to come to understand what that metaphor refers to or the implications of that simile. If all the meanings contained in the one phrase are reasonable, wisdom requires that there be in the community someone who teaches them what, in the whole lot, is the direction of wisdom and not to leave anyone to single out one meaning rather than another, so that the word is one in worship and that differing ceases. If the intended meanings adduced from the one phrase is a single meaning or two, wisdom requires that there exist in the community a person who teaches them the intended aim and the meaning in which there is right guidance and to prevent them from believing any other, since none has the knowledge of what meaning is more worthy of believing than any of the rest due to the human need for a teacher to keep out mutual hatred and contention and to keep uniform the word in worship. If the meanings that are adduced from the outward sense are all erroneous and what is intended by the phrase is not its meaning, but rather it has the function of metaphor and symbol, wisdom requires there to be in the community someone who explains to them what those metaphors and similes refer to, lest they fall into error and believe what they should not. Thus, if there are these three possibilities in this case and all three require that there be someone in the community to guide and to teach, the guide and the teacher is the imam. Therefore, the imamate is obligatory.

The fourth demonstration: Dispositions differ, desires are disparate, events are not predictable or determined, and arrogance, transgression, love of conquest and domination are natural. The course of wisdom thus requires that among people there be a ruler who decides for them about what happens and from whom or from his rule they have no escape nor can they flee his decree. This was the case with the Prophet in his time. God said about him in His statement: 'Indeed, by your Lord, they will not believe until they make you judge their disputes and find no reservation in their souls about what you have determined but accept them fully' [4: 65]. The ruler is the imam. Therefore, the imamate is necessary.

The fifth demonstration: God is just and does not act tyrannically nor unjustly. God singled out the community that existed at the time of the Prophet by the incredible virtue of His having brought into existence among them the Messenger as a safeguard for them against punishment. God noted as much in His saying: 'And God will not punish them while you are with them' [8: 33]. He is also a means for them to seek forgiveness for themselves when they slip up. God confirmed that in His revelation when He said: 'If they, having sinned against themselves, should come to you and they ask forgiveness of God and the Messenger also asks forgiveness for them, they would find God most forgiving and merciful' [4: 64]. As well in His commenting on the account of the hypocrites, when they had appealed to the Messenger to seek forgiveness for them: 'If it is said to them, "Come, let us ask the Messenger of God for forgiveness", they avert their heads and you observe them turning away in arrogance' [63: 5]. That community had the virtue of having among them the Messenger to decide their judgments, instruct them on the waymarkers of their religion and its obligations, prompt them to seek the afterlife, to exert themselves in the way of God, and to ask God to forgive them their sins. None in existence was the like of him among them, but still they are not more favoured than any others, since the Messenger is the Messenger to all people and is the means for the [saving of the] whole. Accordingly, given that God is not unjust to His servants, it is necessary that after the Prophet there come to the community someone who takes up his role and replaces him in being its safeguard and the means whereby it [the community] asks forgiveness of God, who preserves for them the order of things, and who prompts them to do what is best for themselves. God imposed the seeking of a means to Him as a duty when He said: 'O, you who believe, fear God and seek the means to Him' [5: 35]. It is impossible to imagine God not having provided the community such means when He also imposed on them the obligation to seek it. The person who assumes the role of the Messenger is the imam. Therefore, the imamate is necessary.

The sixth demonstration: We maintain that God made Muḥammad the Messenger to all the people, both those of them who existed in his time and those who come into being after his era up to the Day of Resurrection. He ordered him to summon them all to Him in His saying: 'Summon them to the way of your Lord with wisdom and fine words' [16: 125]. The Prophet did what his Lord commanded him to do with his efforts and abilities in speech and in deed all the days of his life. But there remained more people than had already come to and followed him, who had not entered the law of his religion, who were, nevertheless, among those he was obliged to summon with words and efforts. It was well known that the Prophet would not remain in the world forever. Therefore, he set up an appeal to God on behalf of himself to carry on until his religion would appear above all religions, just as God had promised. Thus, given the consequences of the impossibility of the Messenger remaining among creation as a whole until the Day of Resurrection in order to sustain the appeal to them as God commanded, it is necessary that, since it is not possible for him to remain physically, someone assume the place of the Messenger who summons to the abode of Islam by inducement and a warning and in words and efforts so that the command of God will be fulfilled. The person who assumes the place of the Messenger is the imam. Therefore, the imamate is essential.

The seventh demonstration: We hold that, because God said to the Prophet Muḥammad, 'Take of their wealth alms to cleanse them and make them pure' [9: 103], and because Muḥammad was a messenger to those in his own time and as well as whoever was to be born after his death, and yet, even so, he was commanded to take alms payments from the wealth of all Muslims and thereby to make them all pure. Given the impossibility for the Messenger to be present with the entirety of Muslims until the Day of Resurrection in order to take those alms from them and thus to ensure their purity throughout, it is necessary that someone assume the role of the Messenger in taking what he was ordered to take and in purifying the people so that the command of God is upheld. The person who assumes the role of the Messenger is the imam. Hence, the imamate is necessary.

The eighth demonstration: The law closes the gates of sedition through the upholding of its regulations and the ending of the desire for injustice by carrying out its penalties. The law includes actions that are disagreeable, such as killing, crucifying, flogging, stoning, banishment and others. Even though, by nature, humans do not intend to injure and cause pain to themselves, nor be killed if that becomes necessary, or be crucified or any of the rest, they are not stopped from committing the acts of disobedience that merit the application to them of such actions. It is within the possible that, were the methods used in these acts like the methods used in others of those the provisions of which are assigned for the safeguarding of the people, such as prayer, almsgiving and others, if they are not done or are violated, the course of wisdom requires that, as with these actions, there be reliance on someone to uphold them and, in upholding them, maintain them for those deserving them, lest the regulations and penalties be neglected, public security be nonexistent, and the gates of evil opened. The person entrusted with that charge is the imam. Hence, the imamate is necessary.

The ninth demonstration: God made it obligatory to refer what one does not know about, or that in which there is a difference of opinion, to the Messenger. He decreed referring to him in His saying: 'If you quarrel concerning a matter refer it to God and the Messenger' [4: 59]. In regard to what one wanted to know concerning matters that were the subject of contention and difference in respect to issues of religion during the time of the Prophet, the authority was him, but it was not possible nor feasible for him to remain in the world to be among his community to the end so that they could refer to him that in which there occurred a difference or a issue of religion regarding which they did not have sure knowledge. Accordingly, it was necessary to put in the place of the Messenger someone to whom to refer those issues of religion about which there were differences, so that the decision would be his in that matter and the command of God would be upheld. The person who assumes the place of the Messenger is the imam. Thus, the imamate is essential.

The tenth demonstration: Drawing an analogy is to appoint the self as the authority in regard to what one wants to know in respect to that in which there is a difference of opinion and doubt, and to refer to it concerning that matter and to extrapolate from what is there in seeking the latter. God barred the use of analogical reasoning in His statement: 'In whatever matter about which you differ, the ultimate authority belongs to God' [42: 10]. He did not say, 'In whatever matter about which you differ, the authority belongs to you'. Thus, the use of analogy is precluded. And He confirmed it by His indicating to them to whom it should be referred when He said: 'If you disagree about a matter refer it to God and the Messenger' [4: 59]. Thus, since they were barred from using analogy, it is necessary for there to exist among them, after the Prophet, someone to issue rulings in matters about which they differ when it is referred to him. That someone to whom it is referred is the imam. Hence, the imamate is necessary.

The eleventh demonstration: God has spoken of 'The day we shall summon all peoples with their imams' [17: 71]. But, if in every era and time, there were not an imam and the earth were to be without one, even though people successively come into existence, the statement of God would be a lie. It is impossible to imagine that the words of God are a lie. Thus, it is essential that there be an imam for every age in whose name God summons his people. Hence, the imamate is necessary.

The twelfth demonstration: When He said, 'O, you who believe, obey God and obey the Messenger and those in authority among you' [4: 59], God imposed on the believers three acts of obedience in one verse, each linked to the others. Obedience to those in authority is not obedience to the Messenger and obeying the Messenger is not obeying God, but no one can accept the first without the second or the second without the third. Those addressed in the verse are the mass of the believers, both those in the era of the Messenger and those after him; it is not specific. On the part of God, it is impossible to impose on His servant obedience to someone and connect it with obedience to His Messenger and yet not to make that same person exist—that would be to impose an obligation that could not be fulfilled—or not to make him infallible, like the Messenger, and crowned with sacred and sublime traits. With regard to the addressee in the verse being the masses among whom no group is singled out to the exclusion of another, added to the impossibility of God depriving any community of someone they are obligated to obey, it is necessary that there exist for the community someone who is rightly the subject of their obedience, and their following his command in regard to God and the religion of God. The person from whom one takes orders is the imam. Hence, the imamate is necessary.

The thirteenth demonstration: God, the Exalted, high is His glory, created souls and made them alive and able to do good and evil, and He made for them the reward. He was not content, in terms of His own, until he had let them know what He had allocated for them as a reward. This information came on the tongues of His messengers as a warning and admonition. If there were not to be, after the messenger, one imam after another to preserve the messages of God and His command and prohibition, and to report to those communities who come into existence about how God's justice takes the form of both advice and admonition, that would single out the community of the messenger and the people of his time over those who are born into the communities after them. If He singled out for advice and admonition one group over another, the justice of God would prove false, even with a common reward. With respect to the perfection of the justice of God and its certainty, it is necessary for there always to be, after the messenger, an imam who is charged with warning the people of his time and admonishing them, announcing to them glad tidings and cautioning them lest they claim 'there came to us neither announcer of glad tidings nor warner' [5: 19]. When one imam passes on, another takes his place by his command and with his designation. Therefore, the imamate is necessary.

The fourteenth demonstration: The wisdom of the Creator is such that each thing He creates that does not know and lacks ability is under the charge of a thing that does know and has that ability which preserves it and looks after its welfare. Otherwise, creation of it would prove futile. He connects the two, as is the case with the macrocosm, which is this world with its celestial spheres, stars and elements, which He created devoid of knowledge and without power. Then He entrusted them to the closest angels to preserve their proper order and serve as a link between them. These angels have both knowledge and power; otherwise if it were not for them, their creation would prove futile. Another example is the microcosm, which is the individual human, consisting of his hands, legs, head, bowels, which God created ignorant and without power. He gave command of that microcosm to the soul to govern it and preserve its proper order until the end of the time determined for it, and He linked the two, and the soul knows and has power. If it were not for it, the individual would cease to function, just as it does when the soul leaves it. What the lord of the prophets and their seal, Muḥammad, brought on behalf of God as the law, is knowledge by its very existence. This world is the world of legal imposition, a combination of prayer, almsgiving, the pilgrimage and the rest, all taking the form of acts. Acts are deeds and deeds are in their essences without knowledge. Accordingly, wisdom requires, in respect to the obligation of preserving them lest they cease to exist, that it is necessary to give command over them to someone who will preserve and take care of them, as with the other worlds. For that reason, the appointment of the imam is the ultimate obligation. In him the world of law is completed. God declared this principle when He imposed it; He said: 'Today I have perfected for you your religion and I have completed for you My favour' [5: 3]. And he connected the silent prophet with the speaking prophet who said: 'I have left among you the two anchors, the Book of God and my family.' The family functions, with respect to the Book and the law, as does the soul with respect to the world of the individual, and as do the angels with respect to this world. Thus, the imamate is obligatory.

The Second Light

In proof of the infallibility of the imam and its necessity.

The first demonstration: We maintain that the need for the imam is because he occupies the place of the Messenger in regard to those matters of religion and the preservation of its good order that are connected to him. Given that the need for the person who occupies the place of the Messenger is for this reason and yet, if it were possible that he not be infallible, there would be no assurance that, in regard to some or all of his pronouncements, the community would not proceed along a path which is contrary to that of the Prophet. That deviation would lead to injustice and would encourage people to break away and secede from the community. Thus it is necessary that he be infallible, and his infallibility is the reason the community concurs with respect to obedience. Therefore, the imam is infallible. Understand that!

The second demonstration: Because the collection of the alms tax, charitable gifts and the fifth (tithe) goes to the person who occupies the place of the Messenger, as is the case, and because love of money and seeking it is normal, it is essential that that person be infallible so as to be sure of his own restraint and his not spending it otherwise than as God ordered. Thereby, God's command might become an inducement for the people to refuse compliance with it and they might disobey God for that reason. Therefore, the imam is infallible.

The third demonstration: Since the reference for what one wants to understand in regard to issues of religion is, after the Prophet, the imam and, if he did not have infallibility and the ability to be invariably correct, it is possible that he might make a mistake in responding to a question put to him. Thereby, his mistake might lead to error. In that he is the assurance of right guidance, it is necessary that he have infallibility. Therefore, the imam is infallible.

The fourth demonstration: In the law and its provisions, it is not permitted for someone who is himself liable to a penalty to apply such a penalty to another. The carrying out of corporal penalties is the responsibility of the imam. Therefore, it is essential that he have infallibility and that this infallibility keep him from committing an offence that would make him liable to a penalty. And since the community has no way to inflict it on him, having him thus safeguarded from acting like others who do deserve to have the penalty inflicted on them is essential. Hence, the imam is infallible.

The fifth demonstration: The acts of the law are connected to the imam. Were the imam, in regard to infallibility, like others, one could not be sure that he might not pray with the people while being impure or conduct a holy war against a group he unjustly opposes. If that meant that one could not be assured about him, the community, in their prayers and devotions, would be in doubt. Doubt in religion and worship is the road to hellfire. Since the reins of authority are in his hands, it is essential that he have infallibility. Therefore, the imam is infallible.

The sixth demonstration: God imposed obedience to the imam by means of His declaration: 'O, you who believe, obey God and obey the Messenger and those in authority among you.' Thus, He connected it to obeying Him and obeying His Messenger. Wisdom precludes the linking of a pearl with dung, or the noble with the base, or the pure with the unclean. For that reason, it is necessary that the linking of obedience to the imam with obedience to the Messenger who is infallible happens because the one is like the other. If the linking of obedience to the imam with obedience to the infallible Messenger happens because of the one being like the other, and obedience to the Messenger and its being an obligation is because of his being infallible, it is necessary that obedience to the imam is obligatory because of his own infallibility. Therefore, the imam is infallible.

The seventh demonstration: The Messenger is the seat of revelation and the treasure-trove of wisdom and knowledge. The knowledge God sent down to him, by means of which there is salvation, obligated him to convey it to all communities, since he was sent to them as a whole up to the Day of Resurrection. But, given his own departure from the world and the lack of the ability of the community to receive it all in one fell swoop, and given the impossibility of those who are to come into being up to the Day of Resurrection existing altogether, there is no way for him to convey it to the community other than through the teaching of what God sent to him by someone who occupies his place and who fulfils that trust. The person who occupies the place of the Messenger is the imam. Thus, it is necessary that he be trustworthy, reliable, infallible, incapable of perfidy in regard to anything entrusted to him, or of an error in what he is charged with doing. Therefore, the imam is infallible.

The Third Light

In proof of the invalidity of the community choosing its imam.

The first demonstration: We maintain that the application of corporal penalties to the community is the responsibility of the imam and no one else. Given that the application of the penalties, which are a part of the regulations within the comprehensive law, are his responsibility alone and not the community's, the raising to office of the imam, on whom all matters of law depend and whose place is that of the Lord of the worlds, is even more certainly not the responsibility of the community. For that reason, it follows by necessity that a choice made by it has no validity. Therefore, the community's choosing the imam is not valid.

The second demonstration: We maintain that there is no credibility in knowing that the one chosen for a matter is best for it if he is not in fact fully qualified for it. The one chosen for the imamate is not truly and properly suited for it except after having mastered everything required for the imamate, commencing with knowledge of the law, the Book and the legal stipulations. Next comes sure knowledge that the understanding of what is required for the imamate is actually present in the one chosen for it and that he is thus fully qualified for it. But, if the one chosen for the imamate knows all of what is required and if the community that chooses also knows that, the one chosen to be imam is no more appropriate for it than any one else. Those promoted to it are all equal in respect to the reason by which they merit being promoted over the rest. If those put first are equal, the choice and the promotion [of one] by the community is for that reason not valid. Therefore, a choice made by them is invalid.

The third demonstration: We hold that a cause, if present, produces its effect. If the cause of authenticity in regard to the imamate were the consensus of the people and their choice, it would require that whenever a consensus and choice on their part exists, authenticity is a concomitant of that same fact. That being so and yet we have also found that the people altogether without exception—the Jews, Christians, Magians, Sabeans and the rest—agreed unanimously at the time the Messenger was sent, that Muḥammad was a liar, a charlatan, was mad and that he was not a Prophet. They chose someone else over him. But their consensus and choice did not constitute a proof, nor was it a cause for rescinding the prophecy of the Prophet. Thus, since their consensus and their choosing did not constitute a proof or a reason to rescind his prophecy, consensus and choice by the people has no validity. Understand that!

The fourth demonstration: We say, if it were permissible for the community to choose the imam, it would be permitted them to choose judges and appoint their own notary witnesses. If it were permissible for members of the community to select judges and appoint notary witnesses, they would be permitted to control the marriage of orphans and to declare them legally incompetent until such time as they should be regarded as sound. Since that is not permitted to the community, nor are they allowed to declare orphans legally incompetent and control their marriage arrangements, they are not permitted to choose judges or appoint notary witnesses. If it is not permissible for them to chose judges or appoint notaries, it is not permissible for them to choose the imam. Therefore, the community's choosing the imam has no validity.

The fifth demonstration: In the law of God and the legal practice of His Messenger, which remains in force until the Day of Resurrection, it is not valid to raise someone to the place of another—not as deputy, not as guardian, not as successor, not as representative in a claim of right, not in the execution of a matter—based on the statement of someone else, or someone selected other than by him. The place of the imam among the servants of God and in safeguarding, protecting and guiding them is that of the Messenger. From that we determine that the choosing of the imam by the community and their raising him to the position of the Messenger is even more certainly impermissible. Therefore, the community's choosing the imam is not allowed.

The sixth demonstration: Because the imam must be infallible and the infallibility of the imam is not some mark on the face, nor such as to be readily apparent in a person's constitution so that the community would have a means to recognize him, it is inconceivable and incorrect that choosing him is the responsibility of the community. Hence, their choosing is not valid.

The seventh demonstration: The cherubic angels are infallible and incapable of error. When God wanted to create for Himself a deputy on the earth, He said, 'I am to create a deputy on the earth' [2: 30], they preferred that it be their deputy. They said: 'Are you to put on it someone who will corrupt it and shed blood while we sanctify you with praise and venerate you?' [2: 30]. But, despite their infallibility and purity, God refused to let them choose and He rebuked them for their having said what they said. He declared at that point: 'I know what you do not know' [2: 30]. How much more certain that the community, which is not infallible, is precluded from choosing. Therefore, choice by the community is not valid.

The Fourth Light

In proof that the imamate is validated by the designation of God and the choice of the Messenger.[17]

The first demonstration: The prophecy of the prophets who are, in regard to the execution of judgments among His servants, the representatives of God on His earth, is not valid without a designation by God and by His choosing them to take His place in governing, commanding and prohibiting, and prophecy is the foundation of the imamate. The imamate, which is a subsidiary of prophecy and which is a representative of the Messenger and occupies his place, is even more certainly not valid unless based on the choice of God and the choice of His Messenger. Therefore, the imamate is valid only by designation and appointment.[18]

The second demonstration: There is a rule in what God revealed and in the legal practice of His Messenger with regard to relationships among people that appointing someone to the position of another is not valid unless it is by the choice of that other person and by his designation of the one who replaces him. Because the imamate takes the place of the Messenger, God's rule and the rule of His Messenger require that it not be valid unless it is by the choice of the Messenger and by his designation. Hence, the imamate is valid only through designation and appointment.

The third demonstration: God has said: 'Your Lord creates whatever He wants and He chooses; they have no choice in the matter' [28: 68]. Accordingly, that statement makes it necessary for the choice

---

17. In his work *Tanbīh al-hādī wa'l-mustahdī* (p. 232) al-Kirmānī comments about this issue: 'the nobility of the imamate is due to the designation of his righteous forefathers in accord with the requirement imposed under Islam as demonstrated by clear proofs that we have provided in our book known as *al-Maṣābīḥ*, and in the treatise known as *al-Kāfiya* and another known as *Mabāsim al-bishārāt* which confirm what we have set out here in that regard.'

18. *Tawqīf*. Some mss. have here instead *tawfīq*, 'divine favour'. However, the proper term is *tawqīf*, on which see al-Qāḍī al-Nu'mān, *Da'ā'im al-Islām*, ed. A. A. A. Fyzee, 2 vols (Cairo, 1951–61), I, 38ff; English trans. A. A. A. Fyzee, completely revised by I. K. Poonawala, *The Pillars of Islam*, 2 vols (New Delhi, 2002–2004), 49ff.

to be God's, and if the choice is God's, the choice of someone who, for the sustaining of his own position is in need of having his secret thoughts, which no one can know except God, kept unsullied, is even more certainly God's choice. Therefore, the imamate is valid only by the choice of God and the designation of the Messenger.

The fourth demonstration: Because it is God who knows the secrets of creatures, the evil among them as well as the good, and the most suitable person for the imamate is the best and most excellent, and human capabilities lack a means to ascertain these secrets so as to choose the best and most excellent, that fact determines that the choice is God's and the Messenger's to the exclusion of any one else. If the choice is God's and the Messenger's, the imamate is not valid unless it is by their choice. The choice is in the designation. Therefore, the imamate is not valid without the designation and appointment.

The fifth demonstration: The imamate is not some distinctive mark in creatures present and obvious, such as an increase or decrease in some body part, so that the person in whom that distinctive mark is found would be the imam. An example is the long neck in the camel or the existence of a trunk in the elephant, which when present in it, its nature indicates its species. Acknowledgement of the imam is obligatory in religion, but there is no path to religious understanding other than through the Messenger. Hence the imamate is not valid except by his choice, designation and indication. Therefore, the imamate is valid only through his designation and appointment.

The sixth demonstration: The populace at the time the Prophet was sent were unanimously agreed that his prophecy was a lie and a magical trick. If their agreement were the validation of prophecy, his prophecy would have been null and void. But since his prophecy was based on the choice of God, it was not invalidated. Instead, it caused the raising of its banners and paved the way for its expansion. Hence, the imamate is even more surely invalidated by the choosing of the community and most certainly confirmed by the choice of God. Therefore, the imamate is not valid unless by the choice of God and the choice of the Messenger, and that means designation and appointment.

The seventh demonstration: God declared in His Book that it is He who appoints a representative on the earth when He said, 'I am to create a deputy on the earth', and He did not hand responsibility for that to the cherubic angels, who were themselves infallible. Instead, He rebuked them for asking, 'Are you to put on it someone who will corrupt it and shed blood?' He replied, 'I know what you do not know'. Thus, the choosing of representatives is God's. If the choice is His, it is not valid unless He makes that choice and if the designation is His. Therefore, the imamate, which is this representation, is not valid unless it is by the choice of God and the designation of the Messenger.

The Fifth Light

That the imamate after the Prophet belongs to the Commander of the Faithful, ʿAlī b. Abī Ṭālib, God bless him, and to none of the others.[19]

The first demonstration: There are many professions and each of them is divided, whatever its difference and variety, into knowledge and practice. An example is medicine, which is divided into knowledge of the characteristics of medications and the causes of diseases, and into practice, which is the treatment. Another is astronomy,[20] which is divided into knowledge of the configuration of the sphere and its stars and the natures of the planets and their movements and influences, and into practice, which is the [calculation of] the planetary movements[21] and what they determine.[22] Yet another is the science of governing, which is divided into knowledge of the administration of the affairs of kingdoms and their maintenance, the means of raising revenue and collecting it, and maintaining the proper order of affairs, and into practice, which is the infliction of punishment, of beating, imprisoning, executing, dismissing and/or conferring obligation. Knowledge and practice are like instruments. A person

---

19. Al-Kirmānī cites this section briefly in his *Tanbīḥ al-hādī* (p. 228).

20. His term here is simply *al-nujūm* (the stars), and he most likely includes in it both astronomy and astrology.

21. Calculating the positions of the seven planets relative to each other within the twelve astrological houses.

22. That is, predictions corresponding to a given configuration of planets relative to the zodiac.

who has no instrument to use in the knowledge and practice of his profession cannot conceivably do it correctly. Among the basic principles of reason, one is that a person for whom the instrument he uses in his profession is most perfect, he is in that profession more suited for it than any one else. The example is a man whose grasp of medicine and his practice of it is more complete than any one else; he is more suited for it than the rest. The stipulations of Islam that form the prophetic profession are like the others in being divided into knowledge of the manner of religious obligations, what is permitted and what forbidden, the corporal punishments, legal stipulations, revelation, interpretation; and into practice, which are purity, prayer, alms taxation, fasting, pilgrimage, striking with the sword, and what else has a function like these. Knowledge and practice belonged to ʿAlī b. Abī Ṭālib more than to any of the Companions who lived after the Prophet. That judgement determines that he was most suited for governing and most worthy of the imamate. Therefore, the imamate belonged to ʿAlī b. Abī Ṭālib.

The second demonstration: In the matter of the most worthy person to be followed, God Himself commented in His statement: 'So who is most worthy of being followed, the one who guides to the truth or the one who does not guide unless he is himself guided; what is with you that you judge in this way?' [10: 35]. Since after the Prophet, the Companions needed the guidance of ʿAlī b. Abī Ṭālib in the determination of judgements the intention of which were sought from them, ʿAlī b. Abī Ṭālib was the most worthy for the imamate. If he was the most worthy, he was the imam. Therefore, the imamate belonged to ʿAlī b. Abī Ṭālib.

The third demonstration: God said: 'Your guardian is only God, His Messenger and those who are faithful, maintain prayers, pay the alms tax and who bow down' [5: 55]. ʿAlī b. Abī Ṭālib was the person who gave alms during his prostrations.[23] A *walī* (guardian) lexically is both he who is in charge of the affairs of the person of whom he is the guardian and a client of whomever is his patron and he supports.

---

23. On ʿAlī's giving alms while still bowed down for prayer, see Abu'l-Fawāris, *al-Risāla fi'l-imāma*, 13; trans. 30 and the editor's note 56 which supplies the background and references.

Thus it is a bit difficult lexically and visually to tie it in to *muwālā*. But it is false that the intention here is clientage because of the impossibility of construing the verse in that way due to the restriction of the text, which limits the community's guardians to God, to His Messenger and to ʿAlī with regard to the meaning of *muwālā*, despite the statement of God: 'and the believers men and women, some are guardians of others' [9: 91]. Because of that fact, it is proven that, on behalf of God, he designated ʿAlī to take charge of the affairs of the community. Hence, ʿAlī b. Abī Ṭālib is the one designated for the imamate.

The fourth demonstration: God has said: 'The Prophet is dearer to the believer than they are to themselves' [33: 6]. That statement constitutes God's appointment of him as guardian of the believers, to command them and prohibit them, and the prophet took from the believers at Ghadīr Khumm their agreement when he said: 'Am I not dearer to you than you to your own selves?' To which they replied 'Yes' three times. And what he said after taking their agreement were his words: 'So of whomever I am the master (*mawlā*), ʿAlī is his master.' The meaning of that phrase goes back to what they agreed to in regard to God's appointing him guardian over them with the power to command and prohibit with respect to them and their obeying him—regardless of what other meanings language might consider subsumed in this phrase, which might require that other meaning here: namely, 'whoever is his emancipator' or 'his freed slave' or 'the son of his paternal uncle' or 'his successor' or 'his neighbour'.[24] All of these possible meanings in his saying this are precluded in that he followed it with the words 'ʿAlī is his master', which requires his having meant 'Of whoever I am' his emancipator or his freed slave or the son of his paternal uncle, ʿAlī is his emancipator or his freed slave or the son of his paternal uncle. From that we know that his saying 'ʿAlī is his master', right after previously taking their agreement that he [the Prophet] is their master and in conjunction with his saying 'So, of whoever I am the master', is the designation of ʿAlī b. Abī Ṭālib as the guardian of the believers, as the person in charge of matters of their religion, and as the commander and prohibiter among them. It

24. These are the additional meanings of the word *mawlā*.

has the same function in respect to the appointment of a guardian over the believers. Moreover, his saying "'Alī is his master' was followed immediately by his saying and praying: 'O God, make a friend of whoever is his friend and an enemy of whoever opposes him, and support whoever supports him and forsake whoever forsakes him.' This is to confirm the matter. If it were not that the Prophet entrusted the affairs of religion to 'Alī, and if 'Alī were not infallible and not capable of error and mistakes in that for which he is relied on, those who oppose him and do not support him, or forsake him and do not follow his commands but disobey, would not be deserving of the forsaking the Prophet called down upon them along with the animosity of God towards them. Imagining in this something that merits God's animosity and for that necessitating His forsaking of that person because of such abominations, as in this appeal from the Prophet, would be inconceivable if it suggested his being unjust with those who forsake him and to oppose him by having committed what, were he to do it, would be otherwise conceivable and tolerable. But had it been so he would not have called upon Him in such a fashion. As none of the Companions was connected with any of the matters of religion or was infallible, he would not call against them such a heavy penalty. But given that this appeal was of such a kind, it cannot have been required except in the case of someone who was infallible and who was entrusted with the religion after him. Thus, in regard to whatever he should disobey of what the Prophet called upon him to do, this appeal would apply to, and to whoever forsakes him, an interdiction on the community for refusing to obey him and their being oppressed for abstaining from committing to his imamate. It is a confirmation of the designation of 'Alī to the imamate after him by the words "'Alī is his master'. Therefore, 'Alī b. Abī Ṭālib is the one designated for the imamate and he is the imam.

The fifth demonstration: God said: 'Accept what the Messenger brings you and avoid what he forbids to you' [59: 7]. The statement of the Prophet concerning this verse occupies the place of God's words and the Prophet said: "'Alī is to me as Aaron was to Moses except that he is not a prophet after me.' Aaron had, in relation to Moses, several shared attributes. Among them is his being of the same mother and father and also his participation with Moses in prophecy. Another is his having been Moses' deputy in his community during the latter's absence. None of these attributes belong to ʿAlī; he was not from the mother of Muḥammad, nor of his father, and he did not participate with Muḥammad in prophecy. Hence, the statement of Muḥammad that "ʿAlī is to me as Aaron was to Moses except that he is not a prophet after me', following the exclusion of those attributes that are to be rejected in respect to ʿAlī, is the equivalent of his having said "ʿAlī is to me in the succession on my behalf as Aaron was to Moses', because none of the other meanings for the relationship inherent in his statement "ʿAlī is to me as Aaron was to Moses' apply, except that of successorship. Given that no other meaning remains but successorship, and since the Prophet's words 'except that he is not a prophet after me' follow immediately his saying "ʿAlī is to me as Aaron was to Moses', we know for that reason that the denial of prophecy after himself was the indication of the time during which would be his successorship, which was made necessary by his saying "ʿAlī is to me as Aaron was to Moses'. If it were not the time of the succession of ʿAlī after him, he would not have put after his statement that "ʿAlī is to me as Aaron was to Moses', a rejection of prophecy after himself. Thus he said 'except that he is not a prophet after me' and his having left the statement as a whole, such as to be construed to the effect that he was his deputy during his lifetime as the deputyship of Aaron for Moses, occurred during his lifetime. But his having followed his statement with the words 'after me', in regard to denying prophecy, is a designation on his part of the time of ʿAlī's successorship and that of the imams. If it were not so and the purpose in his having specified the time of succession just as he designated him in saying "ʿAlī is to me as Aaron was to Moses', given what exists in the text of the Book about his being the Messenger of God and the seal of the prophets, the Prophet would have had no need to take the trouble of denying prophecy after himself. It was well known that prophecy was sealed with Muḥammad on the basis of the text of the verse and that there would be no prophet after him until the Day of Resurrection, not ʿAlī and not anyone else. That being so, it follows necessarily that the Prophet's denying prophecy after him is an affirmation of the succession to him afterward. Therefore, ʿAlī b. Abī Ṭālib was the person so designated for the imamate and he was the imam.

The sixth demonstration: Because, in designating al-Ḥasan and al-Ḥusayn for the imamate, the Prophet said, 'al-Ḥasan and al-Ḥusayn are imams whether standing or sitting,[25] and their father is better than they'[26] and his having said 'their father is better than they' immediately after referring the imamate to them, we know that the intention of his saying 'better than they' is that 'Alī b. Abī Ṭālib is better than they in what he makes here the attribute of al-Ḥasan and al-Ḥusayn, namely the imamate, when he mentioned the 'two imams'. Therefore, 'Alī b. Abī Ṭālib was the person designated for the imamate and he was the imam.

The seventh demonstration: Everything has attributes, and that with which it shares more attributes and yet is of the same species is more like it than the rest of that same species. An example here are the minerals iron, copper, lead, tin [and] mercury, which have characteristics they share that exist in the others but which are not the same as those in silver. These are purity of substance, persisting over time, resisting the effect of fire, smoothness, forgeability, strength and of great price. These characteristics take the place of gold when gold is non-existent more readily than the others. Another example is many a species of plant which has the ability, with respect to what it shares and what is of the same type in terms of characteristics and attributes, to take another's place more readily than some others, as for example barley, which is most similar to wheat and closer to it than the rest of the edible grains. It takes the place of wheat when the latter is not available more readily than the rest of the grains. Yet one more example are medicines in which some of the same type share a power. When a medicine is not available, another medicine of those that are like it in what they do takes its place more readily than the others, such as gallnuts for constricting and restraining. If it is not available, the acorn is a better replacement than the rest of those that share with it the power to constrict. Or also like pomegranate peels and their ability to act as an astringent. The Prophet, by God's raising him to the rank of prophet caused him to share traits and characteristics, among them revelation, the designation

25. 'Standing or sitting' means openly claiming the imamate or not.

26. Cf. *Da'ā'im*, I, 37; trans. 48. Al-Kirmānī in his *al-Waḍī'a* (f. 20b = p. 82 ed.) again mentions this *ḥadīth* and there comments that it is one of the proofs he offered on this matter in 'our well-known book on the imamate'.

by God, purity, righteousness, piety, courage, generosity, truthfulness, abstinence, justice, mercy, faith, knowledge and others than these. After the Prophet, there was no one who shared with him these attributes except ʿAlī b. Abī Ṭālib. It is as we picture them in tabular form as a method of reckoning and as an *aide-mémoire* at the end of this demonstration, so that it can be seen that these characteristics having existed in him, he took the place of the Prophet and occupied his role more certainly than any other man among the other Companions. Therefore, ʿAlī b. Abī Ṭālib was the imam.

Form to serve as an aide-mémoire *listing the characteristics that existed in the Prophet and which among them existed in the Companions, in order to ascertain who of them was most rightfully the one to replace the Prophet after him. We understand this* aide-mémoire *as a method of reckoning.* [Table I, Plates 1–4]

Muḥammad, the Chosen

1. Names and the Revelation from God: He was revealed to by God.
2. Designation by God: He was designated by God in the tongues of His messengers in God's words in the fifth book of the Torah which indicate him.[27] Moses said: *ʾădōnāy*, 'God', and *missînnay bāʾ wezāraḥ miśśēʿîr lāmô wahôpîaʿ mēhar*, 'from Sinai a radiance shown and a light came from the land of ʿĪṣ to them and appeared

27. Deut. 33: 2. The *Revised Standard Version* reads: 'The Lord came from Sinai, and dawned from Se'ir upon us; He shone forth from Mount Paran, He came from the ten thousands of holy ones, with flaming fire at His right hand.' Abū Ḥātim al-Rāzī, an earlier Ismaili authority, quotes this passage (in Arabic translation) in his *Aʿlām al-nubuwwa* (p. 195) as follows: 'God came from Sinai and shone forth from Sāʿīr and cast a light from mount Paran.' Al-Qāḍī al-Nuʿmān provides a fuller version (again in Arabic) in his *Asās al-taʾwīl* (p. 321): 'God came from Sinai and shone forth from Sāʿīr and announced [reading *istaʿlana*] from mount Paran; and there will come from the myriads of Jerusalem in His right hand a fire which is the law for him.' On this passage and those that follow here from the Hebrew and Syriac Bibles, see the classic study and reconstruction of them by Paul Kraus, 'Hebräische und syrische Zitate in ismāʿīlitischen Schriften', *Der Islam*, 19 (1931), pp. 243–263.

from mount', *pā'rān wa'ātāh mēribăbôt qōdeš mîmînô 'ēš*, 'Tihama and there came from the myriads of Jerusalem [in His right hand] a fire', *dāt lāmô*, 'a likeness for them'.[28]

3. Purity and infallibility: He was pure, purified and infallible; he had not worshipped idols nor images and had bowed down to none other than God in true sincerity.
4. Righteousness: He was righteous and had never committed any act of disobedience or error, had not drunk wine or engaged in corruption.
5. Piety: He was pious and did not covet the property of another, and because of being trustworthy and reliable, he was called 'the Trustworthy', and even prior to this being sent, deposits were deposited with him.
6. Bravery and power: He was brave and intrepid, not frightened by the multitude of unbelievers, and established the call to God, despite the smallness of his numbers, so that His word would be raised high.
7. Generosity: He was generous and kept nothing for himself but gave it for God and God's friends.
8. Abstinence: He was ascetic and did not prefer this world, and held back from it and from being seduced by it, working instead in the way of God.
9. Justice and mercy: He was just and merciful; God referred to him as compassionate and merciful; he said to a man scolding him about the division of funds of the booty: 'If I am not just, who is just, given that I am the Trustworthy of those in the heavens and those on the earth.'
10. Prior in faith: He was prior to those who preceded in faith and the very first of the earliest among them to display the faith, and in it to become stronger and be emulated.
11. Knowing the Book of God: He knew what was and what will be, and what God revealed to him and took pride in it.
12. Knowledge of the interpretation of the Book of God and the Law:

---

28. Although the Hebrew phrase *dāt lāmô* is of uncertain meaning by common consensus, given the normal Arabic rendering of it as 'the law for him', the text here should likely be amended to reflect that difference.

He knew the symbols and what they symbolized in everything he brought.

13. Knowledge of the stipulation in what God revealed: He was a ruler from whose rule there was no escape, nor the choice of someone else in that regard. God says: 'No, by your Lord, they will not believe until they make you the judge of matters about which they dispute, and then find in themselves no restraint concerning what you determine and accept with complete acceptance' [4: 65].
14. Knowledge of the licit and illicit: He knew what was allowed and what [was] prohibited by God and learned from Him.
15. Loved by God: He was beloved by God, the chosen, selected, and he was the dear friend of God;
16. Closeness to God: He was close to God, as near to Him as the middle to the two ends of a bow, or even closer.

The one who appeared on Mount Sinai was Moses, the one who appeared out of the land of ʿĪṣ, which is Syria and the territory of the Greeks, was Jesus, and the one who appeared out of the mountains of the Tihama was Muḥammad. Then it is said in the Torah, in answer to the prayer of Abraham: *ûleyišmāʿēʾl šemaʿtîka wa hīnnēh bēraktî ʾōtô wehirbêtî ʾōtô wehiprêtî ʾōtô* [*bimʾōd*], 'as for Ismāʿīl, I have heard your prayer and I will bless you through him and I will complete my blessing on him and renew my blessing on him through Muḥammad', *bimʾōd meʾōd šenêm ʿāśār neśîʾim yôlîd ûnetatîw*, 'Muḥammad ... twelve tribes the most glorious and most noble born and there will be from him a great nation', *legôy gādôl.*[29] I note that in the Hebrew language the root of 'meʾōd' is 'dhāl' and that it undergoes various changes in meaning by additions that indicate kinds of inflections, such as *ʾôdî*. Its explanation is 'I praise' or 'I thank' and *nôdeh, tôdeh* and *nôdeh*, that is, 'we praise'

29. Genesis 17: 20. The *Revised Standard Version* reads: 'As for Ishmael, I have heard you; behold, I will bless him and make him fruitful and multiply him exceedingly; he shall be the father of twelve princes, and I will make him a great nation.' In al-Qāḍī al-Nuʿmān's *Asās al-taʾwīl* (pp. 320–321), the translation of the same passage runs as follows: 'Your prayer has been heard, and I will answer it and bestow blessings on him and multiply him and increase his power greatly, and there will be born to him a king and I will produce for him twelve mighty princes, and I will make of him a great nation.'

(*naḥmadu*), 'you praise' (*taḥmadu*), 'he praises' (*yaḥmadu*), and the putting of a *mīm* on it, as in *me'ōd*, is in order for it to have the meaning of the passive participle, as is said in Arabic, *muḥammad*, *maḥmūd* or *mashkūr*. If we want to give an order to someone in Hebrew to thank or praise someone else, we say: *hôdēh*. In their language this modification does not alter a root. Therefore *me'ōd* is *Muḥammad*, and thus did God therewith announce him to Abraham.[30]

The Prophet Isaiah said in the Torah:[31] *kî kōh 'āmar 'ădōnāy 'ēlay lēk ha'ămēd hameṣappeh 'ešer yir'eh yaggîd*, 'thus said God to me, go out and set a watchman to give a report of what he sees',[32] *werā'āh rekeb ṣemed pārāšîm rekeb ḥămôr wa rekeb gāmāl*, 'He looked and behold he saw two riders, one of them riding a donkey and the other riding a camel',[33] and he shouted *wayya'an wayyō'mer nāpelāh nāpelāh bābel wekol pesîlê 'eleheyhā [šibbar lā'āreṣ]*, 'Woe, woe to Babylon; he will smash the object of their worship into pieces'.[34] The rider of the donkey was Jesus and the rider of the camel was Muḥammad; that was an announcement and designation of him.

30. In his *Ma'āṣim al-hudā* (f. 45b, ms. 724, IIS, London) al-Kirmānī refers back to this passage, saying there 'and as it is mentioned in the Torah *ûleyišmā'ē'l šema'tîka* on to the end of his words there concerning [the term] *bim'ōd* who is Muḥammad, may God bless him, as we have explained in the book *al-Maṣābīḥ fi'l-imāma*'.

31. Muslim authors included additional parts of the Hebrew Bible in the Torah as part of a 'larger Torah'.

32. Isaiah 21: 6.

33. Isaiah 21: 7.

34. The source for the whole passage is Isaiah 21: 6 to 9 which runs in the *Revised Standard Version* as follows: 'For thus the Lord said to me: "Go, set a watchman, let him announce what he sees. When he sees riders, horsemen in pairs, riders on asses, riders on camels, let him listen diligently, very diligently." Then he who saw cried: "Upon a watchtower I stand, O Lord, and at my post I am stationed whole nights. And, behold, here come riders, horsemen in pairs!" And he answered, "Fallen, fallen is Babylon: and all the images of her gods he has shattered to the ground".' Abū Ḥātim al-Rāzī quotes this passage (*A'lām al-nubuwwa*, p. 196) as follows: 'The Lord said to me, "Go set a watchman to report what he sees"; the one who saw the one on the watchtower said, "Two riders approach, one on a donkey and the other on a camel"; and while we were like that suddenly one of the riders came close and announced: "Woe, woe to Babylon, her gods have been turned upside down and made into scattered ruins on the ground".'

The author of the Gospels said: *m' d't' prqlyṭ' hw d'n' mšdrn' lkwn rwḥ' [d]šrr'*, 'There will come a wise man whom the father sends to you with the Spirit of truth'; *whw nḥkm lkwn šrr' klh*, 'He will teach you all things'.[35]

The author of the Book *Iqlīmas*, attributed to Sham'ūn the Pure,[36] and the author of the Book of Peter said that there will come from the offspring of Ismā'īl a prophet whose name begins with *mīm* and ends with *dāl*, and he will conquer all lands and destroy all the churches in them. All of this is a designation by God of the Prophet through his saints and prophets.

Quss b. Sā'ida al-Iyādī[37] came to Makka and stopped on his Awraq[38] camel at the market of 'Ukāẓ. There he announced the Prophet and the religion to which he would summon: 'O people, he who lives dies and he who dies passes away. Whatever is coming is coming, dark night and the heaven of the zodiac, and stars that shine, seas that accumulate, and sons and daughters, fathers and mothers, the one gone, the one coming, that in the heaven there is a passage

35. John 16: 26: 'But when the Counselor comes, whom I shall send to you from the Father, even the Spirit of truth, who proceeds from the Father, he will bear witness to me.' Added to that or mixed with it is John 14: 26: 'But the Counselor, the Holy Spirit, whom the Father will send in my name, he will teach you all things....' Abū Ḥātim al-Rāzī quotes (*A'lām al-nubuwwa*, p. 196) one of the passages that mention the Paraclete (Counselor or Comforter) as follows: 'I am to depart and the Paraclete will be sent, the Holy Spirit, who will not speak on his own behalf, and he will teach you all things and he will bear witness to me just as I bear witness to him, and he will be sent in my name.' This version, like that of al-Kirmānī, does not match any one passage of John. The phrase 'will not speak on his own behalf' seems to derive from John 16:13.

36. Sham'ūn the Pure is St. Peter. The title *Iqlīmas* evidently is a rendering of Clement/Clementines; see most recently the comments of J. M. F. Van Reeth, in part B of De Smet and Van Reeth, 'Les Citations bibliques dans l'oeuvre de Kirmānī', pp. 154–160.

37. On Quss b. Sā'ida, see 'Ḳuss b. Sā'ida' by Ch. Pellat in *EI2*, and L. Cheikho, *Shu'arā' al-naṣrāniyya* (Beirut, 1920), pp. 211–218. Cheikho offers another, fuller version of the incident described here and the oration, as well as the same verses, see pp. 212–213. However, this incident and Quss's oration are quite famous and it is often quoted in one version or another.

38. A breed of camel.

and that there is on earth a message. What is it to me to witness the people going and not returning, satisfied with the place they stay or they leave it and sleep?' Quss swears by God an oath that on earth there is no religion that honours God more than the religion that guards you in his time; blessedness in his time reaches you who understands him and follows him, but woe to he who opposes him. Then he uttered these verses:

In those of old who have, through the centuries, passed on
  We gain perceptive insights.
When I see that the station to which death arrives
  Has no source from which it comes,
And I see my people toward it pass,
  Both the young and the old,
The person gone will not come back to me,
  Nor will those who remain stay,
I become sure that I, too, without doubt,
  Will go as the people have gone.

God has said in the Qur'ān, 'And Muḥammad is only a messenger; other messengers have passed away before him' [3: 144]; and 'Muḥammad is the Messenger of God and those who are with him have strength against the unbelievers and mercy amongst each other' [48: 29]. He also said, 'Muḥammad was not the father of any one of your men but rather the Messenger of God and the seal of the prophets' [33: 40]; and, 'An unlettered prophet whom you find was mentioned to you in the Torah and the Gospels' [7: 157]; and He said, 'Good tidings of a Messenger to come after me whose name is Aḥmad' [6: 61].

Here is a report about the Companions and, for what character traits of those that are in the table of the Prophet, they are known, except for what was deleted in the process for reasons of brevity due to the limited width of the table. We commence with a reckoning for Abū Bakr in order to come to the end of our purpose. [Table II, Plates 5–12]

Abū Bakr: (1) He did not have revelation from God; (2) He was not chaste because of his having drunk wine in the period of Jāhiliyya and his commission of mortal sins; (3) He was not designated by God or by His Apostle; (4) He was not pure nor purified, he had worshipped idols and had prostrated himself to them and not God; (5) He was not brave or recognized for strength and bravery; (6) He was pious not covetous; (7) He was generous, spending freely; (8) He was not selected by God nor by His Apostle, and he was not dear to either of them nor among those described as such; (9) He was not among those characterized by ascetic restraint; (10) He was not just in the exercise of authority and did not show mercy to the daughter of God's Apostle when he seized her property unlawfully;[39] (11) He came early to Islam; (12) He did not have knowledge of the Book of God nor is one mentioned for that; (13) He was not knowledgeable about what is permitted and what is forbidden and is not cited for that; (14) He was not someone who knew the interpretation; (15) He did not understand how to make judgements and deferred the argument in such matters to ʿAlī; (16) He was not close to God nor to His Apostle.

ʿUmar:[40] (1) It was the same with him; (2) It was the same with him; (3) It was the same with him; (4) It was the same with him; (5) It was the same with him; (6) He had piety; (7) He was generous, spending freely; (8) [blank]; (9) [blank]; (10) [blank]; (11) He came not earlier to Islam as had Abū Bakr; (12) [blank]; (13) He was knowledgeable about what is permitted and what is forbidden; (14) [blank]; (15) [blank].

ʿUthmān: (1) It was the same with him; (2) It was the same with him; (3) It was the same with him; (4) It was the same with him; (5) It was the same with him; (6) He was not pious; (7) He was generous, spending freely; (8) [blank]; (9) [blank]; (10) [blank];

39. On Abū Bakr's refusal to allow Fāṭima to inherit property given her by her father, see 'Fadak' by L. Veccia Vaglieri in *EI2*.

40. Commencing with ʿUmar the entries depend on the successive order of columns and rows in the table, for which see the examples given elsewhere as illustrations of such tables from the manuscripts used for this edition of the text. When al-Kirmānī says here 'It was the same with him' (*tilka sabīluhu*) this phrase refers to the traits listed in the same column one (or more) row(s) above. However, for some of the later names, it is hard to determine the exact alignment of these spaces and thus to know what it refers to. And, in most of the mss., production of these tables has become even less precise with blank spaces replacing the words *tilka sabīluhu*, often misaligned or missing altogether.

(11) He was one of the earliest believers; (12) He was characterized by knowledge of the Book of God; (13) He was not knowledgeable about what is permitted and what is forbidden; (14) [blank]; (15) [blank].

Zayd b. Ḥārith:[41] (1) [blank]; (2) [blank]; (3) [blank]; (4) [blank]; (5) [blank]; (6) [blank]; (7) [blank]; (8) [blank]; (9) [blank]; (10) [blank]; (11) He was among the earliest Muslims; (12) He was one of those characterized by [knowledge of the Book of God]; (13) He was one of those characterized by knowledge of what is permitted and what is forbidden; (14) [blank]; (15) [blank]; (16) [blank].

Ṭalḥa:[42] (1) [blank]; (2) [blank]; (3) [blank]; (4) [blank]; (5) He was courageous; (6) [blank]; (7) [blank]; (8) [blank]; (9) [blank]; (10) [blank]; (11) He was among the earliest Muslims; (12) [blank]; (13) [blank]; (14) [blank]; (15) [blank]; (16) [blank].

al-Zubayr:[43] (1) [blank]; (2) [blank]; (3) [blank]; (4) [blank]; (5) He was courageous; (6) [blank]; (7) [blank]; (8) [blank]; (9) [blank]; (10) [blank]; (11) He was among the earliest Muslims; (12) [blank]; (13) [blank]; (14) [blank]; (15) [blank]; (16) [blank].

Saʿd b. ʿAbd al-Raḥmān:[44] (1) [blank]; (2) [blank]; (3) [blank]; (4) [blank]; (5) [blank]; (6) [blank]; (7) [blank]; (8) [blank]; (9) [blank]; (10) [blank]; (11) He was among the earliest Muslims; (12) [blank]; (13) [blank]; (14) [blank]; (15) [blank]; (16) [blank].

---

41. This is obviously Zayd b. Ḥāritha al-Kalbī, the adopted son of Muḥammad. He died in the year 8/629. On him see 'Zayd b. Ḥāritha' by M. Lecker in *EI2*.

42. Talḥa b. 'Abdallāh, a prominent Companion and an early convert to Islam. He was later to be a rival of 'Alī. On him see 'Talḥa' by W. Madelung in *EI2*.

43. Al-Zubayr b. al-'Awwām, another prominent Companion and an early convert, later an opponent and rival of 'Alī. See 'al-Zubayr b. al-'Awwām' by I. Hasson in the *EI2*.

44. Sa'd (or in at least one manuscript Sa'īd) b. 'Abd al-Raḥmān is not the name of any well-known early Companion of the Prophet and, therefore, it must be the result of some mistake. Possibly al-Kirmānī had in mind both Sa'd b. Abī Waqqāṣ, whose father's name was Mālik (see 'Sa'd b. Abī Waḳḳāṣ' by G. R. Hawting in *EI2*) and also 'Abd al-Raḥmān b. 'Awf, both of whom, as famous early Muslims, certainly fit the context. If so perhaps the two were inadvertently conflated in the course of the transmission of this portion of the table.

Salmān:[45] (1) [blank]; (2) [blank]; (3) [blank]; (4) He was chaste; (5) He was pure; (6) He was pious; (7) He was generous; (8) [blank]; (9) He was dear to the apostle; (10) He was ascetic and among those characterized by it; (11) He was among the earliest Muslims; (12) [blank]; (13) He was knowledgeable about what is permitted and what is forbidden; (14) [blank]; (15) [blank]; (16) He was close to the Apostle owing to his having said: 'For us Salmān is family (*ahl al-bayt*)'.

Abū Dharr:[46] (1) [blank]; (2) [blank]; (3) [blank]; (4) He was chaste; (5) He was pure; (6) He was pious; (7) He was generous; (8) [blank]; (9) He was one of the ascetics and was noted for it; (10) [blank]; (11) He was one of the earliest Muslims; (12) [blank]; (13) [blank]; (14) [blank]; (15) [blank]; (16) [blank].

Miqdād:[47] (1) [blank]; (2) [blank]; (3) [blank]; (4) [blank]; (5) [blank]; (6) He was pious; (7) [blank]; (8) He was generous; (9) He was one of the ascetics, those noted for it; (10) ?? ; (11) He was one of the earliest Muslims; (12) [blank]; (13) [blank]; (14) [blank]; (15) [blank]; (16) [blank].

ʿAmmār:[48] (1) [blank]; (2) [blank]; (3) [blank]; (4) [blank]; (5) [blank]; (6) He was pious; (7) ?? ; (8) He was generous; (9) He was one of the ascetics, those noted for it; (10) ?? ; (11) He was one of the earliest Muslims; (12) [blank]; (13) [blank]; (14) [blank]; (15) [blank]; (16) [blank].

ʿAbdallāh b. Masʿūd:[49] (1) [blank]; (2) [blank]; (3) [blank]; (4) [blank]; (5) [blank]; (6) He was pious; (7) ?? ; (8) He was generous,

45. On him see 'Salmān al-Fārisī' by G. Levi Della Vida in *EI2 Supplement*.

46. Abū Dharr al-Ghifārī, a Companion and one of the earliest Muslims, noted for humility and asceticism. He died in 32/652–53. See 'Abū Dharr' by J. Robson in *EI2*.

47. Al-Miqdād b. 'Amr, a well known Companion and one of the earliest of the Muslims. See 'al-Miḳdād b. 'Amr' by G. H. A. Juynboll in *EI2*.

48. 'Ammār b. Yāsir, a Companion, early Muslim and later a noted partisan of 'Alī. He was killed at the Battle of Ṣiffīn in 37/657. See "Ammār b. Yāsir' by H. Reckendorf in *EI2*.

49. A famous Companion and one of the earliest Muslims, he was a noted reader of the Qur'ān. See 'Ibn Mas'ūd' by J.-C. Vadet in *EI2*.

spending freely; (9) He was one of the ascetics, those noted for it; (10) ?? ; (11) He was one of the earliest Muslims; (12) [blank]; (13) [blank]; (14) [blank]; (15) [blank]; (16) [blank].

ʿAbdallāh b. ʿAbbās:[50] (1) [blank]; (2) [blank]; (3) [blank]; (4) [blank]; (5) [blank]; (6) He was pious; (7) ?? ; (8) He was generous; (9) He was knowledgeable about the Book of God; (10) He was knowledgeable and an expert in legal matters; (11) He understood the principles of legal rulings; (12) He was one of the earliest Muslims; (16) He was close to the Apostle and was the son of his paternal uncle.

ʿAlī b. Abī Ṭālib: (1) [blank]; (2) He had been designated by God and by His Apostle, as we have demonstrated in the 'Light' previous to this one; (3) He was pure and purified, had worshipped neither idol nor graven image and had not prostrated other than to God with a sincerity he was famous for; (4) He was chaste, having never committed an act of disobedience nor a sin, had not drunk wine or encouraged corruption, and was famous for that; (5) He was brave and well known for his leadership, his order never concealed, and proverbs have been made of it; (6) He was pious, not seeking to take the property of anyone by force for the purpose of God nor to impose on God the reproach of blame, and was famous for that; (7) He was generous, God mentioned that in Sūra *Hal atā*[51] as is well known; (8) He was knowledgeable about legal judgments; (9) He was ascetic in this world and was noted for that; (10) He was just and merciful, and his justice became the reason it was expected by those who expected it and he was well known for that; (11) He was one of the earliest of the very first Muslims, being second to the one who [first] believed in God and the Apostle who was Khadīja; (12) He was knowledgeable about the Book of God and all that God

50. Son of the Prophet's uncle al-ʿAbbās, ʿAbdallāh, who was therefore a first cousin of both Muḥammad and ʿAlī b. Abī Ṭālib, was considered one of the most important scholars and authorities of the first Islamic generation. He was also an ancestor of the Abbasids. See "Abdallāh b. al-ʿAbbās' by L. Veccia Vaglieri in *EI2*.

51. Sūra 76 (*Dahr* or *al-Insān*), the first line of which is: *Hal atā ʿalā al-insāni ḥīnun mina'l-dahr* ('Has there come upon man a time when he was a thing unremembered?').

had revealed and was famous for that; (13) He was knowledgeable about what is permitted and what is forbidden, an expert in legal understanding for which he was famous, given that he also knew legal judgments, and for that reason the Prophet said: "'Alī is the best judge among you';[52] (14) He fully understood the interpretation of the Book of God and for that reason the Prophet declared: "'Alī is the master of the interpretation'; (15) He was dear to God based on the Prophet's having said on the day he gave the battle standard to him for the conquest of Khaybar: 'Verily, I give the standard to an impetuous man, not someone who flees. God and His Apostle both love him he who loves God and His Apostle'; (16) He was close to the Prophet and whoever was close to the Apostle was close to God, and he was a member of the 'people of the cloak' (*aṣḥāb al-kisāʾ*) on the day of mutual cursing (*al-mubāhala*),[53] and he was the Prophet's successor and legatee (*waṣī*).

[Circle Table follows immediately, with seven concentric circles from the innermost to the outside: Plates 13–14]

A. The world of the mandate (*ʿālam al-qaḍāʾ*).
B. (1) revelation; (2) designation; (3) purity; (4) chasteness; (5) piety; (6) bravery; (7) generosity; (8) abstinence; (9) justice; (10) precedence; (11) knowledge; (12) knowledge; (13) knowledge; (14) legal authority; (15) dearness; (16) closeness.
C. (1) **Muḥammad** [revelation]: (2) He was designated by God; (3) He was pure, purified; (4) He was chaste; (5) He was pious; (6) He was courageous; (7) He was generous; (8) He was ascetic; (9) He was just, merciful; (10) He was the first of the early Muslims; (11) He knew the Book of God; (12) He knew what is permitted and what is forbidden; (13) He knew the interpretation of the Book of God; (14) He knew the rules of legal judgments; (15) He was dear to God; (16) He was close to God.
D. (1) **Abū Bakr** [no revelation]: (2) missing; (3) missing; (4) missing; (5) He was pious; (6) missing; (7) He was noted [for being generous]; (8) missing; (9) missing; (10) He was one of the earliest

52. This *ḥadīth* appears also in the *Daʿāʾim*, I, p. 92; trans. p. 114.

53. On the *mubāhala*, see Moojan Momen, *An Introduction to Shiʿi Islam* (New Haven and London, 1985), pp. 13–14.

Muslims; (11) missing; (12) missing; (13) missing; (14) missing; (15) missing; (16) missing.

E. (1) **ʿUmar** [no revelation]: (2) missing; (3) missing; (4) missing; (5) He was pious; (6) missing; (7) He was generous, spending freely; (8) missing; (9) missing; (10) missing; (11) missing; (12) He knew what is permitted and what is forbidden; (13) missing; (14) missing; (15) missing; (16) missing.

F. (1) **ʿUthmān** [no revelation]: (2) missing; (3) missing; (4) missing; (5) missing; (6) missing; (7) He was generous, spending freely; (8) missing; (9) missing; (10) He was one of the earliest Muslims; (11) He knew the Book of God; (12) missing; (13) missing; (14) missing; (15) missing; (16) missing.

G. (1) **ʿAlī**, he did not receive revelation: (2) He was designated by God and by His Apostle; (3) He was pure, purified, having committed no sin at all; (4) He was chaste, having never encouraged corruption at all; (5) He was pious having not sought the property of anyone; (6) He was courageous, leading in advance and famous for that; (7) He was generous, so cited by God in His Book and in the practice of the Apostle; (8) He was ascetic and among those so noted; (9) He was just, never bringing on God the reproach of complaints; (10) He was the first of the earliest male believers; (11) He knew the Book of God, both its literal and its figurative meaning; (12) He knew what is permitted and what is forbidden, being an expert in that; (13) He knew the interpretation of the Book of God; (14) He understood legal judgments because of which the Prophet said: "ʿAlī will judge among you'; (15) He was dear to God, owing to the Prophet's declaration about him on the day of Khaybar; (16) He was close to the Apostle of God.

It has become amply clear with these tables that ʿAlī b. Abī Ṭālib combined in himself all of the character traits that were present in the Prophet, except the revelation by which God singled him out as His Prophet. ʿAlī was the most worthy for the place of the Messenger of God after him and he was the imam, rather than any of the rest whose tables are devoid of these character traits. God is the guardian of the believers. This circular table is for he who does not understand the system of reckoning and its applications as in this book, so as to establish also in that way a demonstration.

The Sixth Light

That, after the designation had reached Jaʿfar al-Ṣādiq, the imamate belonged to Ismāʿīl, and his descendants, to the exclusion of any of Ismāʿīl's brothers.

The first demonstration: It is correct that the imamate is valid only on the basis of designation and appointment and that the Prophet's designation came down in favour of ʿAlī b. Abī Ṭālib to the exclusion of all others. From ʿAlī it went to al-Ḥasan, but then after him none of his sons deserved the designation to the imamate because there existed a person the equal of al-Ḥasan in terms of infallibility and purity, and there had been an explicit indication by the Prophet that the imamate was to be his. That person was al-Ḥusayn, and so the designation came to him. Thereafter, subsequent to al-Ḥusayn, the sons of al-Ḥasan did not merit the designation because the offspring of al-Ḥusayn were more worthy of it due to the [principle of] closeness of the womb as in God's statement: 'Those related by the womb are nearer to one another' [8: 75].[54] The designation next followed the progeny of al-Ḥusayn down to Jaʿfar al-Ṣādiq and then Jaʿfar designated Ismāʿīl. The Shīʿa differed about Ismāʿīl with regard to what they held about his having died before Jaʿfar and about Jaʿfar's having pointed afterward to another of his sons. They disagreed also about whether he said: 'Never has God changed His mind as He did in regard to Ismāʿīl.' Subsequent to Jaʿfar b. Muḥammad's designation of Ismāʿīl, with respect to claims about his having designated another of his sons after the death of Ismāʿīl, the situation had three possible outcomes. Either he designated another of his sons following the death of Ismāʿīl, as has been reported, and Ismāʿīl had a son; or he designated him and Ismāʿīl did not have son; or he did not designate another after having issued his previous designation of Ismāʿīl. If the designation [of another] was made and

54. The author's argument here has an almost exact parallel in the *Daʿāʾim*, I, 37; trans. pp. 48–49.

Ismāʿīl had a son, Jaʿfar would have issued a decision contrary to what God revealed should he have thereby given the inheritance of Ismāʿīl, despite his having a son, to his brothers without a cause for depriving the son, as had happened in depriving the son of al-Ḥasan and granting it to the son of al-Ḥusayn. But to imagine something like that of Jaʿfar is inconceivable due to the validity of his imamate and his infallibility. If that is inconceivable, what is attributed to him concerning the designating of another of his sons, after having previously designated Ismāʿīl, is false. If he were to have designated him and Ismāʿīl had no son, and yet [he had done so] with the knowledge and empowerment of God, there would have been a truncation of genealogical descent. But God's knowledge and power would not have permitted a designation in favour of a person whose line would end, given that the imamate is preserved in progeny. That requires that Jaʿfar did not designate Ismāʿīl. However, since we have found that he did designate him, we know that he was not without progeny and lineal succession. And if he was not without progeny and lineal succession, that the imamate belonged to him and to his progeny is proven. If, however, Jaʿfar did not designate anyone after having designated Ismāʿīl, the imamate belonged to Ismāʿīl. If the imamate of Ismāʿīl is established fact, that he had progeny is proven because the imamate is not merited by someone who has no lineal successor since it is preserved through lineal succession. If his progeny is proven, that the imamate belongs to his offspring is also proven. The situation was confined to these three possibilities and yet the three possibilities all require that the imamate belong to Ismāʿīl and to his descendants. Thus, the imamate is proven to have been Ismāʿīl's and his son's. Therefore, the imamate resided in Ismāʿīl and in his descendants.

The second demonstration: We hold that since the imamate resided in the succession of Jaʿfar, the imam would not have designated anyone he regarded as suitable other than a person he knew to be appropriate for it. The first thing to be considered fitting of an imam in regard to his having the imamate is that the person not be infertile. Next, since a person without a successor does not merit the imamate, he should have a lineal successor and progeny. Because the imam Jaʿfar designated Ismāʿīl, from that fact we determine that Ismāʿīl had a son and successor; otherwise he would not have designated him. Since he had a successor, his successor was more worthy of the imamate than his uncles. Therefore, the imamate belonged to Ismāʿīl, and to his successor, to the exclusion of the rest of them.

The third demonstration: Given that the imam is infallible, never having made a mistake, and given that, if Ismāʿīl had not had a son nor successor nor descendants, it would make Jaʿfar's designation of him a mistake, since he was designated, with respect to the infallibility of the imam, that requires that Ismāʿīl had a successor and descendants. If he had descendants and a successor, his successor is more deserving of the imamate than his uncles. Therefore, the imamate after Ismāʿīl belonged to his son, and to his descendants, to the exclusion of everyone else.

The fourth demonstration: The imamate belonged to Jaʿfar and was preserved in his succession and he had four sons: Ismāʿīl, ʿAbdallāh, Muḥammad and Mūsā. ʿAbdallāh was not worthy of it because of being infertile and lacking progeny. That became the greatest evidence of the invalidity of his imamate, that and the absence of having been designated for it. Nor was Muḥammad[55] deserving of it because of his attempting to do that which the words of the Messenger had forbidden and his going against the order not to rebel against the one who guaranteed his safety and who had sheltered him. His disloyalty towards him and his dispatching of swordsmen in the sanctuary where it was forbidden and his claiming in it the imamate, then countermanding his order, frustrating his own *daʿwa,* even though the Prophet had said, 'The imam is he whose *daʿwa* is not refused should you observe him appealing for it in the holy places', and his later denial of himself. All of this becomes the greatest of the evidence for the invalidity of his imamate, that as well as the lack of a designation in his favour. Mūsā

55. This son of Jaʿfar, following the prompting of his own son ʿAlī and other Ḥusaynid rebels led by Ḥusayn b. Ḥasan al-Afṭas, declared himself imam-caliph in Mecca in 200/815. He held his position for only a few months supported sporadically by the Alids and others until his movement was suppressed by the Abbasids. On this incident see the report gathered by al-Ṭabarī (*Ta'rīkh al-rusul wa'l-mulūk*, ed. de Goeje et al., Leiden, 1879–1901, vol. 3, pp. 989–995; Eng. trans. by C. E. Bosworth as *The History of al-Ṭabarī*: vol. 32, *The Reunification of the ʿAbbāsid Caliphate* (Albany, NY, 1987, pp. 30–37), and the comments of al-Masʿūdī (*Murūj al-dhahab wa maʿādin al-jawhar*, ed. ʿAbd al-Ḥamīd, (Cairo, 1964 vol. 4, pp. 26–27).

was also not worthy of it, since he and his offspring do not have those qualifications [which] the presence of the designation cause to exist in the one so designated. Nor does he have a *daʿwa* raising the appeal to the absolute unity of God and knowledge of the interpretation of God's Book and the law of the Messenger, since for those who believe in his imamate, the matter terminates in a person among his descendants who has not existed for upwards of two hundred years, even though the community has need of him, if he were, in fact, the imam. Even so, fear which is a condition for the hiding of one who would be imam is absent; otherwise it might be said that he is afraid. The sword is sheathed that was drawn in the shedding of the blood of the family of Muḥammad and his Shīʿa on the part of the Banū Umayya and the freed war slaves from the family of ʿAbbās. Otherwise, for that reason it could be said that he is a fugitive. Beyond the absence of a *daʿwa* appealing on his behalf, summoning to God for his imamate, which is obligatory and incumbent on him in that he is the imam, he is in concealment. No one is either prophet or imam who has no *daʿwa* and lacks knowledge of the interpretation of issues concerning the Book of God and its explanation about which there is disagreement, and about the licit and illicit and the law on the part of various sectarian claimants to his imamate, even though it is obligatory for him to publish it, if he is, in fact, the imam. The result of all this is great evidence as to the invalidity of his imamate. It proves that the imamate belonged to Ismāʿīl in that it resided in the succession of Jaʿfar, and the doctrine upholding any other of the sons is false. If the imamate of Ismāʿīl is proven, and if it cannot be proven of someone who has no successor, the imamate after Ismāʿīl belonged to his son Muḥammad. Therefore, the imamate after Ismāʿīl belonged to his son.

The fifth demonstration: Everything a power brings into existence is particularized by attributes by which it is distinguished from something else, and the thing that is different in it has no means of being understood other than on the basis of the attributes that single it out in terms of its species and are to be sought in it. If there is no way to understand it as it truly is, other than by referring to the attributes that single it out with respect to its species and are to be sought in it, once its attributes are proven of it and found to be in it, it is correct and proven that it is that very thing. An example here is the thing that differs in its being a citron. If its attributes are referred back in a balance of expression which consist of tables, such as those we have established at the end of this demonstration in regard to the attributes of the species citron, and if its attributes match the tables of the attributes of the species citron perfectly, there is no disagreeing about its being authentically a citron. If, however, its attributes are expressed and it is found that they fill in part of the table but parts are empty, it cannot be doubted that it is not authentically a citron. The matter of the imam in respect to his imamate is quite the same with regard to the imam being the possessor of spiritual character traits and physical good fortune. The authenticity of his imamate is connected to these traits and to that good fortune. If we apply the balance of considerations in the tables we have set up for the attributes of the imam in order to ascertain the validity of the imamate of Muḥammad, Mūsā, ʿAbdallāh (the sons of Jaʿfar), Zayd b. ʿAlī, and the others than these of those cited previously, the tables for them differ by the presences of some traits and the absence of others, except for the table for Ismāʿīl. Thus, it is proven that the imamate belonged to Ismāʿīl. If it is proven to be Ismāʿīl's, his succession, given the lack of a reason to preclude it, is the more certain. Therefore, the imamate belonged to Ismāʿīl and to his lineal successor.

As a prelude to the table for the imamate, here is a table of the attributes of the species citron which makes clear what is not a citron.

Preliminary to the Table of the Imamate. [Tables III and IV, Plates 15–20]

The thing in itself: its shape running to long and ridged on the outside (*mujayyab al-jihāt*); its colour being yellow; its smell being fragrant; the pulp in it is sweet to the taste; the core of it has an acidic taste; it is truly of the species.

The essence of the thing does not differ from it being a citron; its shape runs to long and is ridged on the outside; its colour is yellow; its smell is fragrant; it has a pulp and its taste is sweet; it has a core and its taste is acidic; it is truly a citron.

The essence differs from its being a citron; its shape runs to long; its colour is yellow; it has no fragrant smell; its has no pulp; it has no core; it is not truly a citron but rather a counterfeit.

The essence differs from its being a citron; its shape is spherical; its colour is yellow; its smell is fragrant; its pulp is acidic; it has no core; it is not a citron but rather a quince.

Tables reflecting the validity of the imamate of those who preceded and have passed away to show thereby the falseness of the imamate of those among them who were not imams. [Table V, Plates 21–26]

[1] The names and being from the offspring of prophecy among the lineal descendants of al-Ḥusayn; [2] The existence of an offspring who has received the designation in lieu of the others because, for offspring, that is a cause that precludes the nobility of the imamate; [3] The existence of knowledge of what God revealed as present in the successor who is the one designated; [4] The existence of works in accord with the stipulations of God as present in the successor who is the one designated; [5] The existence of commanding the good and forbidding the bad as present in the successor who is the one designated; [6] The existence of the appeal (*daʿwa*) to obey God as present in the successor who is the one designated; [7] being truly the imam.

Jaʿfar al-Ṣādiq, he was from the offspring of al-Ḥusayn; his successor and the one designated exists and he is al-Ḥākim bi-amr Allāh, Commander of the Faithful; his knowledge of the regulations of God remains as they are present in the one of his successors who has been designated; his works in accord with the regulations of God remain as present in the successor who was designated; his commanding the good and prohibiting the bad remains as present in the one designated; his appeal to obey God remains in force as present in the one among his progeny who is designated; he was truly the imam.

ʿAlī b. Muḥammad, the Ḥasanid ruler of Baṣra,[56] who did not come from the son of al-Ḥusayn; his designated successor does

56. This ʿAlī b. Muḥammad is most likely the leader of the Zanj revolts during the period 255–270/868–883 when he twice ruled Baṣra prior to capture by the Abbasids and execution in 270/883. However, one genealogy put forward for him makes him a descendant of al-Ḥusayn, not al-Ḥasan. See "Alī b. Muḥammad al-Zandjī' by B. Lewis in *EI2*. See also 'al-Zandj. 2: The Zandj Revolts in 'Irāḳ' by A. Popovic in *EI2*. Although there were members of the Ḥasanid line with this name, none could be described as the ruler (*ṣāḥib*) of Baṣra.

not exist; his knowledge did not exist; his works did not exist; his commanding the good and forbidding the bad did not exist; he had no *daʿwa*; he was no imam.

al-Maʾmūn al-ʿAbbāsī,[57] who was not from the progeny of al-Ḥusayn; [this trait] was not present [in him]; [this trait] was not present [in him]; [this trait] was not present [in him]; [this trait] was not present [in him]; [this trait] was not present [in him]; he was no imam.

Zayd b. ʿAlī,[58] who was from the progeny of al-Ḥusayn; [this trait] was not present [in him]; [this trait] was not present [in him]; [this trait] was not present [in him]; [this trait] was not present [in him]; [this trait] was not present [in him]; he was no imam.

Muḥammad b. Jaʿfar,[59] who was a lineal descendant of al-Ḥusayn; [this trait] was not present [in him]; [this trait] was not present [in him]; [this trait] was not present [in him]; [this trait] was not present [in him]; [this trait] was not present [in him]; he was no imam.

ʿAbdallāh b. Jaʿfar, who was a lineal descendant of al-Ḥusayn; [this trait] was not present [in him]; [this trait] was not present [in him]; [this trait] was not present [in him]; [this trait] was not present [in him]; [this trait] was not present [in him]; he was no imam.

Mūsā b. Jaʿfar, who was a lineal descendant of al-Ḥusayn; [this trait] was not present [in him]; [this trait] was not present [in him]; [this trait] was not present [in him]; [this trait] was not present [in him]; [this trait] was not present [in him]; he was no imam.

Ismāʿīl b. Jaʿfar, who was from the offspring of prophecy and was a lineal descendant of al-Ḥusayn; his successor who has been

57. This man is the Abbasid caliph al-Ma'mūn, son of Hārūn al-Rashīd, who ruled from 196/812 to his death in 218/833. On him see 'al-Ma'mūn' by M. Rekaya in *EI2*.

58. Zayd b. ʿAlī was the brother of Muḥammad al-Bāqir and thus, like him, a grandson of Ḥusayn. Zayd's revolt gave rise to the Zaydiyya. He was killed in the year 122/740. See 'Zayd b. ʿAlī b. al-Ḥusayn' by W. Madelung in *EI2*.

59. Muḥammad b. Jaʿfar was, as were ʿAbdallāh, Mūsā and Ismāʿīl, whose names follow here, a son of the Imam Jaʿfar al-Ṣādiq.

designated exists and he is al-Ḥākim bi-amr Allāh, the Commander of the Faithful; his knowledge of what God revealed exists as it is present in his successor who is the one designated; his works in accord with the regulations of God exist as represented in the one designated among his progeny; his commanding the good and prohibiting the bad remains in force as it is performed by the one designated among his progeny; his appeal to obey God remains in force as present in the one designated among his progeny; he was truly an imam.

The sixth demonstration: The imam is needed because he is the preserver of the regulations in the law and the essence of the Book from additions to it or subtractions from it; he is the summoner to Islam by attraction and a warning; he is the representative of the Muslims before their Lord on the Day of Judgment; he is the one who, by his knowledge and explanation, extracts them from issues they fall into disagreement about; he is the one who, on the basis of what God revealed, adjudicates concerning incidents that occur among them and who seeks forgiveness for them and leads them in prayers and purifies them by taking what God ordered that he collect from them as he deems appropriate; he applies to them corporal punishments; he is the one who responds to issues put to him concerning his understanding of matters of religion; he is the conveyor to the community of what the Messenger said, the one who takes his place in regard to all matters connected with the pursuit of the wellbeing of the community. If it were not for these provisions, the imam would not be needed. There would be no preserver of the regulations in the law, no one to extract the people from their disputes when they referred them to him, no one to adjudicate, no one in charge of all we have mentioned as the Messenger's role by his order and thus there would be no imam. The expected person anticipated by all the sects of the Shīʿa who uphold the imamate of Muḥammad [b. Jāʿfar], or ʿAbdallāh or Mūsa, or the others, is not the preserver of the Book, nor the law, nor does he extract the people from their disputes, nor does he adjudicate concerning incidents that befall them, nor seek forgiveness for them, nor lead their prayers, nor make the appeal, nor purify them, nor apply corporal punishments, nor issue responses, nor represent, nor convey, nor take the Messenger's place in all of what by his order is connected to him. Thus, it is proven that he is not the imam. Although it is proven that he is not an imam for that reason, it is even so necessary that the nobility of the imamate and the crown of designation and appointment require, if it were to have been in any one of them, that the authority of the imamate continue in the lineal succession of the one who had a lineal successor. If that succession breaks off for them, while at the same time the existence of the imamate in the lineal succession of Jaʿfar is well established, its authority rests with the lineal succession of Ismāʿīl, and it is thus correct that the imamate belonged to Ismāʿīl and to his lineal succession. Therefore, the imamate belongs to Ismāʿīl and to his lineal descendants to the exclusion of the rest of them.

The seventh demonstration: The Prophet said: 'There will exist in my community what existed in communities that have gone before, as alike as one sandal to another or one arrow feather to another.' God has reported about a group of young men who had faith in their Lord and He increased them in guidance and He strengthened the bonds of their hearts. When they observed that their nation had adopted patrons other than God, they took refuge in a cave and stayed there three hundred and nine years, under the harshest of conditions. God informed His Prophet about it when He said: 'Had you looked upon them you would have surely turned away fleeing and filled with terror at them' [18: 18]. God gave solace to them after the long interval of these harsh conditions. Among the descendants of Muḥammad, who constituted his community, the like of this occurred in truth, arrow feather to arrow feather. The imams after him were subject to suppression, tyranny, fear and concealment, though persons safeguarded and watched over [them], nonetheless tossing and turning on the horizons, now right, now left, for a period of three hundred and nine years, until the time that al-Mahdī billāh Abū Muḥammad rose to take up the holy war in the Maghrib. Therefore, what God reported concerning the story of the inhabitants of the cave was verified for the community of Muḥammad with regard to the progeny of Ismāʿīl, to the exclusion of the progeny of his brothers among the sons of Jaʿfar, by the appearance of al-Mahdī billāh in the Maghrib, and with his rising in pursuit of holy war in the year 309 of the Hijra of the

Prophet,[60] and with the pure imams descended from his son. God thereby removed from the imams the veil of fear and He caused the sun to rise from its western setting, turned the mill of religion on its axis, and restored the truth to his people. Their standards became famous; their banners in defence of their right victorious. Al-Mahdī billāh was the fourth of the male line of Ismāʿīl and of his offspring and his purity. Thus, it is proven that the imamate belonged to Ismāʿīl and to his lineal descendants. Therefore, the imamate was Ismāʿīl's and that of his lineal successor.

The Seventh Light

On the necessity of the imamate of al-Ḥākim bi-amr Allāh, Commander of the Faithful, and the obligation to obey him and follow him over and against all the other doctrines.

The first demonstration: The Muslims agree on the belief in the imamate in two parties: one party upholds the imamate of Abū Bakr and of his precedence. They are the Murjiʾa according to the various subdivision of them, such as the Proponents of Personal Opinion and Ḥadīth, the Ḥanbalīs, the Dāʾūdīs, the Muʿtazilīs, and yet others.[61] Their doctrine and belief is that whoever rises to the position [of imam] who is a Muslim, whether from the Quraysh or is an Abyssinian, and who has the power and authority and support to command the good and prohibit the bad, to apply the corporal punishments, preserve the community, revive the *sunna*, he is the imam, fealty to whom is required, and obedience to him is what the straight path

60. The Hijra date 309 (*tisʿ wa thalāthmiʾa*) for the rise of al-Mahdī is simply wrong since it was 297. How al-Kirmānī could have made such a mistake is not at all clear, a fact that troubled several of the copyists of the text who recognized and commented on the error.

61. For this rather uncommon understanding of the Murjiʾa, see Abū Ḥātim al-Rāzī's *Kitāb al-zīna*, third part on the Islamic sects, edited and published by ʿAbdallāh Sallūm al-Samarrāʾī in his *al-Ghulūw waʾl-firaq al-ghāliya fiʾl ḥaḍāra al-Islāmiyya* (Baghdad, 1972, pp. 229–339), pp. 264–266. The term *irjāʾ* here means 'to put off' (*taʾkhīr*), eg. the imamate of ʿAlī. *Irjāʾ* equals *taʾkhīr* as in this instance and the term Murjiʾa thus applies to all those who uphold the advancement of Abū Bakr over ʿAlī.

demands. He who has the august authority, glorious kingship, established proof, sword unsheathed in support of Islam, commands the good and forbids the bad, applies the corporal punishments, preserves the borders, cares for the populace, revives the *sunna*, safeguards society, endeavours to conduct the holy war, shatters the opposition, extends justice and mercy, without having to mention the condition of the designation and appointment and the nobility of universal high regard, is al-Ḥākim bi-amr Allāh. From that it follows necessarily that he is the imam, fealty to whom is incumbent on them and obedience to him is required of them. The other party uphold the imamate of the Commander of the Faithful, ʿAlī b. Abī Ṭālib. They are the Shīʿa, according to the various subdivisions into which they divide, such as the Zaydīs, the Imāmīs, the Kaysānīs, the Ghālīs, and yet others. These sects further subdivide into two parties: one upholds designation and appointment openly and the other designation in private. Those whose doctrine is the designation in private claim that whoever of the descendants of the Prophet, whether of the Ḥasanid or Ḥusaynid line, but who is a member of the family of Prophet's house, and whoever of them unsheathes his sword and commands the good and prohibits the bad, who is knowledgeable, abstemious, generous, brave, pious, in adherence to the words of the Prophet: 'Truly I leave with you the two anchors, the Book of God and my progeny and family; cleave to them both and you will not go astray as long as you adhere to them.' He also said: 'Whoever does not respond to our summons to the family, God will turn him prostrate in the fire [of hell].' Hence, following him is incumbent on the community and obeying him is required of it. The person whose sword is unsheathed, whose commanding the good and prohibiting the bad is conspicuous, whose knowledge is extensive, his courage, asceticism, and generosity well known, and who is a scion of the pure family and an offspring of prophecy, without mentioning the presence in him of the nobility of designation and appointment, is al-Ḥākim bi-amr Allāh, the Commander of the Faithful. From that fact it follows necessarily that he is the imam, fealty to whom is required of them and obeying him is incumbent and decreed for them. Those who uphold a doctrine of open designation maintain that the imamate after al-Ḥusayn is merited by none except his sons in general and that the nobility of it requires that it be by designation in particular, and that the earth cannot be devoid of an imam who upholds the rights of God, whether visibly and openly or in fear, obscurity and concealment, as said the Commander of the Faithful ʿAlī b. Abī Ṭālib. The imam has a miracle by which his imamate is verified and following him is thus thereby made necessary, and on the basis of it he is distinguished from the others. The one who exists among the lineal descendants of al-Ḥusayn, who uphold the rights of God on His earth, openly to the extent that his sword holds sway over his governors and friends and, to the extent that his command does not prevail, secretly through his deputies, who is foremost in his devotion to guiding to God's absolute unity and summoning through his imamate to divesting Him [of attributes], warning creation of His promise and His threat, extending justice to His servants, commanding what he was ordered of the good and prohibiting what of the bad he was prohibited, who has a miracle, or rather miracles, who informs about events to come before they happen, reveals knowledge that is hidden and the judgements issued in regard to all that the Prophet brought concerning the Book and the law, particularly with respect to the individual letters at the commencement of *sūra*s of the Qur'ān, the path to the examining of which is restricted for the community one and all and even though they desire its interpretation,[62] just as they search for the explanation of other parts, but their personal opinions are nevertheless powerless—this is not to mention the knowledge of *lamiyyāt* which God secures to him and to his like among the imams so that none have access to it save the purified. Thus God said: 'This is a glorious Qur'ān in a hidden book none will touch save the purified' [56: 79] and He said: 'In noble pages exalted and purified by the hands of devout and pious scribes' [80: 13–16]. He who is distinguished in that from the rest, just as he is distinguished in other matters, is al-Ḥākim bi-amr Allāh, Commander of the Faithful, and none other. From this it follows necessarily that it is he whom the earth cannot be without in our time, based on the presence of the condition of someone upholding

62. Twenty-nine *sūra*s of the Qur'ān commence with a first verse composed solely of a letter or a group of letters, the meaning of which has never been adequately explained and has often been treated as a mystery.

the rights of God openly or secretly, miraculous in his knowledge, his informing about the hidden because the imam is he who upholds the rights of God openly, when that is possible, or secretly, not someone who forfeits the rights of God by not upholding them either openly or secretly. If he whom the earth cannot be without his presence and he whose connection through the imamate to the fruit of designation and appointment, which consists of commanding the good and prohibiting the bad and performing the miraculous exists—and he is al-Ḥākim bi-amr Allāh, Commander of the Faithful, and no one else—following him is, according to their own doctrine, required of them, and obedience to him is incumbent on them. Given, then, that the Muslims are two parties and each party requires his imamate according to their own doctrine of it, his imamate is proven. Therefore, al-Ḥākim bi-amr Allāh, Commander of the Faithful, is the imam, obedience to whom is obligatory.

The second demonstration: When Muḥammad summoned the unbelievers to Islam and they summoned him to the worship of images, he made the proof of the falsity of what they, due to their obsession with idols, held against him—the absence in this world and the next of a summons to images. Thus he said: 'What is it to me that I summon you to salvation and you summon me to the fire? You invite me to deny God and to associate with Him what I have no knowledge of; I am summoning you to the Almighty, the All-forgiving. Surely what you summon me to has no appeal in this world or in the next world; our return is to God, and the transgressors, they are the inhabitants of the Fire' [40: 41–43]. The establishment of the appeal to the prophets, and to the imams who take their place, either openly or secretly, is the greatest proof God has. It is the clearest evidence for God. Thus, the establishment of the appeal is the greatest proof, and the appeal for al-Ḥākim bi-amr Allāh, Commander of the Faithful, exists, such that there is no land or region in the territory of Islam that does not have in it his appeal, summoning them to obedience to God through his imamate and to the absolute unity of God by means of him, openly where possible or secretly where not possible. From that fact it follows necessarily that he is the imam to whom obedience is required.

The third demonstration: Given that the imamate is not valid without designation and appointment, and the designation by the Prophet came down upon ʿAlī, and from ʿAlī it came to al-Ḥasan—from him to al-Ḥusayn and from him to ʿAlī [Zayn al-ʿAbidīn] and from him to Muḥammad [al-Bāqir] and from him to Jaʿfar, upholding the successor in place of the predecessor—and the designation has ended up with al-Ḥākim bi-amr Allāh, Commander of the Faithful, and the designation is in him at present, al-Ḥākim bi-amr Allāh, Commander of the Faithful, is thus the imam to whom obedience is an obligation.

The fourth demonstration: The cause for the sake of which the existence of the imam is required is the necessity of preserving the law and the Book from additions to either one or subtractions from them—given that additions and subtractions to them are both possible—and the summons to them and to Islam by exhortation and intimidation, the need of the community for someone to lead them in prayer, to teach them about the waymarkers of their religion, to extract them from their differences, to adjudicate among them in accord with what God revealed, to seek forgiveness for them, to purify them, to apply to them corporal punishments, to respond on matters they refer to him, to convey to them what the Messenger said, to take from them what is due to God as he understands it, to occupy the place of the Prophet in respect to what is before them by his command. The person who preserves the Book and the law with its regulations, who summons to Islam and to them both, and who defends it both by exhortation and a warning, who prays with the people, teaches them the waymarkers of their religion, extracts them from issues about which they differ and which are referred to him, who adjudicates according to what God revealed, who seeks from God forgiveness for he who seeks forgiveness from him, who purifies them, who applies to them the corporal punishments, who responds concerning questions put to him, who conveys what the Messenger has said in its true form, who takes from them what is due to God and expends it as it should be, who occupies the place of the Prophet among the community in accord with his command based on the designating of the person who assumes his place, that person is the imam. Al-Ḥākim bi-amr Allāh, Commander of the Faithful, fulfils all of that, taking thus the place of the Prophet by the designation of the one who came before him, and these functions and character traits are present in him, and he is the imam to whom obedience is required. Therefore, al-Ḥākim bi-amr

Allāh, Commander of the Faithful, is the imam to whom obedience is an obligation.

The fifth demonstration: There is no doubt that the imam must exist for the worship of God and that God never leaves His earth devoid of an imam in each and every time, who upholds the rights of God and who, as His proof to His servants, is the guidance to His absolute unity, who represents them to their Lord 'on the day wherein We summon the people through their imam' [17: 71]. Those who attempt to secure the nobility of the imamate as their own possession and who make a claim to it in our time are al-Ḥākim bi-amr Allāh, Commander of the Faithful; Aḥmad b. Isḥāq from the family of ʿAbbās, who resides in Baghdad; al-Hārūnī al-Ḥusaynī al-Zaydī who resides in Hawsam in the region of Jīlān; ʿUmar al-Nazwānī who resides in Jibāl ʿUmān; the Umayyad who resides in al-Andalus and what is beyond Qayrawān, and those among the offspring of al-Jannābī who call themselves the Lords (*al-Sāda*) in al-Aḥsāʾ.[63] The traits that preclude the meriting of the imamate fill the tables that we have set up at the end of this demonstration in their names, but the table for al-Ḥākim bi-amr Allāh, Commander of the Faithful is devoid of them. From that we determine that al-Ḥākim bi-amr Allāh, Commander of the Faithful, given the falsity of any of the others meriting the imamate and given the impossibility of the earth being without an imam, is the imam to whom obedience is an obligation. Therefore, al-Ḥākim bi-amr Allāh, Commander of the Faithful, is the imam to whom obedience is required of all and sundry.

Tables of traits that prevent [one] being worthy of the imamate in the form of an aide-mémoire *in order to understand from it the invalidity of the imamate of those who claim it and the necessity of its belonging to the one among them who truly has the right to it.* [Table VI, Plates 27–30]

Names: Being not among the lineal descendants of al-Ḥusayn precludes the imamate; being impure in body and soul precludes the imamate; thoughtlessness[64] in the exercise of legal authority

63. For the identities of these claimants to the imamate see the notes to the table that follow at the end of this demonstration.

64. The Arabic term here for thoughtlessness is *ruʿūna*, but many of the

based on ignorance and the utilization of resources for reprehensible purposes precludes the imamate; being devoid of religious knowledge, which consists of understanding what is permitted and what is forbidden and the revelation and the interpretation, precludes the imamate; contempt for the regulations of God and for commanding the good and prohibiting the bad and for maintaining the appeal (*daʿwa*) precludes the imamate; not having the nobility confirmed by the designation and appointment to the place of the Apostle precludes the imamate.

Aḥmad b. Isḥāq, who resides in Baghdad:[65] He is not a lineal descendant of al-Ḥusayn; he is not pure in soul due to his consumption of forbidden things (*suḥt*) and his setting the price of wine that is sold for him on his estates in Baghdad and its hinterland and for the ignorance deeply rooted in him due to the lack of knowledge; the existence in him by his own admission of things connected to the imamate that he does not know and his utilization of resources in ways not religiously commendable; being devoid of the knowledge associated with the religious declaration of God's absolute oneness and his reliance on the leaders of the Postponers (al-Murjiʾa), such as Abū Bakr al-Bāqillānī, and others; contempt for the regulations of God, not commanding the good and forbidding the bad in his own household and entourage, let alone for any other Muslims; being devoid of the designation of the person who occupies the place of the Apostle and instead having been put in office by the august Amir Bahāʾ al-Dawla, may God's mercy be upon him.[66]

---

manuscripts, including those that served as the primary sources for the present edition, have it changed to read *daʿwa*, although the latter word hardly makes sense in the context. Of those I examined directly, only the Hamdani ms. dated 1275/1858 has the reading *ruʿūna* but information supplied from additional mss. in Mumbai confirms it.

65. The Abbasid caliph al-Qādir, who ruled from 381/991 to 422/1031. On him see 'al-Ḳādir biʾallāh' by D. Sourdel in *EI2*.

66. Bahāʾ al-Dawla was the Buyid supreme ruler (*amīr*) in Iraq and then southern Persia as well from 379/989, to his death in Jumādā II 403/December 1012. He was succeeded by his son, Sulṭān al-Dawla. See 'Bahāʾ al-Dawla' by C. Edmund Bosworth in the *EI2 Supplement*. In 381/991 he deposed the Abbasid caliph al-Ṭāʾiʿ and replaced him with the same man's cousin, Aḥmad b. Isḥāq,

al-Ḥārūnī al-Ḥasanī, who resides in Hawsam:[67] He is not a lineal descendant of al-Ḥusayn; he is not pure in body because of leprosy that has taken hold of him, nor in the soul because of his ignorance of God's true oneness; the existence in him of his judging all matters out of ignorance and his responding to questions asked of him with what he has not learned from his own school doctrine or that of any other; being devoid of the knowledge associated with the declaration of God's oneness and his reliance on the statements of the Ḥashwiyya[68] and others like them; the existence in him of contempt for the regulations of God; the lands of the Muslims being devoid of an appeal (*daʿwa*) of his to God; lacking the nobility conferred by designation and appointment, he being like the others who have not inherited the imamate.

ʿUmar al-Nazwānī,[69] who resides in Jabāl ʿUmān: He is not a

---

who took the throne name al-Qādir bi'llāh. Sulṭān al-Dawla was thus the Buyid ruler at the time al-Kirmānī wrote these words. The pious wish that the mercy of God be upon the father indicates that Bahā' al-Dawla had not been dead a long time and that, for some reason, al-Kirmānī wanted to honour his memory. It was Bahā' al-Dawla also who first appointed Fakhr al-Mulk wazir and governor in Baghdad.

67. This person is Abu'l-Ḥasan al-Mu'ayyad bi'llāh Aḥmad b. al-Ḥusayn b. Hārūn, the Zaydī imam in the Caspian region until his death in 411/1020. Al-Kirmānī dedicated a special treatise, *al-Risāla al-kāfiya fi'l-radd ʿalā al-Hārūnī al-Ḥusaynī (or al-Ḥasanī) al-Zaydī* ('The Effective Treatise in Refutation of al-Hārūnī al-Ḥusaynī the Zaydī') against this man who had written his own denunciation of al-Ḥākim and the Ismailis. The *Kāfiya* was published by M. Ghālib in *Majmūʿat rasā'il al-Kirmānī* (Beirut, 1983) pp. 148–182. See also Ivanow, *Rise*, pp. 142–143. Hawsam is a town of eastern Gilan on the coast of the Caspian; see 'Hawsam' by W. Madelung in the *EI2 Supplement*.

68. The term *ḥashwiyya* often refers to the extreme literalist doctrine of the Proponents of Ḥadīth or to those who mindlessly relate *ḥadīths*, even contradictory ones, without attempting to determine if they are valid and reasonable. See the definition given by Abū Ḥātim al-Rāzī in his *Kitāb al-zīna* (section on Islamic sects edited and published by al-Samarrā'ī, p. 267). How it could apply to this man, who was in general a Muʿtazilī, is not readily apparent.

69. This man who is here said to be the Ibāḍī imam at the time is otherwise unknown. His name does not figure in the standard histories of the imams of ʿUmān which, however, do not list anyone as imam for the exact period (about

lineal descendant of al-Ḥusayn; he is not pure of body on account of leprosy that has taken hold of him and settled in most of his limbs, nor in soul due to ignorance; there exists in him by his own admission what he does not know; being devoid of religious knowledge; the existence in him of contempt for the regulations of God, not commanding the good and prohibiting the bad; lack of designation and appointment.

The Umayyad, who resides in al-Andalus: He is not a lineal descendant of al-Ḥusayn; he is not pure due to his being from the Tree of Zaqqūm[70] which are the Umayyad clan; there exists in him by his own admission what is not his business; being devoid of knowledge; there exists in him contempt for the regulations of God in his promoting among his subjects behaviour not that of the Prophet; lacking the designation and appointment.

Those who call themselves the Lords, who reside in al-Aḥsāʾ:[71] They are not lineal descendants of al-Ḥusayn; they are not pure because of drinking wine; there exists among them the expenditure of their funds for purposes not religiously commendable; there exists among them contempt for the regulations of God in their permitting forbidden acts; they are devoid of religious knowledge; they lack the designation and appointment.

Al-Ḥākim bi-amr Allāh, the Commander of the Faithful: He is a lineal descendant of al-Ḥusayn; he is pure in body and soul; spending of his funds is for religiously commendable purposes and its benefit; he knows what is permitted and what is forbidden, and legal affairs and decisions; he commands the good and prohibits the bad; he was designated by his pure forefathers who were offspring of the Apostle.

403/1012 to 405/1014) in question, perhaps because the authors of these accounts did not know who it was.

70. A tree in hell with fruit that are the heads of devils; see Qurʾān 37: 62, 44: 43–46, and 56: 52.

71. He refers to the Qarmatians in Bahrain who are, according to what al-Kirmānī says about them, at this time completely excluded from the Ismaili fold. For their relations with the Fatimids in the period just prior to this, see Daftary, *The Ismāʿīlīs*, p. 194.

The sixth demonstration: The characteristic of what might be claimed but for which there exists no evidence or proof is that it is not true, and the characteristic of what might be claimed and for which there exists evidence and proof is that it is true. What al-Ḥākim bi-amr Allāh, Commander of the Faithful, claims about his being an ʿAlid, Ḥusaynid, the one designated, knowledgeable, just, pious, commander of the good and prohibiter of the bad, brave, ascetic, the sum of virtuous qualities, chosen by God, is established on basis of evidence and proofs. Testimony as to the validity of his claim comes from Ḥasanid and Ḥusaynid descendants of ʿAlī in the Holy Cities[72] publicly and, from those who are not in his kingdom, it comes from Ḥasanid and Ḥusaynid descendants of ʿAlī whose testimony is otherwise prevented by continuous stream of statements from those who disapprove of it whether out of some desire or some fear. But those whose testimony approves are not less than the testimony of the others; by contrast, resisting they commit themselves in fealty to him and his imamate in private. The existence of evidence of his justice, which unites the elite and the masses and which has caused his repute to emanate far and wide, and evidence of his piety, which none deny, is his refraining from taking the property of people by force and his abstaining from expropriating what is not his out of mercy, so that strangers who die and others who have no heir present and who leave what they leave, he does not brandish the lance of his piety seeking their money, nor does he employ it to further the sin of greed through the oppressing of women and men. He commands that it be deposited in the Warehouse of Deposits,[73] the policy for the erecting of which was a consequence of

72. Al-Kirmānī notes in his treatise called *al-Kāfiya* (pp. 173–174) that, even during the incident when the Amir of Makka Abu'l-Futūḥ al-Ḥusaynī rebelled against the authority of al-Ḥākim and claimed the imamate for himself, he did not deny that of al-Ḥākim which he might have if he doubted its authenticity.

73. On the *dār al-wadīʿa*, as a repository for funds and property left in trust by travellers who had died within the Fatimid empire but whose heirs were not present there to make a claim for it immediately, we have no other reference. However, al-Ḥākim is known to have created a *dīwān al-mufrad* in the year 400/1009–1010, which had the specific purpose of collecting and holding the estates of those who had been executed by the government. J. Van Ess questioned whether the two institutions might be the same (*Chiliastische Erwartungen und*

the goodness of his justice in safeguarding the property of Muslims and in searching for the heirs and giving to them what was due them. There is ample evidence of his commanding the good and prohibiting the bad, which none can deny, in the way he lives, devoting his nights and days to strengthening the word of truth, aiding the oppressed, building mosques, tearing down churches, preserving the communal prayer, applying the regulations of the law and confirming them and the corporal punishments, extending justice to the masses, and acting with respect to them with clemency and charity to the extent that the countries whom the protection of his orders include are in the cradle of security at home, neither evil nor sadness touches them. There is evidence for his prohibiting the bad, reports of which have spread far and wide, from his closing down sources of depravity and dissolution, which are permitted quite openly in their cities by those who claim the imamate among the family of Umayya and the family of ʿAbbas. There is much evidence of his *jihād* in the service of God and his preservation of the borders, and his familiarity with the commoners and his discouraging the word of the false and what pertains to short-changing the law that his ancestor Muḥammad brought. There is also considerable evidence of his knowledge of the Book and the law and religious affairs and the unequivocal interpretations of it in matters concerning which mankind has no ability, nor were those in the nations that preceded who were the specialists in the explanation of it; of those some have been spread by his trusted followers and his friends in the various districts [of the Islamic world]. He has explained symbols with answers that put spirits at ease and cause doubting to cease. As evidence of his asceticism, report of which has spread in the cities, there is his riding a donkey and wearing rough clothing, eating grits, all despite the great position that God conferred on him. There is also good evidence of his bravery, which cannot be hidden and mention of which has spread throughout the world. His riding about alone in spite of the great position God gave him is no secret and, despite the knowledge among his troops and his

---

die Versuchung der Göttlichkeit: Der Kalif al-Ḥākim (386–411 H.) (Heidelberg, 1977), notes 300 and 301, citing al-Maqrīzī's *Ittiʿāẓ*, II, pp. 81 and 82, for evidence of the *dīwān al-mufrad* and this treatise of al-Kirmānī for the *dār al-wadīʿa*). But, given the lack of additional information about either one, it is hard to be certain that they were the same.

men, both small and great, that his riding has as its only purpose to kill them for their disobedience and previous error from other times, they are unable to act, as would not be the case with anyone other than him in a similar situation. Even with the great concern caused by his riding without many men or a force of his own, fear does not prevent him from doing that, nor is he held back by imagining what might befall him from his enemies should he be by himself and he does not lose courage. Finding himself in the middle of them without men, knowing that individuals among his soldiers and staff have sworn more than once to kill him and that they had distributed among them a large sum to encourage capturing him, the army was incapable of finding him. How much more so would cowardice hobble a man alone other than him, but weakness did not overcome him because of them. Instead, dread was cast into their hearts and these men scattered on different paths, all of this showing that God is supporting and safeguarding him. The evidence of his generosity is [such] that no day passes by nor week nor month but he disperses huge sums of dinars in relief of those in need and to support those seeking help. From this we determine that he is the guarantor of what is true, and if it is true, he is the truthful, and the truthful by the words of God: 'be with those who are the truthful' [9: 119] requires being in his company and following him. Therefore, al-Ḥākim bi-amr Allāh, Commander of the Faithful, is the truthful imam, and following him and obeying him is obligatory.

The seventh demonstration: Each thing cannot be detached from the definition by which it is distinguished from what is other than it, and what has a definition distinguishing it from what does not participate in its definition is not within its domain nor can it be a part of its group. If we are to confirm the definition of the imamate, the imam is someone among the offspring of prophecy, who is not infertile, who is knowledgeable about the Book and the law and the stipulations in it and practice of it, both the outward and the inner, and acts upon it, who has been designated by the person who takes the place of the Messenger, who commands the good and prohibits the bad, who summons to God through his imamate by being the person who himself summons to God. Whoever commands the good and prohibits the bad, who has been designated on behalf of the Messenger, is pious and knowledgeable and is among the offspring of prophecy and is not infertile, he is the imam. A person cannot be the imam who is not from the pure offspring since God preserves the imamate in the chosen offspring; nor can someone be the imam among that offspring who has no lineal successor through whom to preserve the imamate, since it is preserved in the lineal succession; nor can he be from that offspring who has a lineal successor but has no knowledge, since the community has need of that knowledge; nor can he be of the offspring, have a lineal successor, knowledge, but is not pious and instead practices corruption generally through the absence of piety; nor can he be of the offspring, have lineal succession, knowledge, function piously, but has not been designated to occupy the place of the Messenger, and one who has been designated cannot be someone who does not command the good and prohibit the bad, who does not summon to the obedience of God through his imamate, since the designation is the cause for commanding and prohibiting and summoning to God. Commanding and prohibiting and summoning to God are the fruits of the designation. Al-Ḥākim bi-amr Allāh, Commander of the Faithful, matches this definition like no one else and as we show in the tables at the end of this demonstration to illustrate this point. From all this, it is clear that he is the imam, obedience to whom is obligatory. Therefore, al-Ḥākim bi-amr Allāh, Commander of the Faithful, is the imam, obedience to whom is an obligation.

Tables for the definition of the imamate to make clear who fits its definition and who does not fit the definition and to verify that the imamate belongs to which one among them by right. [Table VI, Plates 27–30]

The names: Being from the offspring of prophecy and a descendant of al-Ḥusayn; being not infertile and having the knowledge of the Book of God and the law of the Apostle, both literally and by interpretation; doing what the Prophet established as regulations, duties, practice, acts of piety, courage and all kinds of virtuous traits; the existence of the designation by the person who occupies the place of the Apostle; commanding the good and forbidding the bad and the result appears because of him; the appeal (*daʿwa*) to God and to His absolute oneness through his activities.

Aḥmad b. Isḥāq: He is not infertile; he relies on al-Bāqillānī and others of the leaders of the Murji'a; he is not characterized by that; put in office by the august Amir Bahā' al-Dawla, son of ʿAḍud al-Dawla; does not command the good and forbid the bad; he has no *daʿwa*.

al-Ḥārūnī al-Ḥusaynī: He is not infertile; with him there is no knowledge of the Book of God and the law of the Apostle; he is not mentioned as having this trait; he was not put in office nor also someone appointed to it; he has no *daʿwa*, does not command the good and forbid the bad; he appears in person before no one.

ʿUmar al-Nazwānī: He is not infertile; [blank]; [blank]; [blank]; [blank]; he does not show himself to anyone neither at prayer time nor on any other occasion.

The one awaited among the lineal descendants of Mūsā according to the belief of the Twelvers; his followers admit that he has had no offspring until now and it is he who is awaited; [blank]; [blank]; he was not designated nor is he also from those who were designated; [blank]; he has no *daʿwa*, neither commands nor forbids but rather the opposite.

Al-Ḥākim bi-amr Allāh, who descends from the offspring of al-Ḥusayn; he is from the offspring of prophecy and is a descendant of al-Ḥusayn; he is not infertile owing to the existence of his progeny, and he knows the Book of God and the law of the Apostle, both literally and by interpretation; he performs what the Prophet established, combining all the traits we have explained above; he has been designated by pure forefathers back through ʿAlī b. Abī Ṭālib to Muḥammad, the Chosen; he maintains the commanding of good and forbidding of the bad, the effect of which is the good and not the bad; he maintains the appeal to God and to His absolute oneness by supporting agents (*dāʿīs*) in all the lands of Islam.

It thus becomes clear from this that the one who fits the definition of the imamate is al-Ḥākim bi-amr Allāh, Commander of the Faithful, and none of the rest of those who claim it, and that obedience to him is incumbent on the community in its entirety. Therefore, we have fulfilled what we promised to do at the outset of the book, in accord with the grace of God and the excellent oversight of His guardian on His earth, on him be peace. We add that we have restricted the demonstrations assembled for each 'light' to the number mentioned in it and did not lengthen it by additions or by the objections an objector might bring to each topic and the response to them, because we will take up all that in a book other than this one which is to follow. And also because we are wary of falling into a weariness that narrows the breast and blunts the spirits to the point that the desire for study ceases and the benefit of it is lost. Otherwise the favour of God is more than can be counted. Also, this book is an introduction to what will come in our book called *The Comfort of Reason*[74] which will present the sciences in a way that is more appropriate for the grade by grade advancement in religious understanding.

Here then we have put the seal on our book with thanks to God, the Lord of the universe, and with prayers for the best of the prophets and their seal, Muḥammad, the Chosen, and for the light of those who inherit and their lord, ʿAlī, the Approved, and on the pillar of religion, the rightly guiding imams, who are the lights in the darkness. And with peace and greetings to them and to the Imam Abū ʿAlī al-Manṣūr al-Ḥākim bi-amr Allāh, Commander of the Faithful, and on those expected until the Day of Judgment. (May God single out our lord and master, the Imam al-Mustanṣir billāh Maʿadd Abū Tamīm, Commander of the Faithful, the imam of our time, with the most excellent of blessings and peace. God suffices us; how blessed a keeper is He.)[75]

---

74. Al-Kirmānī's *Rāḥat al-ʿaql.*

75. This final sentence is obviously an addition that reflects the work of a copyist and is not a part of al-Kirmānī's original text. Most likely it indicates the period when this treatise entered the literature of the Yemeni *daʿwa* where it was subsequently preserved. Note that the copyist cites only al-Mustanṣir and not either al-Ẓāhir, who preceded al-Mustanṣir, or al-Mustaʿlī, who succeeded him. Later copyists kept this citation and did not add to it the names of the imams of their time. The Ṭayyibīs believe that al-Mu'ayyad fi'l-Dīn al-Shīrāzī, chief of the central *daʿwa* under al-Mustanṣir, arranged to have Fatimid Ismaili works transferred to the Yemen and that the *dāʿī* Lamak b. Malik was the person largely responsible for the task. Accordingly, it could well be that Lamak was the first of the Yemeni *dāʿī*s to have copied this treatise and that all copies in the Yemen derive from his.

Bibliography

Abu'l-Fawāris Aḥmad b. Ya'qūb. *ar-Risāla fi'l-imāma*, ed. and English trans., Sami Nasib Makarem as *The Political Doctrine of the Ismā'īlīs (The Imamate)*. Delmar, New York, 1977.

Adang, Camilla. *Muslim Writers on Judaism and the Hebrew Bible: From Ibn Rabban to Ibn Hazm*. Leiden, 1996.

al-Anṭākī, Yaḥyā b. Sa'īd, *History*, ed. 'Umar 'Abd al-Salām Tadmūrī. Tripoli, 1990.

Assaad, Sadik A. *The Reign of al-Hakim bi Amr Allah (386/996–411/1021): A Political Study*. Beirut, 1974.

Baumstark, A. 'Zu den Schriftzitaten al-Kirmānīs', *Der Islam*, 20 (1932), pp. 308–313.

Blois, François de. 'The Oldest Known Fāṭimid Manuscript from Yemen', *Proceedings of the Seminar for Arabian Studies*, 14 (1984), pp. 1–7. (off-print)

Bosworth, C. Edmund. 'Bahā' al-Dawla', *EI2*.

——'Mazyad, Banū', *EI2*.

Bruijn, J. T. P. de. 'al-Kirmānī', *EI2*.

Bryer, David R. 'The Origins of the Druze Religion', *Der Islam* 52 (1975), pp. 47–84, 239–264; 53 (1976), pp. 5–27.

al-Bustī, Abu'l-Qāsim. *Kashf al-asrār wa-naqd al-afkār*, ed. 'Ādil Sālim al-'Abd al-Jādir, in his *al-Ismā'īliyyūn*. Kuwait, 2002, pp. 187–369.

Canard, Marius. 'La Destruction de l'Eglise de la résurrection par le calife Hâkim et l'histoire de la descente du feu sacré', *Byzantion* 35(1965), pp. 16–43, reprinted in his *Byzance et les Musulmans du Proche Orient*. London, 1973, article XX.

Cheikho, L. *Shu'arā' al-naṣrāniyya*. Beirut, 1920.

Cortese, Delia. *Ismaili and Other Arabic Manuscripts: A Descriptive Catalogue of Manuscripts in the Library of The Institute of Ismaili Studies*. London, 2000.

——*Arabic Ismaili Manuscripts: The Zāhid 'Alī Collection in the Library of The Institute of Ismaili Studies*. London, 2003.

Daftary, Farhad. *The Ismā'īlis: Their History and Doctrines*. Cambridge, 1990.

De Smet, Daniel. 'Le Verbe-impératif dans le système cosmologique de l'ismaélisme', *Revue des Sciences Philosophiques et Théologiques*, 73 (1989), pp. 397–412.

——'Le *Kitâb Râḥat al-'Aql* de Ḥamîd ad-Dîn al-Kirmânî et la cosmologie ismaélienne à l'époque fatimide', *Actas Orientalia Belgica*, 7 (1992), pp. 81–91.

——'*Mīzān ad-diyāna* ou l'équilibre entre science et religion dans la pensée ismaélienne', *Acta Orientalia Belgica*, 8 (1993), pp. 247–254.

——*La Quiétude de l'Intellect: Néoplatonisme et gnose ismaélienne dans l'oeuvre de Ḥamîd ad-Dîn al-Kirmânî (X^{e}/XIe s.)*. Louvain, 1995.

——'Perfectio prima—perfectio secunda, ou les vicissitudes d'une notion, de S. Thomas aux Ismaéliens Ṭayyibites du Yémen', *Recherches de Théologies et de Philosophie Médiévales*, 66 (1999), pp. 254–288.

De Smet, Daniel, and J. M. F. Van Reeth. 'Les citations bibliques dans l'oeuvre du *dā'ī* ismaélien Ḥamīd ad-Dīn al-Kirmānī', in U. Vermeulen and J. M. F. Van Reeth, ed., *Law, Christianity and Modernism in Islamic Society: Proceedings of the Eighteenth Congress of the Union Européenne des Arabisants et Islamisants, 1996*. Louvain, 1998, pp. 147–160.

Djebli, Moktar. 'al-Sharīf al-Raḍī', *EI2*.

Donohue, John J. *The Buwayhid Dynasty in Iraq, 334H/945 to 403H/1012: Shaping Institutions for the Future*. Leiden, 2003.

Encyclopaedia of Islam. New ed. cited as *EI2*. Leiden, 1960–2006.

Ess, Josef van. *Chiliastische Erwartungen und die Versuchung der Göttlichkeit: Der Kalif al-Ḥākim (386–411 H.)*. Heidelberg, 1977.

——'Biobibliographische Notizen zur islamischen Theologie: Zur Chronologie der Werke des Ḥamīdaddīn al-Kirmānī', in *Die Welt des Orients*, 9 (1977–78), pp. 255–261.

Gacek, Adam. *Catalogue of Arabic Manuscripts in the Library of The Institute of Ismaili Studies*. vol. 1. London, 1984.

Ghālib, Muṣṭafā. *A'lām al-Ismā'īliyya*. Beirut, 1964.

——*al-Ḥarakat al-bāṭiniyya fi'l-Islām*. Beirut, 1982.

Goriawala, Mu'izz. *A Descriptive Catalogue of the Fyzee Collection of Ismaili Manuscripts*. Bombay, 1965.

Halm, Heinz. *Die Kalifen von Kairo: Die fatimiden in Ägypten, 973–1074*. Munich, 2003.

al-Hamdānī, Ḥusayn. *al-Maqālat kitāb al-riyāḍ l'l-shaykh Aḥmad al-Kirmānī*. Hyderabad, 1358/1939.

Ḥusayn, Muḥammad Kāmil. *Ṭā'ifat al-durūz*. Cairo, 1962.

Ibn al-Athīr. *al-Kāmil fi'l-ta'rīkh*, ed. C. J. Tornberg. Leiden, 1851–1876 (Beirut reprint).

Ibn al-Dawādārī. *Kanz al-durar*, vol. 6, ed. Ṣ. al-Munajjid. Cairo, 1961.

Ibn Isḥāq. *The Life of Muhammad: a Translation of Ibn Isḥāq's Sīrat Rasūl Allāh*, trans. Alfred Guillaume. Oxford, 1974.

Ibn al-Jawzī. *al-Muntaẓam*, vol. 7. Hyderabad, 1939.

——*al-Wafā' fi-aḥwāl al-muṣṭafā*, ed. M. 'Abd al-Wāḥid. Cairo, 1966.

Ibn Kathīr. *al-Bidāya wa'l-nihāya fī ta'rīkh*. Cairo, 1932– .

Ibn Khaldūn. *The Muqaddimah: An Introduction to History*, trans. F. Rosenthal, 3 vols. New York, 1958.

Ibn Khallikān. *Wafayāt al-a'yān*, trans. W. MacGuckin de Slane, *Ibn Khallikan's Biographical Dictionary*, 4 vols. London, 1842–1871.

Ibn Qutayba. *Dalā'il*, in Ibn al-Jawzī's *al-Wafā bi-aḥwāl al-muṣṭafā*. [Cairo], 1966.

Ibn Taghrībirdī. *al-Nujūm al-zāhira fī mulūk Miṣr wa'l-Qāhira*. Cairo, 1348–1391/1929–1972.

Idrīs 'Imād al-Dīn. *'Uyūn al-akhbār*, vol. 6, ed. M. Ghālib. Beirut, 1984.

Ivanow, W. *Ismaili Tradition Concerning the Rise of the Fatimids*. London, etc., 1942.

——*Ismaili Literature: A Bibliographical Survey*. Tehran, 1963.

Jiwa, Shainool. 'Fāṭimid-Būyid Diplomacy during the Reign of al-'Azīz Billāh (365/975–386/996)', *Journal of Islamic Studies*, 3 (1992), pp. 57–71.

al-Kirmānī, Ḥamīd al-Dīn. *al-Aqwāl al-dhahabiyya*, ed. Ṣalāḥ al-Sāwī. Tehran, 1977.

——*Kitāb ma'āṣim al-hudā wa'l-iṣāba fī tafḍīl 'Alī 'alā al-ṣaḥāba* (ms. D(724), The Institute of Ismaili Studies).

——*Kitāb al-riyāḍ*, ed. 'Ā. Tāmir. Beirut, 1960.

——*Kitāb tanbīh al-hādī wa'l-mustahdī* (ms. D(723), The Institute for Ismaili Studies; ms. Fyzee Collection, Bombay University Library, Goriawala, no. 57).

——*Majmū'at rasā'il al-Kirmānī*, ed. M. Ghālib. Beirut, 1987. (Contains *al-Durriyya, al-Nuẓum, al-Raḍiyya, al-Muḍī'a, al-Lāzima, al-Rawḍa, al-Zāhira, al-Ḥāwiya, Mabāsim, al-Wā'iẓa, al-Kāfiya*, and two treatises, *Fi'l-radd 'alā man ankara [yunkiru] al-'ālam al-rūḥānī* and *Khazā'in al-adilla*, not by al-Kirmānī).

——*al-Maṣābīḥ fī ithbāt al-imāma*, ed. M. Ghālib. Beirut, 1969.

——*Rāḥat al-ʿaql*, ed. M. Kāmil Ḥusayn and M. M. Ḥilmī, Cairo, 1953; ed. M. Ghālib. Beirut, 1983.

——*al-Risāla al-durriyya fī maʿnā al-tawḥīd*, ed. M. K. Ḥusayn, Cairo, 1952; ed. M. Ghālib in *Majmūʿat rasāʾil al-Kirmānī*, pp. 19–26. (ms. Tübingen University)

——*al-Risāla al-lāzima fī ṣawm*, ed. Muḥammad ʿAbd al-Qādir ʿAbd al-Nāṣir, in *Majallat Kulliyyat al-Ādāb, Jāmiʿat al-Qāhira*, 31 (1969), pp. 1–52; ed. M. Ghālib, in *Majmūʿat rasāʾil*, pp. 61–80.

——*al-Risāla al-nuẓum fī muqābalat al-ʿawālim*, ed. M. K. Ḥusayn, Cairo, 1952 with *al-Durriyya*; ed. Ghālib, in *Majmūʿat rasāʾil*, pp. 27–34.

——*al-Risāla al-raḍiyya*, ed. M. Ghālib, in *Majmūʿat rasāʾil*, pp. 35–42.

——*al-Risāla al-waḍīʾa fī maʿālim al-dīn*, ed. Muhammad ʿIsā al-Hurayrī. Kuwait, 1987 (ms. Fyzee Collection, Bombay University Library).

——*al-Risāla al-wāʿiẓa*, ed. M. K. Ḥusayn, in *Majallat Kulliyyat al-Ādāb, Jāmiʿa Fuʾad al-Awwal*, 14, part 1, (1952), pp. 1–29; ed. M. Ghālib in *Majmūʿat rasāʾil*, pp. 134–147.

——*Risālat mabāsim al-bishārāt*, ed. M. K. Ḥusayn, in his *Ṭāʾifat al-durūz*, pp. 55–74; ed. M. Ghālib, in his *al-Ḥarakat al-bāṭiniyya fiʾl-Islām*, pp. 205–233, and in al-Kirmānī, *Majmūʿat rasāʾil al-Kirmānī*, pp. 113–133.

Kraemer, Joel L. 'The Death of an Orientialist: Paul Kraus from Prague to Cairo', in Martin Kramer, ed. *The Jewish Discovery of Islam* (Tel Aviv, 1999), pp. 181–223.

Kraus, Paul. 'Hebräische und syrische Zitate in ismāʿīlitischen Schriften', *Der Islam*, 19 (1931), pp. 243–263.

Lazarus-Yafeh, Hava. *Intertwined Worlds: Medieval Islam and Bible Criticism*. Princeton, 1992.

Madelung, Wilferd. 'Das Imamat in der frühen ismailitischen Lehre', *Der Islam*, 37 (1961), pp. 43–135.

——'The Assumption of the Title Shahanshah by the Buyids and "The Reign of the Daylam (*Dawlat al-Daylam*)"', *Journal of Near Eastern Studies*, 28 (1969), pp. 84–108 and 168–183.

——'A Treatise on the Imamate of the Fatimid Caliph al-Manṣūr bi-Allāh', in Chase F. Robinson, ed., *Texts, Documents and Artefacts: Islamic Studies in Honour of D. S. Richards* (Leiden, 2003), pp. 69–77.

——'Imāma', *EI2*.

al-Majdūʿ, Ismāʿīl b. ʿAbd al-Rasūl. *Fahrasat al-kutub waʾl-rasāʾil*, ed. ʿAlī Naqī Munzavī. Tehran, 1966.

al-Maqdīsī, Muṭahhar b. Ṭāhir. *Kitāb al-badʾ waʾl-taʾrīkh (Le livre de la création et de l'histoire de Motahhar ben Tahir el-Maqdisi)*, ed. M. Cl. Huart.

Paris, 1899–1916.
al-Maqrīzī, Taqī al-Dīn Abu'l-ʿAbbās Aḥmad b. ʿAlī. *Ittiʿāẓ al-ḥunafāʾ bi-akhbār al-aʾimma al-Fāṭimiyyīn al-khulafāʾ*, vol I, ed. J. al-Shayyāl, Cairo, 1967, vols. II and III, ed. M. H. M. Aḥmad. Cairo, 1971 and 1973.
al-Masʿūdī, Abu'l-Ḥasan ʿAlī b. al-Ḥusayn. *Murūj al-dhahab wa maʿādin al-jawhar*, ed. ʿAbd al-Ḥamīd. Cairo, 1964.
Momen, Moojan. *An Introduction to Shiʿi Islam*. New Haven, 1985.
al-Naysābūrī, Aḥmad b. Ibrāhīm. *Kitāb ithbāt al-imāma*, ed. M. Ghālib, Beirut, 1984; ed. and tr. Arzina Lalani. London (forthcoming).
——*Istitār al-imāma*, ed. W. Ivanow, in the *Majallat Kulliyyat al-Ādāb bi'l-Jāmiʿa al-Miṣriyya*, 4, part 2 (1936), pp. 93–108; English trans. in Ivanow, *Rise of the Fatimids*.
——*Risāla al-mūjaza al-kāfiya fī adab al-duʿāt*, in Ḥātim b. Ibrāhīm al-Ḥāmidī's *Tuḥfat al-qulūb wa turjat al-makrūb*, ed. Abbas Hamdani, London (forthcoming).
al-Nuʿmān b. Muḥammad, al-Qāḍī Abū Ḥanīfa. *Asās al-taʾwīl*, ed. ʿĀrif Tāmir. Beirut, 1960 (mss. The Institute of Ismaili Studies).
——*Daʿāʾim al-Islām*, ed. A. A. A. Fyzee, 2 vols. Cairo, 1951–61; English trans. A. A. A. Fyzee, completely revised by I. K. Poonawala, *The Pillars of Islam*, 2 vols. New Delhi, 2002–2004.
Poonawala, Ismail K. *Biobibliography of Ismāʿīlī Literature*. Malibu, CA, 1977.
——'Idrīs b. al-Ḥasan', *EI2 Supplement*.
al-Rāzī, Abū Bakr Muḥammad b. Zakariyāʾ. *Rasāʾil falsafiyya*, ed. P. Kraus. Cairo, 1939.
al-Rāzī, Abū Ḥātim. *al-Aʿlām al-nubuwwa*, ed. Ṣalāḥ al-Ṣāwī and G. R. Aʿwānī. Tehran 1977.
——*Kitāb al-iṣlāḥ*, ed. Ḥasan Mīnūchihr and Mahdī Moḥaghegh. Tehran, 1998.
——*Kitāb al-zīna*, section on Islamic sects edited by ʿAbdallāh Sallūm al-Samarrāʾī, in his *Al-Ghuluww wa'l-firaq al-ghāliya fi'l-ḥaḍāra al-Islāmiyya*. Baghdad, 1972, pp. 225–312.
Saleh, Abdel Hamid. 'Ibn Khalaf', *EI2*.
al-Sijistānī, Abū Yaʿqūb. *Ithbāt al-nubuwwa* (or *al-nubuwwāt*), ed. ʿĀrif. Tāmir. Beirut, 1966 (ms. Fyzee Collection).
——*Kitāb al-iftikhār*, ed. I. K. Poonawala. Beirut, 2000.
——*Kitāb al-maqālīd* (ms. Hamdani Library).
——*Kitāb al-yanābīʿ*, ed. with partial French trans. by H. Corbin, in his

Trilogie ismaélienne, Tehran and Paris, 1961. See also Walker, *The Wellsprings of Wisdom.*

Sourdel, D. 'al-Ḳādir bi'llāh', *EI2*.

Stern, S. M. 'Fāṭimid Propaganda among Jews according to the Testimony of Yefet b. 'Alī the Karaite', in his *Studies in Early Ismā'īlism*. Jerusalem and Leiden, 1983, pp. 84–95.

al-Ṭabarī, Abū Ja'far Muḥammad b. Jarīr. *Ta'rīkh al-rusul wa'l-mulūk*, ed. Jan de Goeje et al. Leiden, 1879–1901, vol. 3; Eng. trans. C. E. Bosworth as *The History of al-Ṭabarī*: vol. 32, *The Reunification of the 'Abbāsid Caliphate*. Albany, NY, 1987.

Van Reeth, J. M. F. '*Al-Qumāma* et le *Qā'im* de 400 AH: le trucage de la lampe sur le tombeau du Christ', in U. Vermeulen and D. De Smet, ed., *Egypt and Syria in the Fatimid, Ayyubid and Mamluk Eras*, II. Louvain, 1995, pp. 171–190.

Walker, Paul E. 'The Doctrine of Metempsychosis in Islam', in W. Hallaq and D. Littles, ed. *Islamic Studies Presented to Charles J. Adam*. Leiden, 1991. pp. 219–238.

——'The Ismaili *Da'wa* in the Reign of the Fatimid Caliph al-Ḥākim', *Journal of the American Research Center in Egypt*, 30 (1993), pp. 161–182.

——*Early Philosophical Shiism: The Ismaili Neoplatonism of Abū Ya'qūb al-Sijistānī*. Cambridge, 1993.

——*The Wellsprings of Wisdom: A Study of Abū Ya'qūb al-Sijistānī's* Kitāb al-Yanābī'. Salt Lake City, UT, 1994.

——*Abu Ya'qub al-Sijistani: Intellectual Missionary*. London, 1996.

——'Fatimid Institutions of Learning', *Journal of the American Research Center in Egypt*, 34 (1997), pp. 179–200.

——*Ḥamīd al-Dīn al-Kirmānī: Ismaili Thought in the Age of al-Ḥākim*. London, 1999; Persian trans. Tehran, 2000; Arabic trans. Damascus, 2000.

——'"In Praise of al-Ḥākim": Greek Elements in Ismaili Writings on the Imamate', in Emma Gannagé et al., ed. *The Greek Strand in Islamic Political Thought: Proceedings of the Conference at the Institute for Advanced Study, Princeton 16–27 June 2003*. Special issue of *Mélanges de l'Université Saint-Joseph*, vol. 57 (2004) pp. 367–392.

William of Tyre. *Historia rerum in patribus transmarinis gestarum*, English trans. E. A. Babcock and A. C. Krey as *A History of Deeds Done Beyond the Sea*. 2 vols. New York, 1943.

Index

List of Tables and Plates*

Table I

[7th demonstration (*burhān*), 5th light (*miṣbāḥ*), 2nd part (*maqāla*)]:

The characteristics that existed in the Prophet.

Table II and Circular Table

[end 7th demonstration, 5th light, 2nd part]:

A report about the Companions and, for what character traits of those that are in the table of the Prophet, they are known.

Tables III and IV

[end 5th demonstration, 6th light, 2nd part]:

A table of the attributes of the species citron that makes clear what is not a citron; and A table reflecting the validity of the imamate of those who have passed away to show thereby the falseness of the imamate of those among them who were not imams.

Plate 15:	Citron etrog (*utrūj*)
Plate 16:	Table III and IVa (ms. Ar. 1226)
Plate 17:	Table IVb (ms. Ar. 1226)
Plate 18:	Table III (ms. Ar. 130)
Plate 19:	Table IVa (ms. Ar. 130)
Plate 20:	Table IVb (ms. Ar. 130)

Table V

[end 5th demonstration, 7th light, 2nd part]:

Tables of traits that prevent being worthy of the imamate.

Plate 21:	Table Va (ms. Ar. 1226)
Plate 22:	Table Vb (ms. Ar. 1226)
Plate 23:	Table Vc (ms. Ar. 1226)
Plate 24:	Table Vd (ms. Ar. 1226)
Plate 25:	Table Va-b (ms. Ar. 130)
Plate 26:	Table Vb-d (ms. Ar. 130)

Table VI

[end 7th demonstration, 7th light, 2nd part]:

Tables for the definition of the imamate in order to make clear who fits its definition and who does not fit and to verify that the imamate belongs to which one among them by right.

Plate 27:	Table VIa (ms. Ar. 1226)
Plate 28:	Table VIb (ms. Ar. 1226)
Plate 29:	Table VIc (ms. Ar. 1226)
Plate 30:	Table VIa–c (ms. Ar. 130)

*Plates are from manuscripts in the Library of The Institute of Ismaili Studies; picture of the citron courtesy of The Wellcome Library, London.

Plates

al-Maṣābīḥ fī ithbāt al-imāma

الاسماء والكون بين ذرية النبوة ونسل الحسين عليه السلام	الكون لا عطاء العلم بالكتاب والسنة وشريعة الرسول ظاهرا وتاويلا	العمل بما جاء به النبي من الاحكام والفرائض والسنن من الورع والتقى	وجود النص من القائم مقام الرسول صلى الله عليه وعلى آله	الامر بالمعروف والنهي عن المنكر وظهور الاتقية	الدعوة الى الله والى الحق جهرة بالامثلة
احمد بن اسحاق	ليس بعظيم	[illegible]	ليس بموصوف بذلك	[illegible]	[illegible]
الهادي الحسين	ليس بعظيم	[illegible] عمله	[illegible]	[illegible]	[illegible]
[illegible]	غير عظيم				[illegible]
[illegible]	[illegible]			[illegible]	[illegible]
الحاكم بامر الله امير المؤمنين [illegible] الحسين	كان الاعظم [illegible]	عالم بالكتاب والشريعة الرسول ظاهرا وتاويلا	عالم بما جاء به النبي جامعا [illegible] فيما يصنع	[illegible]	[illegible]

Plate 30: Table VIa-c (ms. Ar. 130)

Plate 29: Table VIc (ms. Ar. 1226)

السّعيد

ليس هو عالم بكتاب ربه

لا دعوة له	ولا ظهور شخصه لاحد
لا يأمر بمعروف ولا ينهى عن منكر	لا دعوة له ولا يأمر بالمعروف ولا ينهى عن منكر
منصوب للامير بها والدولة بعضد	ليس بمنصوب ولا هو ايضا لمنصوب علم
ليس في موضع يليق بذلك	ليس منكور بعض الخصال
معوله على الباقلاني وغيره من رؤساء المرجئة	لا يوجد عنده علم من كتاب الله وشريعة الرسول صلعم
ليس بعقيم	غير عقيم
احمد بن رزق	الهاروني الحسين

Plate 28: Table VIb (ms. Ar. 1226)

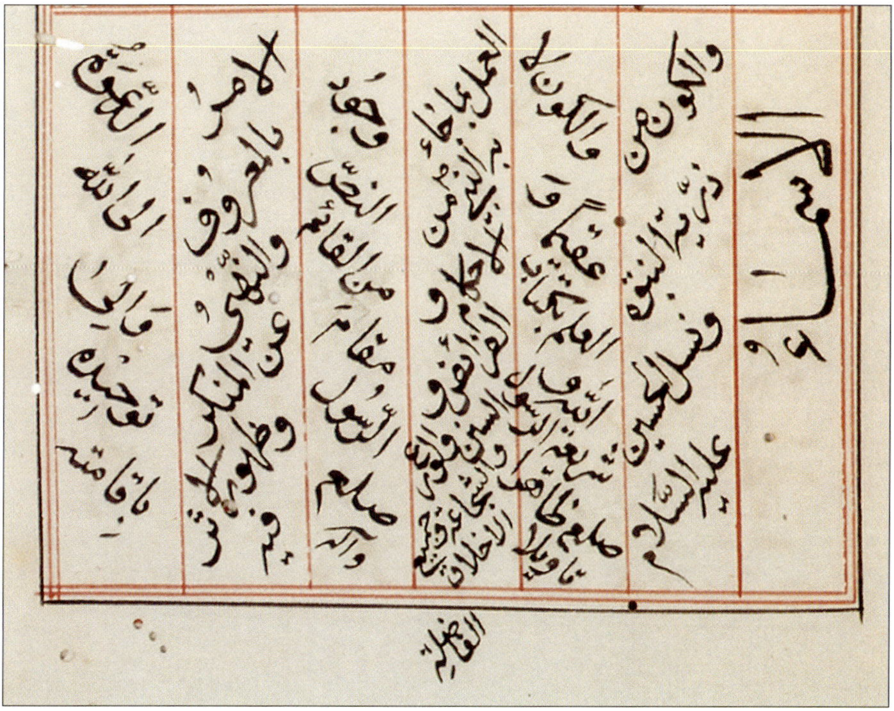

Plate 27: Table VIa (ms. Ar. 1226)

بالجهل عن منكر

عمر [illegible] المقيم بجبال عمان	كان من غير نسل الحسين عليه السلام	غير طاهر [illegible] المتمكن منه في اكثر [illegible]	موجود فيه [illegible] بعلمه	خالي من العلوم الدينية	موجود [illegible] باحكام لا يامر بمعروف ولا ينهى	خالي من النص والتوفيق
الاموي المقيم بالاندلس	كان من غير نسل الحسين عليه السلام	غير طاهر لكونه من شجرة القوم الذين هم بنو امية	موجود فيه دعاء ما ليس من شانه	خالي من العلوم	[illegible]	خالي من النص والتوفيق
المسمون انفسهم السادة المعمور بالاحسان	كائنون من غير نسل الحسين عليه السلام	غير طاهر لتشربهم الخمر	موجود فيهم [illegible] امر الدين	خاليون من العلوم	[illegible]	خاليون من النص والتوفيق
الحاكم بامر الله امير المومنين سلام الله عليه	من نسل الحسين عليه السلام	طاهر [illegible]	متفقه [illegible] في محامد الدين وصلاحه	عالم بالحلال والحرام والقضايا والاحكام	امر بالمعروف والناهي عن المنكر	منصوص عليه من اباىٔه الطاهرين من ذرية الرسول صلى الله عليه وعلى اله وسلم

Plate 26: Table Vb-d (ms. Ar. 130)

جدول الحد الامر ليبين من الحد بحدها ومن لم يحد و يتحقق
ان الامامة لمن منهم

احمد ابن اسحاق المقيم ببغداد

الهادي الحسيني المقيم بهوسم

Plate 25: Table Va-b (ms. Ar. 130)

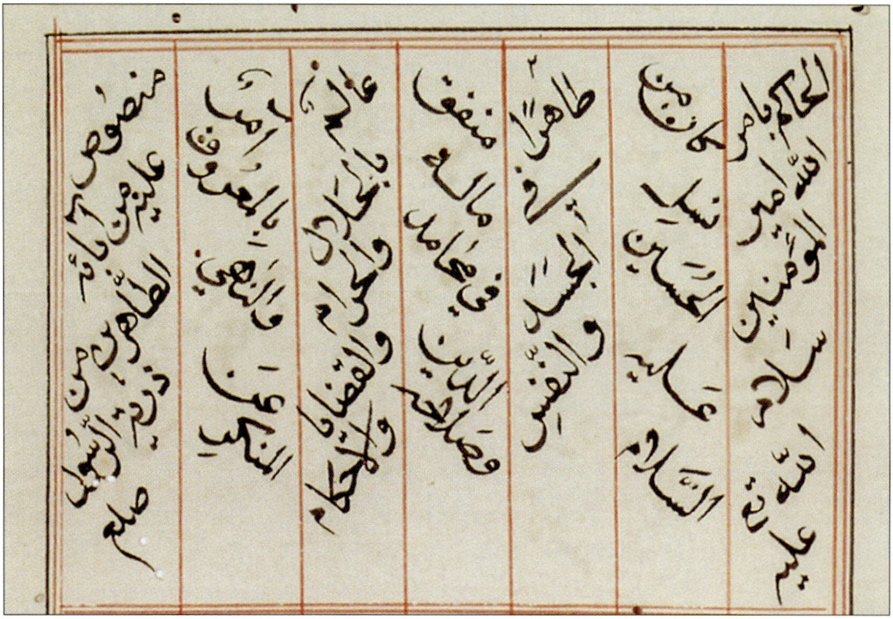

Plate 24: Table Vd (ms. Ar. 1226)

المصابيح في إثبات

الإمامة

لأحمد حميد الدين الكرماني

المصابيح في إثبات الإمامة

تأليف

أحمد حميد الدين الكرماني

الحمد لله بديع الوجود وما حواه، ومخترع الأزل وما عداه، الذي شهدت لوامع الأنوار القدسية في ذوات العقول الرضية بأنه كان ولا وجود ولا عدم، ونطقت الآثار[1] الأزلية في ذوات الأنفس الزكية بأنه[2] كان ولا حدث ولا قدم، المُقَرّ على ذاته دوحة الوجود والأزل، وأول واقع من الاختراع في الأول الذي اتخذه الجهلاء[3] معبوداً، وأشركوا بالله من حيث ظنّوه توحيداً، بأنه لا إله منه ومن دونه من المبدعات إلا فاطره، عزّ ببديع فعله ذلك عن التشبيه، وتكبّر بعظيم صنعه عن التحديد، وتعالى عمّا يقول الظالمون علواً كبيراً. أحمده بما دلنا عليه من أسمائه العظام وأعبده من تلقاء أوليائه[4] مصابيح الظلام، وأشهد أن لا إله مما وقع تحت الإبداع وحصره سمة الوجود والاختراع إلا هو إلهًا متقادسًا عن الصفات، متجاللاً عن السمات، متعاززاً عن الموصوفات، متنازهًا عن الموسومات. وأشهد أن محمداً عبده ورسوله الذي اصطفاه، وانتجبه واجتباه، فأيّده

[1] الآثار: + العلوية، هـ و ٧٤ (الهامش)

[2] بانه: انه، ٤٨

[3] الجهلاء: الجهال، پ

[4] اوليائه: اوليائه الكرام، ز

بموادّ البركات القدسانية، وأمدّه بفيض السعادات[١] النفسانية، فشرّع الشريعة وأحكم قواعدها، وبسط الحكمة وأعلن أوابدها، وأدى الأمانة بنصب الأعلام، ونصح الأمة باتّباع الإمام، صلى الله عليه صلاة متضاعفة ما تعاقب الملوان، واختلف الجديدان، وعلى أبرار عترته أئمة الهدى، ومصابيح الدجى، الذين نوّر الله بهم عرصات الحنادس، ودفع ببركاتهم تمويهات الأبالس، أفضل السلام والتحيات.

أما بعد: فإنني لما رأيتُ سيّد العظماء، وزين السادة[٢] الأجلاء، وقائد الجيوش النجباء، فخر الملك[٣] وزير الوزراء، أطال الله بقاءه، مخصوصًا من الله بالفطنة والفهم، ممنوحًا عن الدراية والعلم، متوّجًا بشرف الولاية النبوية، معتصمًا بالعصمة العلوية، متديّنًا بمحبّة العترة الطاهرة آل طه ويس، وتخيّلتُ أن بعضًا من الشياطين[٤]، الذين يوسوسون في صدور الناس من الأبالسة الملاعين، قد تمكن من[٥] عالي مجلسه وألقى إليه من الكلام ما أثّر في نفسه صداً عن سبيل الله وجرأة على الله وإخلالاً بطاعة الله وجحوداً لآيات الله، ثم لم يكن في خدمته من كان له انبعاث في إظهار ما وصل إليه من مواد البركات، من جهة أولياء النعمة وسادات الأمة الذين افترض الله طاعتهم، سلام الله على العابر والغابر والقائم منهم فينا والناظر، بعثتني[٦] حمية الدين، وصدق الولاء واليقين، وقضية ما أرجع إليه في الله من صحة الاعتقاد وحكم ما افترض الله عليّ في سبيله من الجهاد، على أن أقرّر وجوب الإمامة وصدق مقامات آل طه ويس من الأئمة، عليهم من الله التحية والسلام، وصحة إمامة

---

[١] السعادات: السعادة، ز و ٧٤

[٢] السادة: السادات، هـ و ز

[٣] الملك: الملوك، ز

[٤] بعضا من الشياطين: بعض الشياطين، ٤٨

[٥] من: في، ٧٤

[٦] بعثتني: بعثني، ٧٤

القائم في عصرنا منهم مولانا أمير المؤمنين عبد الله ووليه المنصور أبي علي الحاكم بأمر الله، سلام الله عليه وعلى آبائه[١] الأئمة الطاهرين، وافتراضَ طاعته واتّباعه بمقدار اليسير الذي تناهى إليّ من أنوارهم، وآتي عليها ببراهين نيرة لا تردّ، ودلالات بينة لا تُهدّ، وأن أجعل ذلك إليه في كتاب ليقف عليه وينظر منه على صحة المذهب الشريف والاعتقاد، ويتصوّر لديه رجاحة أهل الطاعة بما شملهم من فضل الله بالاستمداد، ففعلتُ وسمّيتُ الكتاب بكتاب المصابيح في إثبات الإمامة لصاحب الزمان عليه السلام إذ المُورَد فيه من الدلالات كالمصابيح التي هي كالرجوم للشياطين[٢]، وجعلته في مقالتين: إحداهما في إثبات المقدمات التي يحتاج إليها في إثبات الإمامة؛ وثانيتهما في الإمامة. [و]أنا أستعين بالله وبوليه عليه السلام في إتمام ذلك وأستمدّ المعونة منه ومن حسن رأفة وليه[٣] وأسأله العصمة والتوفيق لإيراد الشيء كما أخذتُه من أوليا ء النعمة عليهم السلام.

والمقالتان تجمعان أربعة عشر مصباحًا يشتمل جميعها على مائة برهان وخمسة براهين.

المقالة الأولى

في إثبات المقدمات وهي سبعة مصابيح

المصباح الأول: في صدر الكتاب وبيان العلة الداعية إلى تقديم المقدمات وترتيبها في برهان واحد.

المصباح الثاني: في إثبات الصانع، يشتمل على سبعة براهين.

---

[١] آبائه: -، پ و ٧٤ و ٤٨

[٢] القرآن ٦٧: ٥: «ولقد زيّنّا السماء الدنيا بمصابيح وجعلناها رجوما للشياطين»

[٣] رافة وليه: رافته ولبه، ٤٨

المصباح الثالث: في إثبات النفس وأنها جوهر حيّ باقٍ غير عالم في بدء وجودها، يشتمل على عشرة براهين.
المصباح الرابع: في إثبات صورة[١] السياسة الربّانية التي هي الجزاء وأن داره غير دار[٢] الدنيا، يشتمل على عشرة براهين.
المصباح الخامس: في إثبات وجوب[٣] الشرائع والرسوم التي هي العمل، يشتمل على سبعة براهين.
المصباح السادس: في إثبات وجوب التأويل الذي هو العلم، يشتمل على سبعة براهين.
المصباح السابع: في إثبات الرسالة ووجوبها، يشتمل على سبعة براهين.

المقالة الثانية

في إثبات الإمامة ووجوبها[٤] وهي سبعة مصابيح

المصباح الأول: في إثبات الإمامة ووجوبها، يشتمل على أربعة عشر برهانًا.
المصباح الثاني: في إثبات وجوب عصمة الإمام، يشتمل على سبعة براهين.
المصباح الثالث: في إثبات بطلان اختيار الأمة الإمام، يشتمل على سبعة براهين.
المصباح الرابع: في إثبات كون صحة الإمامة[٥] بالنصّ من الله تعالى

---

[١] صورة: صور، پ
[٢] دار: -، ٧٤ و ز
[٣] وجوب: وجوب وجود، پ، ٧٤، ز
[٤] وجوبها: -، هـ و ٧٤
[٥] الامامة: الامام، ز و هـ و ٧٤

واختيار الرسول، يشتمل على سبعة براهين.

المصباح الخامس: في أن الإمامة بعد النبي صلى الله عليه وآله[١] لأمير المؤمنين علي بن أبي طالب عليه السلام من دون غيره، يشتمل على سبعة براهين.

المصباح السادس: في أن الإمامة[٢] بعد مجيء النصّ بها إلى جعفر بن محمد الصادق عليه السلام لإسماعيل وذريته[٣] عليهم السلام من دون إخوته، يشتمل على سبعة براهين.

المصباح السابع: في إثبات وجوب إمامة صاحب الزمان الإمام الحاكم بأمر الله أمير المؤمنين سلام الله عليه وافتراض طاعته على المقالات كلها، يشتمل على سبعة براهين.

ابتداء المقالة الأولى[٤]:

المصباح الأول

في صدر الكتاب والبيان عن العلة الداعية إلى تقديم المقدمات وترتيبها على ما رتّبت له في برهان واحد

البرهان الأول: نقول إن الأشياء كلها لا تخلو من أصول يُرجع[٥] إليها في إثباتها، ومن علل تتقدم عليها وبها تصح أعيانُها، ومن قوانين

---

[١] صلى ... وآله:-، ز

[٢] الامامة: اثبات الامام، ز

[٣] وذريته: في ذريته، ٤٨

[٤] ابتداء المقالة الاولى:-، هو ٧٤

[٥] يرجع: ترجع، پ، ٤٨

عليها يُتكلم في إيجابها، ومتى لم تكن تلك القوانين ممهّدة، ولا تلك العلل مقرّرة، ولا تلك الأصول مثبتة، كان الكلام على فروعها غير مفهوم، ولا معلوم، وكان يعرض تسرّع السامع إلى دفعها لاشتباه القواعد عليه فيها. وإذا كانت الأصول مثبتةً والعلل مقرّرةً كان إيجاب الفروع لازمًا لا محيص عنه، كالنار التي هي علة الإحراق والإسخان متى وُجدت كان إحراقها وإسخانها واجبًا لازمًا لا ينكر، وكالسراج الذي هو سبب الضوء في الظلمة متى وجد كان الضوء واجبًا لا يُدفع، وكالجزاء الذي إذا ثبت كان العمل واجبًا[١]. ولما كانت إمامة الإمام وخلافته لا تصح إلا بصحة كون[٢] الرسول ورسالته، وامتناع بقائه، ولا رسالة للرسول[٣] إلا بصحة وجود المرسِل والمرسَل إليه جميعًا، وكون المرسَل إليه عاجزاً عن الوصول إلى المرسِل مع كونه قادراً على قبول الرسالة والعمل بها، ووجوب الجزاء على الطاعة والعصيان لاستحالة استخلاف الخليفة من المستخلِف مع بقائه وارتفاع توهّم غيبته، وامتناع وجوب إرسال الرسول من المرسَل مع عدم مَن يُرسل إليه أو كون المرسل إليه عاجزاً، لا استطاعة له، ولا قدرة على قبول الرسالة والعمل بها، أو[٤] وجود المرسل إليه السبيل إلى المرسل بغير واسطة، أو بطلان الجزاء على قبول المرسل إليه الرسالة وطاعته فيها أو نبذها، وكان كل واحد من هذه الأسباب التي[٥] لا تصح الرسالة التي هي علة الإمامة إلا بها، وكانت هذه الأسباب كل سبب منها[٦] هي[٧] علة لما دونه ومتعلقًا بما سواه، وكانت كلها كالأصول، احتجنا إلى

[١] واجبا: + لا ينكر، ز و هـ
[٢] كون: -، ز
[٣] للرسول: الرسول، پ
[٤] او: و، ٤٨
[٥] التي: -، هـ
[٦] وكانت هذه الأسباب كل سبب منها: -، هـ و پ
[٧] هي: -، ز و ٤٨ ، هـ و پ

تقديم الكلام عليها أولاً ليكون لنا إلى المراد طريقًا، ولما نُورده من الغرض في تقرير الإمامة وإثباتها تصديقًا، فكان[١] الأولى بتقديم الكلام عليه إثبات الصانع الذي هو المرسِل وتعلق وجود الكل[٢] بوجوده الذي لولاه لكان الأيسية لا. ثم إثبات أنفس البشر للحاجة في إيجاب الرسالة إلى وجود من يرسل إليه أولاً وكونها جوهراً شريفًا حيًا قادراً غير عالم في بدء وجودها قابلاً للآثار بعلم واختيار، باقيًا بعد فناء الأشخاص. ثم إثبات صورة السياسة الربّانية التي هي الجزاء للوجوب[٣] في الحكمة تمايز الرب من المربوب مع كون الأنفس مختارة قادرة على فعل الخير والشر. ثم إثبات الشرائع والأعمال لحاجة الأنفس في استحقاق الجزاء إلى أعيان الأعمال الشريفة الموضوعة المشابهة[٤] لعاملها[٥]. ثم إثبات التأويل الذي هو العلم لحاجة الأنفس إلى إعلامها ثوابها وعقابها ومعادها بما تراه وتدركه من جهة الحس وتعريفها الحكم والمعاني التي تجيئها[٦] من جهة خالقها بالرسالة المضمنة[٧] أعيان الأعمال التي هي أدلة محسوسة على ما لا يرى. ثم إثبات الرسالة التي هي آخر المقدمات، فإنه إن لم يجب في الحكمة إيجاد أعيان الأعمال ليقع بالعمل بها استحقاق الجزاء، ولم يلزم منها نصب الأمثلة لامتناع وقوع معرفة الأنفس إلا بها المعاد، ولم يفترض فيها إقامة الوسيلة لامتناع الله تعالى عن الرؤية، لم تقع الحاجة إلى الرسول الذي يمثّل الأمثلة ويرسم الأعمال ويكون الوسيلة. ثم الانتقال إلى الكلام على الإمامة التي هي الغرض في هذا الكتاب إذ

---

[١] فكان: وكان، هـ و ز و پ
[٢] الكل: الكلام، هـ
[٣] للوجوب: الموجوب، پ و ز (الهامش، خ)
[٤] المشابهة: المتشابهة، پ ، ٧٤؛ الشابهة، هـ
[٥] لعاملها: لعالمها، پ و هـ؛ لمعالمها، ٤٨
[٦] تجيئها: تحتها، ز و ٤٨
[٧] المضمنة: المتضمنة، پ و ٤٧ و هـ

بامتناع بقاء الرسول في هذا العالم وجبت الإمامة ليصير ذلك كله كالسلسلة بعضها متّصل ببعض، ففعلنا وجعلنا المصابيح جامعةً لبراهينها على ما هي مختصة به بحسب الحاجة، والله الموفق للصواب.

المصباح الثاني
في إثبات الصانع

البرهان الأول: نقول إنّ السبيل إلى معرفة ما يُراد معرفته من طرق ثلاثة: إما من جهة الحس على ما ينقسم إليه من سمع وبصر وشم و ذوق ولمس، وهو المأخوذ به أولاً في معرفة ذوات الأشياء، وإما من جهة العقل على ما توجبه قضاياه وتقاسيمه بواسطة الحس[1]، وإما من جهة البرهان والاستدلال الذي يقوم من بين الحس والعقل جميعًا. ولما كان الصانع لا بذي كيفية فيكون مُدركًا بحس[2]، ولا بذي سمة فيكون معقولاً بعقل، كان السبيل إلى إثباته من جهة إقامة البراهين من بين الحس والعقل على صنعه الذي هو أكبر شهادة.[3] وإذا كان ذلك كذلك وكُنّا إذا عللنا العالم ودللنا على حدثه كان بحدوثه وجوب المحدث الصانع كالمضروب الذي إذا قامت الشهادة عليه وجب به ضرب وضارب، قلنا: إن علة الشيء في وجوده غير عين الشيء كما نرى[4] عيانًا أن علة وجود حركة الطاحونة غير الطاحونة، وعلة وجود حركة أشخاص الحيوان غير الأشخاص إذ لو كانت ذواتها علة لحركتها لكانت أبداً متحركة لوجود ذواتها، ولكانت حينئذ لم

---

[1] الحس: الحسية، ٤٨

[2] بحس: بالحس، ٧٤

[3] قارن القرآن ٦: ١٩ «قل أي شيء أكبر شهادةً»

[4] نرى: ترى، ٤٨

تكن علة بل كانت عين الشيء، ولما كنّا نراها باقية بعد الحركة لا تتحرك صح أن علة وجود الأشياء غير ذواتها، ولما صح أن علة وجود الأشياء غير ذواتها، وكان العالم بما يحويه ذاتًا واحدة بمعنى أنه من حيث الجسمية شيء واحد، وكان البعض منه متحركًا والبعض ساكنًا، ثبت أن حركة المتحرك وسكون الساكن لا من قِبَل ذاته، إذ لو كان من قبل ذاته لكانت الأبعاض كلها متحركة أو ساكنة إذ الذات ذات واحدة، وإذا ثبت أن حركة المتحرك منه وسكون الساكن منه لا من قبل[1] ذاته وجب أن يكون من محرِّك مسكّن يحفظ نظام الكل وترتيبه، وهو غيره، والمحرّك[2] المسكّن هو الصانع، إذاً الصانع ثابت.

البرهان الثاني: لما كان العالم بكليته جسمًا ذا أجزاء وأبعاض معدودة متغايرة بالأشكال والصور مثل ما نُعاين أن صورة الأفلاك والكواكب التي هي أبعاض العالم غير صورة الماء، وصورة النار وشكلها غير صورة الأرض والهواء، وصورة أشخاص المواليد غير صورة الهواء والأفلاك، وكل ذلك على تباين صوره منتضد، والبعض بالبعض متّصل[3] كالباب الذي كله خشب وهو ذو أبعاض وأجزاء، وصورة بعض أجزائه التي هي الألواح مخالفة لصورة الأجزاء الأخرى[4] التي هي[5] الأعمدة[6] وغيرها، وكل[7] ذلك على تباين الصورة[8] متّصل والبعض بالبعض منتضد، ومعلوم أن كل شيء جمعه[9] والشيء الآخر معنىً من المعاني[10] فهو في

---

[1] قبل: -، ز
[2] والمحرك: فالمحرك، پ
[3] متصل: تصل، هـ
[4] الاخرى: الاخر، ٤٨، پ؛ -، ٧٤
[5] هي: -، هـ
[6] الاعمدة: اعمدة، ز
[7] وكل: فكل، پ
[8] الصورة: صورت، هـ؛ صورته، ٧٤؛ صورة، ٤٨
[9] جمعه: جميعه، هـ

ذلك المعنى، وإن كان كل واحد منهما يختصّ بمعانٍ أخر[1]، مثله وشكله، ولما وجدنا معنىً تخالُف الأجزاء والنضد قد جمع العالم والباب، وكان الباب لم تجتمع أجزاؤه إلا بفعل فاعل، كان العالم، في أن أجزاءه، لم تجتمع إلا بفعل فاعل مِثْله[2]. إذاً العالم مصنوع مُحْدَث والمحدَث يقتضي مُحْدِثًا صانعًا، فالصانع ثابت.

البرهان الثالث: لما كان في المشاهد أن عالم اللغات على أنواعها من لغة العرب والفرس والعبراني والسرياني والنبط[3] والروم والزنج والترك[4] وغير ذلك مؤلف من أجزاء معلومة معدودة، مثل الحروف البسيطة التي هي[5] ا، ب، ت، ث، وبها تمكن العبارات[6] عما في النفس من صُوَرِ[7] المحسوسات والمعقولات بالنطق، وكانت هذه الحروف لا تأتلف من ذواتها إلا بمؤلف يُؤلفها فيقدّم واحداً ويؤخّر آخراً، مثل قولنا فِضّة الذي لم يكن تقدّم الفاء الذي هو في أصل الحروف بعد الضاد على الضاد الذي هو في الأصل[8] قبل الفاء إلا بتقديم مقدّم وتأخير مؤخّر، وكان العالَم عالَمُ الجسم مماثلاً في كونه أجزاءً معلومةً وأعيانًا متغايرة وصوراً مختلفة لعالَم[9] اللغات والنطق، كان منه العلم بأن ائتلاف أجزائه مع العلم بأنها غير قادرة على حركة ولا هي حية ولا عالمة، فيتوهّم أنها ائتلفت بذاتها

---

[10] معنى من المعانى: يعني من المعاني آخر، هـ

[1] بمعان أخر: بمعنى آخر، هـ، ز

[2] كان العالم في...كان العالم في اجزاءه اذا العالم مصنوع: كان العالم في ان اجزائه لم تجمع الا بفعل فاعل مثله اذ العالم مصنوع، ز

[3] والنبط: والقبط، پ

[4] والترك: + والنوبة، ز

[5] هي: -، هـ

[6] تمكن العبارات: تمكن العبارة، ٧٤، پ

[7] صور: صورة، پ

[8] الاصل: اصل الحروف، هـ، ٤٨

[9] لعالم: لعلم، ز

واجتمع إلى بعض بعضها[١] لو كان جائزاً وكونها مع ائتلافها متضادة متنافرة، لم تكن إلا بفعل فاعل وجمع جامع، وإذا كان ائتلافها[٢] لم يكن إلا بفعل فاعل، والفاعل[٣] هو الصانع، فالصانع ثابت.

البرهان الرابع: لما كان سمة ما لا يستحيل عما عليه عنصره ولا يتغيّر ولا يقبل الفعل أن يكون لا مفعولاً[٤]، وكان سمة ما يقبل الفعل الذي به يستحيل من حال إلى حال ويدخل عليه التغييرات[٥] أن يكون مفعولاً، وكان العالم بأفلاكه ونجومه ومواليده لا نراه على حالة[٦] واحدة من أن تكون الكواكب أبداً طالعة أو غاربة أو أن يكون أبداً نهاراً أو ليلاً أو أن[٧] تكون الموجودات من المواليد أبداً باقية على حالتها[٨]، وكانت الاستحالة من حال الكينونية والطلوعية والنهارية إلى حال الفسادية والغروبية والليلية فيه موجودة، كان من ذلك العلم بأنه[٩] من قبيل ما يقبل الفعل الذي به يستحيل ويتغيّر، وإذا كان من قبيل ما يقبل الفعل كان مفعولاً، وإذا كان مفعولاً اقتضي فاعلاً، والفاعل هو الصانع. إذاً الصانع ثابت[١٠].

البرهان الخامس: لما كان العالم محسوساً مُدركًا، وكان لا يخلو بجميع ما فيه من خمسة أقسام: إما مُبصَراً وهو مدرك البصر، وإما مسموعًا وهو مدرك السمع، وإما مشمومًا وهو مدرك الشم، وإما مذوقًا

---

١ الى بعض بعضها: بعضها الى بعض، ٤٨، هـ
٢ ائتلافها: ائتلافه، ز، ٧٤
٣ والفاعل: فالفاعل، ٤٨
٤ ولا يتغير...لا مفعولا: -، هـ
٥ التغييرات: التغيير، هـ، ٤٨؛ التغير، ٧٤ و پ
٦ حالة: حالته، پ
٧ ان: -، هـ، ٤٨
٨ حالتها: حالها، ٧٤
٩ بانه: بان، هـ
١٠ اذا الصانع ثابت: فالصانع اذا ثابت، ٤٨؛ فالصانع ثابت، ز

وهو مدرك الذوق، وإما ملموسًا وهو مدرك اللمس، وكان لو كان العالم بأقسامه هذه يستحق القدمة لكان الذي يدركه، وهو مدركه[١]، أولى بأن يستحق القدمة إذ من قضايا العقل أن الذي يُدرك[٢] أجلّ من مدركه[٣]، وأن الذي يحوي أعلى[٤] من المحوي، وكانت القوى التي بها يُدرَك العالَم التي هي المشاعر الخمسة محدثة، فالعالَم المدرَك أولى بأن يكون مُحدَثًا.
إذاً العالم محدث، والمحدَث يقتضي مُحدِثًا، والمحدِث هو الصانع[٥]، فالصانع ثابت.

البرهان السادس: لما كانت الأشياء لا تدرِك إلا ما كان من عنصرها، ولا تُدرك[٦] ما علا عليها إلا ما كان دونها، وكان المحدَث[٧] لا من عنصر القديم، ولا هو عال عليه، كان من ذلك الحكمُ بأن العالم لو كان قديمًا لكان غير مدرَك ولا محسوس بحواسّ محدَثة، ولما كان مدركًا محسوسًا ملموسًا مبصراً مذوقًا بحواس محدثة مفعولة قد علت الحواس بإدراكها إياه، وكان لا عالم الطبيعة إلا ذلك، كان منه العلم بأنه محدث مثله والمحدَث يقتضي محدِثًا. إذاً للعالم صانع، فالصانع ثابت.

البرهان السابع: لما كان العالم ذا أجزاء وأبعاض، وكان كل بعض يختص[٨] بمعنى هو في البعض الآخر معدوم من ضياء ولطافة وكثافة وشفافة ونور وظلمة، وكان لو كان[٩] العالم قديمًا لا يتقدمه صانع صنعه ورتبه كما هو لكان لا يكون اختصاص جرم الشمس بأن يكون مضيئًا

---

١ مدركه: مدرك، ٤٨، پ
٢ يدرك: يدركه، ٤٨
٣ مدركه: المدرك، ز
٤ اعلى: اولى، ٧٤
٥ هو الصانع: صانع، ٧٤؛ الصانع، پ
٦ تدرك: -، هـ
٧ المحدث: محدث، هـ
٨ يختص: مختص، هـ، ز، ٧٤
٩ كان: +، هذا، هـ، ز

أولى من جرم الأرض، ولا اختصاص جرم الماء بأن يكون رطبًا سيّالاً أولى من النار، ولا اختصاص الهواء بأن يكون لطيفًا أولى من الأرض، ولا اختصاص جرم الأرض بأن يكون كثيفًا ثقيلاً أولى من الهواء والنار، وكان، لما كان الاختصاص في أبعاضه موجوداً، كان منه الإيجاب بأنه لعلة صار البعض مختصًا بمعنى هو في الآخر معدوم، وإذا حصلت العلة وجب أن يكون له فاعلاً فعله، إذ لولا[١] الفاعل وتخصيصه كل بعض ما هو مختص به لكان مع عدم الفاعل لا يجب اختصاص شيء منه بمعنى دون آخر[٢] ولكانت الأبعاض كلها شيئًا واحداً[٣] إما كثيفًا أو لطيفًا أو مضيئًا أو[٤] مظلمًا. إذاً للعالم صانع، فالصانع ثابت.

المصباح الثالث

في إثبات النفس وأنها جوهر حي قادر غير عالم في ابتداء وجود ذاتها باق بعد فساد الجثة بما تكسبه من العلم[٥] والعمل

البرهان الأول: لما كان حركة كل متحرك لا تخلو إما أن تكون من داخل وإما أن تكون من خارج، وكان ما كان حركته من خارج إما مجروراً

---

[١] لولا: +كان، هـ، ز

[٢] آخر: الآخر، ز و ٤٨

[٣] شيئا واحدا: شيء واحد، ز

[٤] او...او...او: اما...اما...اما، ٤٨

[٥] العلم: العلوم، ٧٤، ز

جراً أو[١] مدفوعًا[٢] دفعًا، وبطل أن تكون حركة شخص[٣] البشر بجر أو دفع، ثبت أن حركته من داخل، و[لما كان] ما كان حركته من داخل إما طبيعيًا وإما من محرك مختار، وكان ما كان طبيعيًا لا يسكن البتة، كحركة النار، وما كان من محرك مختار تارة يتحرك وتارة يسكن، وبطل أن تكون حركة الشخص طبيعيًا لا يسكن البتة، ثبت أن حركته من محرِّك مختار، والمحرِّك المختار نسمّيه نفسًا. إذاً النفس ثابتة.

البرهان الثاني: لما كان لشخص البشر قوة وغضب وامتعاض من مثل ما يُفعل بالموتى من غسلهم وتحنيطهم وتكفينهم وسد منافذهم، وكان في حال الموت لا يغضب ولا يمنع إذا فعل به ذلك، ويبطل[٤] منه غضبه ومنعته[٥] من غير بطلان ذاته أو جارحة من جوارحه، كان من ذلك العلم بأن غضبه لا من ذاته ولا من قوته إذ لو كان من ذاته لكان غاضبًا[٦] مانعًا ممتعضًا بوجود ذاته، ولما[٧] لم يكن من ذاته كان من غيره، والغير هو الذي نسمّيه نفسًا. إذاً النفس ثابتة.

البرهان الثالث: لما كان سكون كل ساكن لا يخلو إما أن يكون بالطبع وإما أن يكون بالقهر، وكان[٨] ما كان سكونه بالطبع لا يكون زوال سكونه[٩] إلا بتحريك محرِّك، مثل حجر الطاحونة الذي إذا تركه المحرِّك له عاد إلى حال سكونه، وما[١٠] كان سكونه بالقهر لا يدخل السكون عليه إلا بإمساك

---

[١] او: + اما، ٤٨، هـ
[٢] مجرورا...مدفوعا: مجرور...مدفوع، هـ، ز، پ، ٤٨، ٧٤
[٣] شخص: اشخاص، ٤٨
[٤] يبطل: بطل، ٧٤
[٥] منعته: منعه، ٤٨
[٦] غاضبا: غاضبانا، ٤٨ و پ
[٧] ولما: وما، ٤٨
[٨] وكان: فكل، ٧٤ و ٤٧
[٩] سكونه: + بالطبع، ز، ٤٨، هـ
[١٠] وما: وكان ما، ز

مُمسك، مثل ارتعاد القصبة في الماء الجاري التي لا تسكن إلا بإمساك مُمسِك، وإذا تركها المُمسِك عادت إلى حال حركتها، وكان[١] شخص البشر سكونه عند الموت لا بقهرَ قاهر ولا بإمساك مُمسِك إياه، ثبت أن سكونه بالطبع، ولما كان سكونه بالطبع لزم أن زوال سكونه حين كان متحركًا لم يكن إلا بتحريك محرِّك إياه، وأن سكونه حين كان ساكنًا لم يكن إلا في ترك المحرِّك تحريكه إياه، وإذا لزم أن زوال سكونه بتحريك محرِّك إياه وسكونه في ترك المحرِّك تحريكه، ثبت أن له في حال حركته محركًا إذا تركه لم يتحرك، والمحرِّك هو الذي نسمّيه نفسًا. إذاً النفس ثابتة.

البرهان الرابع: نقول إن كل شيء اتّحد بحد شيء فهو عينه ومثله، ولما كان حد الجوهر أنه قابل للمتضادات من غير استحالة عن ذاته وكانت النفس المحركة لشخص البشر قابلة للمتضادات، مثل العلم والجهل، والشجاعة والجبن، والسخاء[٢] والبخل، من غير استحالة عن ذاتها، وكان كل قابل للمتضادات من غير استحالة عن ذاته[٣] جوهراً، كانت النفس جوهراً، وإذا كانت جوهراً كانت باقية قائمة بذاتها، إذاً النفس جوهر باق.

البرهان الخامس: لما كان طبيعة الجوهر أن يكون حاملاً وطبيعة العرض أن يكون محمولاً، والجوهر أن يكون قابلاً والعرض أن يكون مقبولاً، والجوهر أن يكون مكانًا والعرض أن يكون متمكنًا، وكانت النفس مما يحمل، لا مما يُحمل، ويَقبل لا مما يُقبل، ويُتمكن منه، لا مما يتمكن، كان منه الإيجاب أنها موصوفة بصفة الجوهر، وإذا كانت موصوفة بصفة الجوهر في كونها حاملة لا محمولة وقابلة لا مقبولة ومكانًا لا متمكنة، كانت جوهراً، فإذاً النفس جوهر، وإذا كانت جوهراً كانت قائمة باقية لا تبيد.

---

[١] وكان: واذا كان، پ، ز

[٢] السخاء: السخاوة، هـ

[٣] وكان كل قابل...عن ذاته:-، ز، پ

البرهان السادس: لما كان العلم صورة الشيء على ما هو به من حال هليته ومائيته وكميته وكيفيته ولميته، والعالِم هو المتصوّر بهذه المعارف، وكانت أنفس البشر عند ابتداء نشوئها، لو أمسكت[١] عن تعليمها معارف الأشياء واحداً بعد واحد بالزمان والمدة لكانت لا تعدو البهائم ولا تعرف شيئًا تتميز به عنها كما نشاهده من حال الأطفال وغيرهم في خلوّهم من علم ما دنا منهم إدراكه بجسمهم فضلاً عما نأى عنهم إدراكه بنفوسهم[٢] إلا بدليل وهادٍ ومعلم، كان من ذلك العلم بأنها عاطلة الذات من صور الأشياء وتعلمها[٣]، خالية من معارفها، إذ لو لم تكن خالية عاطلة لكانت تعرف الأشياء وتعلمها بوجود ذاتها، وتستغني عن الاكتساب والتعلم، ولاستحقت[٤] اسم العالمية، كما أنها لما كانت حية بوجود ذاتها لم تعدم الحياة واستحقت اسم الحياة، ولم تحتج إلى اكتساب ما به تصير حية لكونها حية[٥]، وكما أنها، لما كانت قادرة فاعلة بوجود[٦] ذاتها من حركة وقدرة عليها، لم تعدم القدرة والفعل، واستحقت اسم القادرية والفاعلية، ولم تحتج إلى اكتساب ما به تصير قادرة وفاعلة لكونها قادرة وفاعلة، ولما كانت عاطلة الذات من العلم خالية ثبت أنها غير عالمة، وإذا ثبت أنها غير عالمة وكانت مكانًا للمعارف بكونها جوهراً، ثبت أنها محتاجة إلى العلم لتمامية ذاتها. إذاً النفس في ابتداء وجودها غير عالمة وهي محتاجة إلى التعليم.

البرهان السابع: لما كان الموت ترك النفس استعمال كل الأعضاء التي يجمعها الشخص من يد ورجل وعين وأذن وأنف ولسان، وغير ذلك مما

---

[١] امسكت: امسك، ز، ٧٤، ٤٨

[٢] بنفوسهم: بانفسهم، ٤٨

[٣] وتعلمها: وتعليمها، ٧٤

[٤] ولاستحقت: واستحقت، ٤٨، ٧٤

[٥] لكونها حية: -، پ، هـ

[٦] بوجود: لوجود، ٤٨

في الأحشاء والبطن، وتحريكها، وكانت الأشخاص تستحق اسم الحياة باستعمال النفس أبعاضها، كانت النفس التي بها تكون حياة غيرها أولى أن تكون حية في ذاتها، إذاً النفس حية، وإذا كانت حية كانت باقية لا تبيد.

البرهان الثامن: لما كان فساد كل شيء مما يضاده، إما بالمجاورة وإما بالمخالطة، وكان كل ما يجلّ عن أن يجاور أو يخالط غير متوهم فيه الفساد، وكانت النفس ليست بذي أجزاء مركبة فيداخلها ويخالطها غيرها، ولا بذي نهايات[١] وجهات في ذاتها[٢] فيجاورها سواها، كانت النفس مما لا يجاور ولا يخالط، وإذا كانت مما لا يجاور أو يخالط[٣] فغير متوهم فيها الفساد، إذاً النفس باقية لا تفسد ولا تبيد.

البرهان التاسع: لما كان البقاء والسرمد لعالَم الوحدة، وكان ما كان له بقاء فبقاؤه بما يمتدّ إليه من فيض هذا العالَم الذي هو عالَم الوحدة، وكان ما يمتدّ إليه فيض هذا العالَم، أعني عالَم الوحدة، مما يكون قبوله بعلم واختيار، نهايته إلى البقاء، وما يكون قبوله ذلك بغير علم ولا اختيار نهايته إلى الانسلاخ منه والفساد، وكانت الأنفس قبولها ذلك الفيض من جهة التعليم بعلم واختيار، وجب أن يكون نهايتها، مُثابةً كانت أو معاقبةً، الي البقاء إذا كانت هي والمادّة الممتدّة إليها التي هي المعارف من عالَم الوحدة، قد صارت شيئًا واحداً، فإذا كانت قد صارت شيئًا واحداً كانت نهايتها إلى البقاء، وإذا كانت نهايتها إلى البقاء فغير متوهّم فسادها، إذاً النفس باقية لا تبيد.

البرهان العاشر: لما كان كل شيء نشوؤه بشيء، فمصيره إلى ذلك

---

[١] نهايات: نهاية، ٤٨، ز

[٢] ذاتها: ذواتها، هـ

[٣] ولا يخالط واذا...او يخالط:-، ز، ٧٤؛ ولا مما يخالط، هـ

الشيء كما نشاهده[١] عيانًا من مصير المواليد الثلاثة التي هي الحيوان والنبات والمعادن إلى ما منه نشأت الذي هو الأمهات الأربعة، وكانت الأنفس نشوؤها وتربيتها من مبدأ وجودها بالعلم، وكان العلم لا من عالَم الطبيعة، بل هو من عالَم القدس الذي هو دار البقاء، كانت النفس مصيرها بما نشأت عليه من العلم[٢]، رذلاً كان أم شريفًا، إلى البقاء، وإذا كان مصيرها إلى البقاء فهي باقية لا تبيد. إذاً النفس باقية لا تبيد، فاعرفه[٣].

المصباح الرابع

في إثبات صورة السياسة الربانية التي هي[٤] الجزاء ووجودها وأن دارها غير دار الدنيا التي هي العالم الطبيعي، يشتمل على عشرة براهين

البرهان الأول: لما كان الله تعالى قد جعل جوهر النفس حية قادرة على فعل الخير والشر والطاعة والمعصية، وكان، لو كان طاعتها ومعصيتها وفعلها الخير والشر شيئًا واحداً لا فرق بينهما، ولا سياسة قائمة تمتاز بها النفس الخيرة الطائعة من النفس الشريرة العاصية، [لما كان] يظهر الآمر من المأمور والمنعِم من المنعَم عليه والسابق من المسبوق، ولا يتبيّن الرب من المربوب ولا العبد من المعبود، ولا يظهر شرف الخالقية

---

[١] نشاهده: نشاهد، ز، پ، ٧٤، ٤٨
[٢] العلم: العلوم، پ، ٧٤، ٤٨
[٣] فاعرفه:-، ز، پ
[٤] هي: + دار، پ

ولا مجد الربوبية لكون الأنفس من جهة الحياة والقدرة والعلم والاختيار والإدراك في أفق عالم الربوبية، وكان في الحكمة ومنها أن تكون آثار الربوبية قائمة، وجب أن تكون السياسة التي بها يتعلق مجد الربوبية قائمة فتكون فاصلة فرقانًا بين الرب والمربوب، وهي الجزاء. إذاً الجزاء ثابت.

البرهان الثاني: لما كان نوع البشرية مكلّفين تحت الأمر والنهي، وكانت أشخاصه[١] لا يقع منها بمجرّدها فعل تستحق به مدحًا ولا ذمًّا إلا بالأنفس التي هي تستعملها[٢]، وكان الأحق منهما، من الشخص والنفس، بنسب[٣] الفعل إليه النفس لاستعمالها إياه، وكان الشخص باستعمال النفس إياه في إيقاع الأفعال التي تخالف السياسة النبوية يُقطَع جزاء على ذلك الفعل، مثل قطع اليد والرجل عند السرقة وضرب الرقبة عند القتل، واليد جزء من الشخص لا جزء من النفس، كانت النفس أولى بأن تكون مجازاة في ذاتها على ما كان منها من خير أو شر. إذاً الجزاء ثابت.

البرهان الثالث: لما كان عدل الله تعالى تامًا، وكان ما خلقه من نوع البشرية مخصوصًا بالتمييز من[٤] غيره، وكان النوع ذا أشخاص والأشخاص ذوات أنفس، وكانت هذه الأنفس منها ما يُؤثر لذّات المعقولات الآجلية النفسانية على لذّات المحسوسات العاجلية، فيمتنع عن طلبها ثقة بنيل ما آثره، وإن كان آجلاً، ومنها ما يؤثر لذات المحسوسات العاجلية على لذات المعقولات النفسانية الآجلية، وينكبّ على طلبها شكًا منه في الآجلية وثقة بالعاجلية، وكان النقص لو كان لا ثواب لهذه

---

[١] اشخاصه: اشخاص، ٤٨

[٢] تستعملها: مستعملها، هـ، پ، ٤٨، ٧٤

[٣] بنسب: ينسب، ٧٤، ٤٨

[٤] من: عن، هـ

الأنفس التي هجرت في طاعة الله لذاتها وطلبت ما عنده، ولا عقاب للأنفس التي أقبلت على طلب العاجلة، وأعرضت عن أمر[١] الله تعالى مع إرساله تبارك وتعالى الرسل لتحذيرهم[٢] الغرور بالعاجل الفاني في عدل الله تعالى متوهمًا، وكان عدل الله منزهًا عن أن يُتوهم فيه نقص، كان من ذلك الإيجاب بأن للأنفس جزاء. إذاً الجزاء واجب ثابت.

البرهان الرابع: لما كانت رحمة الله تعالى تامة، وكان الله قد أرسل الرسل ليمنع[٣] عباده عن[٤] اللذات والشهوات المردية الدنية، وكان لو كان لا وجود لما هو خير من اللذات المحسوسات الدنية النقص، لِما منعهم من اللذات بما لم يكن له أصل لاحقًا برحمته، وكانت رحمة الله منزهة عن أن يتوهم فيها نقص، كان من ذلك العلم بأن للأنفس في ترك المنهي عنه من اللذات العاجلية وفعل المأمور به ما هو خير منها لها، وهو جزاؤها على تركها وفعلها. إذاً الجزاء واجب ثابت.

البرهان الخامس: لما كان الله تعالى أبدع عالَم العقل والنفس فجعله داراً فائضة منها بركات كلمة الله تعالى على ما هو دونه فيضًا ودافعة إلى الأنفس كرامات وحدانية الله تعالى دفعًا، وكانت جواهر الأنفس في قبول ما يلمع في ذواتها بما تكتسب علمًا وعملاً كالمرايا تهيُّأً ومصيرها بكونها مما يجانس عالَم العقل والنفس إليه، وجب من حيث كون الأنفس قابلة وعالم العقل والنفس داراً فائضة أن يكون لها في مصيرها بعد اكتساب العلم والعمل[٥] قبول لفيض عالم العقل والنفس، إن كانت خيرة نيرة فالمقبول على ما هو عليه لذة وبه مسرة كالصحيح، وإن كانت شرة شمرة فالمقبول بالعكس على ما هو عليه ألماً وبه غمًا كالمريض، وإذا كان

---

[١] امر: اوامر، پ، ز

[٢] لتحذيرهم: لتحذير، ز

[٣] ليمنع: لتمنع، ز؛ ليمتنع، ٤٨

[٤] عن: من، ٤٨

[٥] والعمل: بالعمل، هـ، ز

لها قبول فالمقبول هو الجزاء على سابق العلم والعمل. إذاً الجزاء واجب ثابت، فاعرفه.

البرهان السادس: لما كان ما لم يُبدعه الله فلا صورة له في الوجود أصلاً ولا في الإمكان إيجاده ولا في الاستطاعة إحداثه، وكان عالم العقل والنفس سابقًا في الإبداعية على عالَم الحس الذي هو الدنيا، على ما أوردنا برهانه في كتاب «راحة العقل»، لزم أن صورة الأشياء كلها الموجودة في عالم الحس مما يتعلق بالحكمة وهي التي أبدعها الله في عالم النفس، وإذا لزم ذلك وكان في العالم موجوداً صورُ السياسات ومؤاخذة الجاني بجنايته ومعاقبته[1] على ذنبه، ثبت أن في عالم النفس جزاء. إذاً الجزاء واجب ثابت.

البرهان السابع: لما قامت البراهين على صدق رسالة الأنبياء عليهم السلام، وكانوا عن آخرهم أعلموا أممهم أن لهم قيامة وحشراً ونشراً[2] وجزاءاً وحسابًا على الخير والشر، وكان سيد الأنبياء وخاتمهم محمد المصطفى صلى الله عليه وآله قد أخبر بمثل ذلك عن الله تعالى بقوله: «لِيَجْزِيَ الذِّينَ أَسَاؤُوا بِمَا عَمِلُوا وَيَجْزِيَ الذِّينَ أَحْسَنُوا بِالحُسْنَىَ» [٥٣:٣١]، وقوله: «فَمَنْ يَعْمَلْ مِثْقَالَ ذَرَّةٍ خَيْراً يَرَهُ وَمَنْ يَعْمَلْ مِثْقَالَ ذَرَّةٍ شَرّاً يَرَهُ» [٩٩: ٧ و٨]، وقوله: «إنّي جَزَيْتُهُم اليَوْمَ بِمَا صَبَرُوا أَنَّهُم هُمُ الفَائِزُونَ» [٢٣: ١١١] وجب أن يكون للأنفس جزاء. إذاً الجزاء واجب ثابت.

البرهان الثامن: لما كان العدل يقتضي أن يكون الجزاء بعد الاستحقاق، خيراً كان أم شراً، وكان الاستحقاق لا يقع إلا بالعمل، وجب أن يكون العمل متقدمًا على الجزاء، وإذا وجب أن يكون العمل متقدمًا على الجزاء، وكان البشر في الدنيا رهين العمل، كان من ذلك العلم بأن الدنيا دار العمل، وإذا كانت الدنيا دار العمل لم تكن بدار الجزاء. فإذاً

[1] معاقبته: معاقبه، ز
[2] ونشرا: ونشورا، ز

الدنيا ليست بدار الجزاء، فاعلم.

البرهان التاسع: لما كان الجزاء لا يكون إلا بسابق الاكتساب، وكان الاكتساب، إما أن يكون بالعمل أو بالفكر، وكان لا سبيل للنفس إلى اكتساب بالعمل إلا من جهة الأشخاص وأبعاضها، ولا[١] إلى اكتساب بفكر واعتقاد إلا من جهة التعاليم وموضوعاتها، وكانت الأشخاص والتعاليم لا تكون إلا في الدنيا، كان من ذلك العلم بأن الدنيا دار الاكتساب، وإذا كانت دار الاكتساب فليس بدار الجزاء. فإذاً الدنيا ليست بدار الجزاء، فاعرفه.

البرهان العاشر: لما كانت أنفس البشر موجودة الذات ثابتة، وكانت متهيئة لقبول ما يلمع في ذاتها من صور الموجودات بكونها مكانًا للصور العلمية وقيامها جوهراً قابلاً لم تخل مع كونها[٢] بهذه الصفة في وجود ذاتها من وجهين: إما أنها كانت موجودة الذات قبل الأشخاص المهيأة لها لنشوئها ويقال عليها نفس، أو لم تكن بموجودة الذات قبل الأشخاص، فإن كانت موجودة الذات قبل الأشخاص ويقال عليها نفس لم يخل كونها من وجهين: إما أنها كانت في عالم النفس أو في عالم الجسم لكونها ما شمله الوجود في هذين العالمين، فإن كانت في عالم النفس وكان عالم النفس ذا صور من معارف الأكوان السابقة والتالية والمتعاقبة مجردة وفيوض فائضة علمية، فكون النفس في تهيئها للقبول يقتضي أن تكون تلك المعارف التي هي صورَ[٣] مجردة وفيوض فائضة قد لمعت في ذاتها فصارت محمولة موجودة فيها وهي بها عالمة، ونراها خالية من ذلك بكونها عاجزة عن ذكر ما كان من أحداث أو يكون من أكوان، مع قدرتها

[١] ولا: + سبيل، ٧٤
[٢] كونها: + مكانا، ٤٨
[٣] صور: صورة، هـ، ٤٨

على الفكر[١] فيما تحويه ذاتها من صوَر الموجودات والكائنات من جهة التعليم، ونجدها غير مفكرة ولا عالمة ما لم تكتسب العلم من جهة المعلمين، وإذا كانت خالية محتاجة في العلم إلى الاكتساب بطل أنها كانت في عالم النفس. وإن[٢] كانت في عالم الجسم لم يخل كونها[٣] من وجهين: إما أنها كانت قائمة بذاتها أو قائمة بغيرها، فإن كانت قائمة بذاتها وكان لا يقوم بذاته ما لا يكون جوهراً باقيًا، وكان لا يكون جوهراً باقيًا ما لا يقبل كلمة الله تعالى التي هي المعارف بعلم لكون الكلمة علة لجوهرية الحوهر في قيامه بذاته وبقائه، وبطل أنها قد قبلت كلمة الله تعالى التي هي المعارف بعلم بخلوها من العلم والمعرفة فتكونَ جرهراً، وإذا لم تكن جوهراً بطل أن يكون لها قيام بذاتها، وإذا لم تكن قائمة بذاتها بطل هذا الوجه، وإن كانت قائمة بغيرها فقيامها بغيرها، إما أن يكون بالمجاورة أو بالمخالطة أو بالإحاطة، وبطلت الوجوه الثلاثة بكونها لا مما يجاوِر أو يجاوَر، ولا مما يخالط أو يخالَط، ولا مما له جهات يحيط أو يحاط بوجودها، [و]لا مما يتجزأ فيجوز المخالطة، ولا مما له جهات فيجوز المجاورة، ولا مما له علم فيحيط بالأجسام أو هو جسم فيحيط بجسم أو [يحيط] به جسم، وإذا بطلت الوجوه الثلاثة بطل أنها كانت في عالم الجسم، وإذا بطل كونها من هذين العالمين ثبت أنها لم تكن موجودة الذات ويقال عليها نفس، وإذا ثبت أنها لم تكن موجودة الذات ويقال عليها نفس قبل الأشخاص، ثبت أن وجودها رهين بوجود الشخص المهيأ لها للارتياض والاكتساب، وإذا ثبت أن وجودها رهين بوجود الشخص ثبت أنها لم تكتسب قبله علمًا ولا عملاً. وإذا لم تكتسب

[١] الفكر: الفكرة، هـ

[٢] وان: واذا، پ؛-، هـ

[٣] كونها:-، پ، ٧٤

فمحال أن تكون[١] الدنيا لها دار جزاء. إذاً الدنيا ليست بدار الجزاء.

المصباح الخامس

في إثبات الشريعة وأعيان الأعمال ووجوبها قائمة ثابتة، يشتمل على سبعة براهين

البرهان الأول: لما خلق الله تعالى نوع البشرية واختصّه من بين خلقه بالفضيلة، وأوجب عدله إيجاب الجزاء، وكان استحقاق الجزاء لا يكون إلا بالأعمال[٢]، وجب أن يكون للبشر أعيان لأعمال[٣] شريفة لائقة بعبادة[٤] الله تعالى ليكون له بها استحقاق الجزاء. إذاً الأعمال ثابتة واجبة.

البرهان الثاني: لما كانت الأخلاق للأنفس كالصور للمحسوسات، حسنة كانت أم قبيحة، وكانت الفضيلة للأنفس في الحسن منها الذي هو العدل والرحمة وكظم الغيظ والشجاعة والعبادة والصدق والسخاء والعفة والورع والطهارة والديانة، لا في القبيح منها الذي هو الجور وقلة الرحمة وسرعة الغضب والجبن طلبًا للبقاء في الدنيا والتهاون بالعبادة والكذب والغدر والبخل وارتكاب الكبائر والطمع وقلة مراقبة الله تعالى، وكانت أنفس البشر في حال الصبا تكتسب الأخلاق الدنية بالطبع واستمرارُ عادتها[٥] بها يكسبها[٦] رذالة، وكانت العادات التي هي الأفعال علة

[١] تكون: كون، ٤٨
[٢] بالاعمال: بالعمل، ٧٤
[٣] لاعمال: الاعمال، ٤٨
[٤] بعبادة: لعبادة، پ
[٥] عادتها: عاداتها، ٧٤، هـ
[٦] يكسبها: تكتسبها، ٧٤، ٤٨؛ تكسبها، ز، پ، هـ

لاستحكام صور الأخلاق، حسنة كانت أم قبيحة، في الأنفس وجب من حيث وجوب طلب الفضيلة وامتناع الأمر في اكتساب الأنفس الفضائل وسلبها ما اكتسبته في حال الصبا من الرذائل إلا بلزوم العبادات[١] أن تكون أعيان العبادات التي بها تكتسب الأنفس فضائل الأخلاق موجودة فيما بين البشر، فيكون للأنفس في لزومها شرفُ الكمال. إذاً العبادات[٢] التي هي الأعمال في رياضة الأنفس واجبة، والأعمال هي الشرائع وأحكامها وسننها.

البرهان الثالث: لما أبى الله تعالى إلا عمارة الآخرة وخراب الدنيا كما قال رسول الله صلى الله عليه وسلم، وكانت عمارة الآخرة من جهة أنفس البشر التي تتوفر على العبادة، وكان بقاء أشخاص نوع البشرية والتوفر على العبادة في الدنيا بعموم الأمن واحتقان الدماء وانحفاظ الفروج والأموال، وكان ذلك كله لا يكون إلا بكون رسوم فيما بينهم مرتسمة[٣] يجرون على منهاجها ويأخذون بأحكامها، وكان لو لم تكن الرسوم والوضائع وأحكامها لا يكون أحد بامرأة له تكون في داره أولى من الآخر ولا بمال ولا ذخيرة أولى من الآخر، وكانت تتّقد نيران الفتنة بالقتل وسفك الدماء وسبي الذراري واستباحة الفروج ومصير القوي قاهراً لغيره، فيكون[٤] ذلك مؤديًا إلى البوار والهلاك وانسداد أبواب بيوت عبادة الله تعالى بالاشتغال[٥] عنها بالذب عن الحريم والأموال، وجب من طريق الحكمة في استيفاء حكمة الله فيما صنعه وذرأه ليعمر[٦] الآخرة أن يكون

---

[١] العبادات: العادات، ٧٤، هـ

[٢] اذا العبادات: اذ العبادات، ز، ٤٨؛ اذ العادات، هـ

[٣] مرتسمة: مرسمة، ز، پ، ٤٨؛ سمة، هـ

[٤] فيكون: ويكون، ٧٤، هـ

[٥] بالاشتغال: باشتغال، پ؛ بالاثتقال، هـ

[٦] ليعمر: لتعمر، ز، ٧٤، ه؛ لتتعمر، پ، ٤٨

فيما بين البشر رسوم وأحكام يجرون على قضاياها[١] فتنسد أبواب الفتن. إذاً الرسوم التي هي الشرائع والأعمال واجبة.

البرهان الرابع: لما كان نوع البشر لا استطاعة له في قبول كل الحكمة دفعة واحدة، وكان غير ممكن أن يبقى رسول الله صلى الله عليه وسلم فيما بينهم فيعلّمهم يومًا بيوم ما ينزله الله من الحكم، ولا في استطاعة من يقوم مقام الرسول ويسد مسده في التعليم أن يعلّم من غير قانون يرجع إليه في تعليم الحكمة، وجب أن يكون بين الأمة قانون للحكمة[٢] موضوع يكون مرجع القائم مقام الرسول إليه في التعليم، والقانون هي الكُتب والشرائع والرسوم والوضائع. إذاً الرسوم التي هي الشرائع واجبة.

البرهان الخامس: لما كان الفيض من عالَم القدس لا ينقطع عن المؤيدين خصوصًا وكان شيئًا روحانيًا ليس في استطاعة البشر نيله إلا من كانت نفسه متهيئة للقبول، وكان الذي يناله برفيع حدّه إذا لم يقيد تلك الحِكَم والمعارف التي لاحت في نفسه المؤيدة من فيض عالَم القدس بما يكون محسوسًا لائقًا به من الحروف والوضائع فيكون للبشرية وصلة إليها كما فعل البارئ تعالى بلطيف صنعه من إبداع الأطعمة اللذيذة الروحانية اللطيفة الممتنعة عن الدرك إلا من جهة الأجسام التي تحفظها الأجسام المحسوسة، فعقدها بها ليصل البشر بها إليها لئلا تبطل الحكمة في الإفاضة ببطلان الانتفاع بها، وجب أن يكون الفيض الذي هو الحِكم والمعارف الواصل إلى أنفس المؤيدين من الرسل عليهم السلام بالوحي مودعًا[٣] الرسوم المقومة والأقوال المهذبة ليصل البشر إلى الانتفاع به، والرسوم والأقوال من الرسل هي الشرائع والكتب. إذاً الشرائع واجبة.

البرهان السادس: لما كان كل شيء موجود لا يخلو من أن يكون قائمًا

---

[١] قضاياها: منهاجها، پ

[٢] للحكمة: الحكمة، ٤٨

[٣] مودعا: + في، پ

بالفعل، كالإنسان الموجود صورته في نطقه وفعله، وكعين الدم الموجود صورته في الحيوان، وكالنخل القائم صورته في جذعه وسعفه وشماريخه وكالنار الموجود صورتها في[1] إحراقها وإسخانها، أو قائمًا بالقوة، كالنطفة التي هي في القوة إنسان، وكالنبات الذي هو في القوة دم في الحيوان، وكالنواة التي هي في القوة نخل وكالزند الذي هو في القوة نار، وكان ما كان قائمًا بالقوة بالإضافة إلى القائم بالفعل رذلاً دنيًا وكان لا يشرف عنصره إلا بالخروج إلى الفعل، وكان لا يكون خروجه إلى الفعل إلا بالاستحالة عما عليه صورته في حال كونه في القوة، وكانت الاستحالة التي بها يفارق صورة كونه في القوة لا تكون إلا بالفعل، وكانت أنفس البشر قائمة في قواها من العلم والمعرفة والنطق والتمييز وغير ذلك بالقوة لا بالفعل، على ما يوجد عليه حال الصبيان والأطفال، كان من ذلك العلم بأن الأنفس ما لم تخرج إلى الفعل فلا شرف لها، ولما كان ما في قوته أن يشرف بالفعل، فتركه على حالته في القوة ليس من الحكمة، وكان إخراجه إلى الفعل بالفعل من الحكمة، وجب من حيث وجوب فعل الحكمة على الحكيم أن يخرجها إلى الفعل بالفعل، والفعل[2] هو العمل، وخير الأعمال[3] ما كان مؤديًا إلى عبادة الله تعالى. إذاً الأعمال التي هي سنن الأنبياء وهي رياضة الأنفس وإخراجها إلى الفعل واجبة.

البرهان السابع: لما كان كل ما لا يكون للنفس مما لا يرى ولا يحس مثال له محسوس من جهة الحس لا يمكنها دركه، مثل هيئة الأفلاك وتراكيبها التي لا سبيل للنفس إلى تصوّرها إلا من جهة الصور الهندسية الواقعة تحت الحس التي هي أمثلة لها من جهة الحس، وكانت الدار الآخرة

---

[1] في:-، ٤٨، ٧٤، هـ
[2] والفعل: فالفعل، ز
[3] الاعمال: العمل، ٤٨

التي هي عالم النفس غير محسوسة ولا مرئية، وهي دار المعاد، وكان البشر مدعوّين إليها ومخاطَبين عليها، وعنها وجب من حيث ندب البشر لطلبها ومعرفتها أن يكون لهم أمثلة[١] لماَ يُدعون إليه من جهة الحس ليدركوه، كما أنه لو كان معرفة هيأة الأفَلاك وتراكيبها فريضة وكان البشر مدعوين إلى تصوّرها لكان يجب مع امتناع معرفتها إلا من جهة الصور الهندسية المحسوسة أن تكون أمثلتها التي هي الصور الهندسية موجودة فيما بينهم كلهم، والأمثلة هي الشرائع والرسوم الوضعية. إذاً الرسوم والشرائع[٢] التي هي أمثلة للنفس من جهة الحس لعالم النفس واجبة.

المصباح السادس

في إثبات التأويل لما يرد من جهة الرسل من التنزيل والشريعة الذي هو العلم، ويشتمل على سبعة براهين[٣]

البرهان الأول: لما كانت العقول والأنفس لا سبيل لها إلى معرفة المعاد وما قد غاب عن الحواس إلا من جهة الأمثلة المحسوسة التي يرسمها الرسل عليهم السلام ومن تلقاء وضائعهم وتعليمهم، وكان سيّد الأنبياء وخاتمهم محمد المصطفى صلى الله عليه قد أفاد الأمثلة المحسوسة التي هي الحكمة البالغة، وجب أن تكون هذه الحكمة مضمونة[٤] في أفقها لتقبلها وموافقة لقضاياها فتتمسك بها وملقحة إياها أنوارها

[١] امثلة: مثال، ز، پ، ه؛ مثل، ٧٤؛ امثل، ٤٨

[٢] الرسوم والشرائع: الشرائع، ز، هـ

[٣] الذي هو...سبعة براهين:-، هـ، پ، ٧٤

[٤] مضمونة: كذا في پ و هـ٢؛ مضمونًا، ه، ٤٨، ز، ٧٤

فلا تنسلخ منها، ولما كان ما جاء به محمد صلى الله عليه وسلم من القرآن والشريعة مخالفًا ظاهره لأحكام العقل مثل قول الله تعالى: «وَإِذْ أَخَذَ رَبُّكَ مِن بَنِي آدَمَ مِن ظُهُورِهِم ذُرِّيَّتَهُم وَأَشْهَدَهُم عَلَىٰ أَنْفُسِهِم أَلَسْتُ بِرَبِّكُم قَالُوا بَلَىٰ» [٧: ١٧٢]، واستحالة إخراج الذراري مثل الذر على ما جاء في التفسير من أهل الظاهر، وأخذ إقرارها بأن الله تعالى ربهم مع الموجود في حكمة الله[١] تعالى أن لا يقبل قول الصبيان فضلاً عن الأطفال وقول الأطفال فضلاً عن الذر لكونهم غير مكلفين ولا مؤاخذين، ومثل قول النبي صلى الله عليه وسلم: «بين قبري ومنبري روضة من رياض الجنة» واستحالة القول مع كون الموضع في الظاهر خاليًا مما وصفه به من الروضة، وجب من حيث أن الرسول حكيم لا تتّجه عليه سمة الجهالة أن لا يتعرى ما جاء به من معان توافق العقول وتقبلها ويصح بها كون التنزيل[٢] حقًا منطويًا على الحكمة، وتلك المعاني هي التي نسمّيها تأويلاً وباطنًا وشرحًا وبيانًا. إذاً التأويل واجب.

البرهان الثاني: نقول إن النبي صلى الله عليه وآله دعا إلى الله تعالى بالحكمة كما أمره بقوله تعالى: «أُدْعُ إلىَ سَبِيلِ رَبِّكَ بِالحِكْمَةِ وَالمَوْعِظَةِ الحَسَنَةِ» [١٦: ١٢٥] وأن من توهم في الرسول غير ذلك كان كافراً، ولما كان لا يجوز توهم غير ذلك، وقد وجد في الظاهر أنه عليه السلام دعا إلى الله وإلى عبادته بفعل ما لو فعله إنسان في غير الموضع الذي أمر بفعله فيه لقيل أنه مجنون ولاعب وساه، مثل أعمال الحج ومناسكه العجيبة وكان لا يتعلق بظاهر هذه الأفعال من مخاطبة الحجر والعدو على أطراف الرجل التي هي القدم بالتهرول والإمساك عن تقليم الأظافير وحلق شعر الرأس ورمي الأحجار حكمة، وجب من حيث كونه عليه السلام داعيًا بالحكمة أن لا يخلو ما دعا إليه من تلك الأفعال من

[١] حكمة الله: حكمه، ٧٤، هـ
[٢] التنزيل: + بل، پ، ٧٤

معان توافق الحكمة، وتدل العقول بمعرفتها على ما فيه نجاتها ولقاحها بأنوار القدس، وتلك المعاني نسميها تأويلاً وباطنًا وبيانًا ومعنى وتفسيراً. إذاً التأويل واجب.

البرهان الثالث: لما كان في عدل الله تعالى أن لا يؤاخذ أحداً بجرم غيره فقال جل ثناؤه: «وَلاَ تَزِرُ وَازِرَةٌ وِزْرَ أُخْرَىَ» [٦: ١٦٤ وغيرها]، وكان من ترسيم الرسول[١] صلى الله عليه وسلم وشرعه أن يؤخذ العم بجرم ابن أخيه إذا قتل خطأ، وكان ذلك خلافًا لعدل الله تعالى وما أمر به، وكان غير متوهم في الرسول صلى الله عليه وسلم أن يفعل ما يخالف عدله ورحمته ولا أن يأمر بما يناقض أمر الله تعالى، وجب أن يكون ذلك وما كان مثله لمعنى وحكمة يجانس عدل الله تعالى ورحمته من جهة العقول، والمعنى الذي يجانس عدل الله ورحمته من جهة العقول[٢] هو التأويل الذي نسميه باطنًا وشرحًا وتفسيراً. إذاً التأويل واجب.

البرهان الرابع: لما كان من الحكيم العاقل من البشر مستحيلاً مخاطبةُ الموات التي لا حياة لها ولا ثواب ولا عقاب ولا آلة لها في قبول الأمر والنهي والجواب، فضلاً من المتعالي المتقادس رب السموات والأرضين، وأخبر الرسول عليه السلام عن الله تعالى بأنه خاطب السموات والأرض بقوله تعالى: «ثُمَّ اسْتَوَىَ إِلَىَ السَّمَاءِ وَهِيَ دُخَانٌ فَقَالَ لَهَا وَلِلأَرْضِ ائْتِيَا طَوْعًا أَوْ كَرْهًا قَالَتَا أَتَيْنَا طَائِعِينَ» [٤١: ١١]، وكان الله عليمًا حكيمًا والسموات والأرض موات لا عقل لهما[٣] ولا آلة للنطق، وجب من حيث استحالة مخاطبة الموات من الحكيم أن يكون لأمره السموات والأرض وجوابهما له معنى يحقق قول الله تعالى ويقبله العقل في الحكمة[٤]، وذلك

---

[١] الرسول: النبي، ٧٤

[٢] والمعنى الذي...من جهة العقول:-، ب، ٤٨، ٧٤

[٣] لهما: لها، ٧٤

[٤] في الحكمة:-، ز

المعنى الذي نسميه التأويل. إذاً التأويل واجب.

البرهان الخامس: لما قال الله تعالى: «إِذْ يُغَشِّيكُمُ النُّعَاسَ أَمَنَةً مِنْهُ وَيُنَزِّلُ عَلَيْكُم مِنَ السَّمَاءِ مَاءً لِيُطَهِّرَكُم بِهِ وَيُذْهِبَ عَنكُم رِجْزَ الشَّيْطَانِ وَلِيَرْبِطَ عَلَى قُلُوبِكُم وَيُثَبِّتَ بِهِ الأَقْدَامَ» [٨: ١١]، وكان معلومًا أن رجز الشيطان هو الكفر والشك والشبهة والنفاق والجهل والضلال وما يجري مجرى ذلك الذي يكون في القلوب والأوهام والنفوس[١]، وكان إذا كان رجز الشيطان في القلوب والأوهام فغير متوهم أن يطهرها الماء النازل من السماء المحسوس المشروب لامتناع الأمر في ذلك، وكان لو كان الماء الذي ذكره هو الماء الطبيعي كان كل أحد طاهراً من مؤمن وكافر، وجب أن يكون لهذا الماء معنى لولاه لكان من الله مستحيلاً أن يقول شيئًا هو بخلافه، وذلك المعنى نسميه تأويلاً وتفسيراً وشرحًا وباطنًا. إذاً التأويل لذلك ولِما كان مثله واجب.

البرهان السادس: لما أوجب الله تعالى التأويل لِما جاء به الرسول صلوات الله عليه بقوله تعالى: «هُوَ الَّذِي أَنزَلَ عَلَيْكَ الْكِتَابَ مِنْهُ آيَاتٌ مُحْكَمَاتٌ هُنَّ أُمُّ الْكِتَابِ وَأُخَرُ مُتَشَابِهَاتٌ فَأَمَّا الَّذِينَ فِي قُلُوبِهِم زَيْغٌ فَيَتَّبِعُونَ مَا تَشَابَهَ مِنْهُ ابْتِغَاءَ الْفِتْنَةِ وَابْتِغَاءَ تَأْوِيلِهِ وَمَا يَعْلَمُ تَأْوِيلَهُ إِلاَّ اللهُ وَالرَّاسِخُونَ فِي الْعِلْمِ يَقُولُونَ آمَنَّا بِهِ كُلٌّ مِن عِندِ رَبِّنَا وَمَا يَذَّكَّرُ إِلاَّ أُولُو الأَلْبَابِ» [٣: ٧]، وكان معارضة من يعارض فيقول: إن التأويل لا يعلمه إلا الله وإن «الراسخون في العلم» ابتداء لا محمول على ما تقدم من الخطاب، باطلة بوجود ما يسقط معارضته من قول العرب عند الاختصار والإيجاز إذ قال لغيره: لا يسلم عليك إلا فلان وفلان يعتذر، ولا يعلم الطب إلا فلان وفلان يناظر عليه، ولا يعلم النحو إلا فلان وفلان يتعمق فيه، ولا يجيئك إلا فلان وفلان راكبًا، بمعنى أن كليهما يسلمان

---

[١] والاوهام والنفوس: اوهام النفوس، ز

ويعتذر أحدهما وكليهما يعلمان الطب ويناظر عليه أحدهما وكليهما يعلمان النحو ويتعمق فيه أحدهما وكليهما يجيئان وراكبًا[١] أحدهما، وجب أن يكون التأويل واجبًا ويعلمه الراسخون في العلم. إذاً التأويل واجب.

البرهان السابع: لما كان لا سبيل إلى تعريف ما لا يرى ولا يحس إلا بالعبارة عنه بما يرى ويحس، وكان إخبار الرسول عليه السلام عما لا يرى ولا يحس من الله تعالى والجنة ونعيمها والجحيم وعذابها، لزم أن يكون إخباره وعبارته عما عنه أخبر وعبّر مما لا يرى ويحس بما يرى ويحس[٢]، كما أخبر صلى الله عليه وآله عن الجنة التي هي الدار الآخرة وهي غير مرئية ولا محسوسة بالبساتين والأنهار والأشجار والثمار والمياه وعن كون ما فيها بالولدان والأكواب والأباريق وحور العين واللؤلؤ المكنون وجميع النعم الطبيعية التي كلها مرئية محسوسة، وكما أخبر عن الجحيم وعذابها وهي غير مرئية ولا محسوسة بالنار والإحراق والماء الحميم والغل والسلسلة والقيد وجميع الآلام الطبيعية التي كلها مرئية محسوسة، وإذا[٣] لزم ذلك كان ما قال وفعل ودعا إليه من الآخرة جاريًا مجرى الأمثال في التشبيه، والأمثال تقتضي الممثَّلات، والممثَّلات هو المعبَّر عنه بالتأويل. إذاً لِما جاء به الرسول صلى الله عليه وآله عن الله تعالى ودعا إليه من التنزيلَ والشريعة تأويل، فالتأويل واجب.

---

[١] راكبا: الراكب، ز، پ

[٢] بما يرى ويحس: مما يرى ويحس، ز

[٣] وإذا: فاذا، ز؛ واذ، ٧٤

المصباح السابع
في إثبات الرسالة ووجوبها

البرهان الأول: لما خلق الله تعالى الخلق ولم يجعل نوع البشرية في معرفة ما يحتاج إليه مثل البهائم والطيور وغيرها من أنواع الحيوان التي تعرف مصالحها ومعارفها من ذاتها بالطبع، كالوزة في السباحة والفرّوج[١] في النقر والخُطّاف في طلب حجر اليَرَقان إذا رأى بفراخها صفرة لون، بل جعله محتاجًا إلى التعليم، مثل ما نشاهد من حال الطفل الذي لولا تعليم أبويه إياه والمعلمين لكان لا يعرف شيئًا ولا يعدو البهائم، وكانت الأنفس عاطلة الذات رذلة بخلوها من المعارف وهي متهيئة لقبول ما يفاض عليها فيشرف عنصرها، وكان تركها على حالتها هذه مع تهيئها للقبول لا من الحكمة، وجب من حيث وجوب فعل الحكمة على الحكيم وكونه غير مرئيٍ الإفاضة على أكثرها تهيؤاً وأقربها إلى القبول جوهراً، فيكون القابل بقبوله ذلك الفيض قائمًا مقام الحكيم المفيض في التعليم والهداية، وإفاضة الفيض هي إرسال الرسل، والمفاض عليه هو الرسول. إذاً الرسالة واجبة.

البرهان الثاني: لما كان للموجودات الواقعة تحت الوجود خالق، وكان البشر من جملتها مختصًا بالتمييز[٢] والثواب والعقاب، حَكَمَ العقلُ بأن يكون باحثًا عن معرفة خالقه ومصالحه، ولما كان العقل موجبًا على البشر معرفة خالقه، وكان[٣] لا سبيل له إلى أن يعرف أن خالقه هل هو محسوس فيطلبه أو معقول فيبحث عنه، وكان ذلك مؤديًا إياه إلى الحيرة والضلال،

---

[١] الفروج: الفروخ، هـ، ز، پ، ٤٨، ٧٤

[٢] بالتمييز: بالتميز، ز، ٤٨

[٣] وكان: ولكن كان، ز

وجب من تمام الرحمة أن يكون لله تعالى لما كان ممتنعًا عن الرؤية فيتولى بذاته هدايتهم إلى المعارف به[١] فيما بين البشر، واسطة بينه وبينهم يهديهم ويعرّفهم معرفة خالقهم، والواسطة هو المتولي لأداء المعارف التي هي الرسالة. إذاً الرسالة واجبة.

البرهان الثالث: لما كانت الأنفس في ابتداء نشوئها غير عالمة[٢] بذاتها، وكانت للآخرة أنشئت التي هي دار الجزاء وكانت هاتيك الدار مع جلالتها واحتوائها على ما لا عين رأت ولا أذن سمعت ولا خطر على قلب بشر غير مرئية فتراها وترغب فيها، وجب من تمام رحمة الله تعالى أن يكون لها باعث يعلّمها خيرها ويرغبها في خيراتها ويعبّر عنها بالمحسوسات ليقرب إلى الأفهام تصورها، والباعث هو الرسول المؤيَّد. إذاً الرسالة واجبة.

البرهان الرابع: لما كان كل شيء لا يتّحد بحد شيء فهو مباين منه مفارق له، وكان ما يتحد بحد غيره فهو في أفقه ومن جملته وصورته، وكانت الأنفس مصيرها إلى العالم النفساني بطاعتها لله تعالى ولرسوله، ولا سبيل لها إلى الاتّحاد بحده والتصوّر بصورته من ذاتها فتكون في أفقه، وإذا فارقت عالم الأشخاص لزمت ما اتّحدت بحده، وجب في الحكمة وتمام الرحمة أن يكون بها[٣] موكّلاً مَن يفيدها نقوش العالم النفساني فتتّحد بحده، والذي يفيد نقوش العالم النفساني هو المؤيد، والمؤيد هو الرسول. إذاً الرسالة واجبة.

البرهان الخامس: لما كان البشر قد خصه الله تعالى من بين الحيوان، بدلاً عن الأسلحة فيها من مخاليب ومناقير وأنياب وحوافر وغيرها،

---

[١] به: -، ز
[٢] عالمة: عاقلة، ٤٨
[٣] بها: لها، پ. ٤٨. ز

بالتمييز[١] ولطف التدبير والقدرة وحسن الخيرة، وكان في طباعه طلب الرياسة وعقدها على الغير وحبّ الغلبة والقهر، وكان لا يؤمَن منهم، مع ما قد أعطوا من فضل العلم والحيلة[٢] والقدرة، أن يبغي بعضهم على بعض ويسعوا في الأرض بالفساد، وجب من طريق الحكمة أن يتوسطهم من جهة الله تعالى مَن يأمرهم وينهاهم ويحفظ نظامهم لتندفع[٣] غائلة بعضهم عن بعض، والمتوسط الذي يأمر وينهى عن الله تعالى هو الرسول. إذاً الرسالة واجبة.

البرهان السادس: لما كانت الحاجة ماسة في بقاء البشر إلى الرسوم المقومة والأحكام المبسوطة ليجروا على أحكامها ومنهاجها فتحقن[٤] دماؤهم وأموالهم وفروجهم وإلا كان لا يكون أحد بشيء يملكه من مال وذخيرة وامرأة أولى بها من غيره، وكانت الرسوم لا تترسم من ذواتها إذ هي فعل والفعل لا يكون إلا من فاعل، وجب كون فاعل يفعل الرسوم ويرسّمها ويأمر وينهى ويجري بالبشر على قضاياها، والفاعل هو المؤيد من جهة الله تعالى المطاع، والمؤيد هو الرسول. إذاً الرسالة واجبة.

البرهان السابع: لما كان كل نوع من الأنواع الواقعة تحت كل جنس يتناهى في نوعيته إلى ما هو أشرف من سائره ويكون هو المقدم عليها والرئيس لها بتخصيص الله تعالى إياه بالفضيلة، كأنواع المعدنيات التي تناهت فيما كان يذوب وينطرق إلى الذهب وفيما كان حجراً لا يذوب ولا ينطرق إلى الياقوت[٥]، وكأنواع النبات التي تناهت فيما كان من الحبوب المغذية إلى الحنطة وفيما كان من الثمار إلى التمر، وكان البشر نوعًا من أنواع الحيوان، وجب أن يتناهى إلى ما هو أشرف من سائرهم وأعلم من

---

[١] بالتمييز: بالتميز، ز، ٤٨

[٢] والحيلة: والحكمة، پ

[٣] لتندفع: ليدفع، ز، پ

[٤] فتحقن: فتحتقن، ز، پ، ه؛ فتتحقن، ٧٤

[٥] الياقوت: + الاحمر، پ

جماعتهم، وهو رئيسهم بتخصيص الله عز وجل إياه بالفضيلة كغيره في كل نوع، والمتناهَى إليه هو مَن يكون مؤيداً من الله عز وجل بما يوحي إليه، والمؤيد هو الرسول. إذاً الرسالة واجبة.

المقالة الثانية من كتاب المصابيح في الإمامة

المصباح الأول من المقالة الثانية

في إثبات الإمامة ووجوبها

البرهان الأول: لما كان الرسول صلى الله عليه وآله قد أورد عن الله حكمة بالغة وكان لازمًا له عليه السلام أداؤها إلى من كان رسولاً إليه

من نوع البشرية الكائن منهم في الوجود في[١] أيامه ومَن يجيء إلى الكون من البشر إلى يوم القيامة بالتوالد بعده، وكان مَن كان في أيامه من البشر لا استطاعة لهم في قبول كل الحكمة دفعة واحدة، ولا كان في المقدور أن يكون مَن يجيء إلى الكون من البشر إلى يوم القيامة موجوداً جملة، ولا كان مقدراً[٢] أن يبقى الرسول في العالم بقاءً سرمداً إلى أن تنصرم الأمم يؤدي[٣] إليهم أمانة الله، وجب أن ينصب مَن يقوم مقامه في أداء الأمانة والنص على غيره أبداً إذا حان انتقاله، ومَن ينصب لذلك هو الإمام. إذاً الإمامة واجبة.

البرهان الثاني: لما كان ما جاء به النبي صلى الله عليه وآله من الكتاب الكريم والشريعة المشروعة والسنن المفروضة والرسوم الدينية والأقوال المهذبة ممكنًا الزيادة فيه والنقصان منه، وفي الاستطاعة تغيير رسومه وأحكامه والإحداث فيه، وكان إذا كان ممكنًا الزيادة فيه، والنقصان منه وفي الاستطاعة تغيير رسومه وأحكامه إذا زيد أو نقص أو غير، أدّى ذلك إلى الجور والظلم والعسف وامتداد أيدي الظلمة إلى المحظورات ومصيره علة لظهور الضلالات وعموم الخوف وعدم الأمن، وجب من طريق الحكمة أن يكون بها موكّلاً مَن يحفظها على وجهها ويمنع من الزيادة والنقصان والتغيير منها ويجري بالأمة على سننها فتكون أوامر الله طرية وكلمته عالية وشأفة الشر مستأصلة والموكل هو الإمام المختار من جهة الله تعالى. إذاً الإمامة واجبة.

البرهان الثالث: لما كان ما جاء به النبي صلى الله عليه وآله من التنزيل والشريعة بلغة العرب، وكان ذلك مقدَّراً على احتمال معان شتى

---

[١] في:-، هـ، ٤٨

[٢] مقدرا: مقدورا، ز، پ

[٣] يؤدي: ويؤدي، ٧٤، پ

إذ كانت اللفظة الواحدة من كلام العرب تؤدي معاني شتى[١] كثيرة لكونه أمثالاً تحتمل معاني ورموزاً تؤدي أغراضًا، وكان[٢] ممكنًا أن يؤوَّل كل آية وكل خبر على حسب ما يريده المؤوِّل ومطرداً ذلك في العقول، على حسب ما نشاهده من الأمة في تفرد كل فريق منها في آية من القرآن وخبر من الأخبار استدلالاً على صحة نحلته بمعنى غير المعنى الذي يستدل به الفريق الآخر على صحة مذهبه، مثل قول الله[٣] تعالى: «مَا مَنَعَكَ أن تَسْجُدَ لِمَا خَلَقْتُ بِيَدِي» [٣٨: ٧٥]، وذهاب المعتزلة في ذلك إلى تصحيح مذهبهم بقولهم أن المراد بقوله «بيدي» القدرة والقوة، وذهاب قوم آخرين إلى أن ذلك يريد به النعمة والمنة، وذهاب قوم آخرين، وهم[٤] المجبرة على أصنافها، في تصحيح مذهبهم إلى أن المراد بذلك اليد التي هي أحد أجزاء الجسد[٥] وأبعاضه. وكان كل أقاويلهم حقًا لا ينكر لأن قولنا «يد» يؤدي من المعاني إلى ما أوردته كل فرقة من الأمة واحتجت به، وكان في كونه مقدراً على ما يؤول منه بحسب مراد المؤول مشابهًا للثوب الذي هو مقدَّر على ما يقع الفصل منه من فاصله بحسب هواه، فواحد يريد أن يقطع منه قميصًا لحاجته إليه وكان ذلك ممكنًا، وآخر يريد أن يقطع منه سراويل لحاجته إليه وكان ذلك ممكنًا، وآخر يريد أن يقطع منه صُدرة أو جوربًا أو قباءاً لحاجته إليه وكان ذلك كله ممكنًا، وكالنار أيضًا فواحد له مسرجة وفتيلة يشعل فيها وواحد له شمع يشعل فيه، وواحد له حطب يشعل فيه. وكان ذلك لا يخلو من ثلاثة أوجه: إما أن يكون جميع المعاني التي يؤديها ظاهر اللفظ مما جاء به النبي صلوات الله عليه رشاداً وهو واجب معرفته على وجهه، وإما أن يكون المقصود من المعاني الكثيرة

---

[١] شتى: -، ٤٨، پ

[٢] وكان: -، ز، ٤٨

[٣] قول الله: قوله، ز

[٤] قوم اخرين وهم: -، ٧٤، هـ

[٥] الجسد: البدن، غ، پ، ٧٤، هـ

التي تؤديها اللفظة الواحدة معنىً واحداً أو اثنين وباقيها ضلال وواجب معرفته ليتجنب[١]، وإما أن يكون جميع المعاني التي يوجبها ظاهر اللفظة كلها ضلالاً، والمقصود في اللفظ غير معانيه التي يؤديها ظاهره، فيجري اللفظ حينئذ مجرى التشبيه والأمثال وواجب معرفة ممثّلات[٢] تلك الأمثال ومعاني تلك التشبيهات. فإن كان المعاني التي تضمنها اللفظ الواحد كلها رشاداً، فتقتضي الحكمة أن يكون فيما بين ظهراني الأمة مَن يعلّمهم وجه الحكمة في الجميع، ولا يترك أحداً ينفرد بمعنى دون الآخر لتكون الكلمة واحدة في العبادة والخلاف زائلاً، وإن كان المقصود من المعاني التي يؤديها اللفظ الواحد معنى واحداً أو اثنين، فالحكمة تقتضي أن يكون موجوداً بين الأمة مَن يعلّمهم الغرض المقصود والمعنى الذي فيه الرشاد ويمنعهم عن اعتقاد غيره، إذ لا علم لأحد بالمعنى الذي هو أولى باعتقاده من غيره لحاجة البشر إلى المعلّم ليرتفع التباغض والتنازع وتجتمع الكلمة في العبادة، وإن كانت المعاني التي يؤديها ظاهر اللفظ كلها ضلالاً والمقصود باللفظ غير معانيه ويجري اللفظ مجرى الأمثال والرموز، فالحكمة توجب أن يكون بين الأمة مَن يبيّن لهم ممثّلات[٣] تلك الأمثال والتشبيهات لئلا يضلوا أو يعتقدوا غير الواجب. وكان إذا كان لا يخلو من ثلاثة أوجه، وأوجبت الوجوه الثلاثة كون مَن يهدي ويعلّم بين الأمة، فالهادي والمعلم [هو] الإمام. إذاً الإمامة واجبة.

البرهان الرابع: لما كانت الطباع مختلفة والأهواء متفاوتة والحوادث غير معلومة ولا محصورة، وكان في الطبع الاستطالة والتعدي وحبّ القهر والغلبة، وجب من طريق الحكمة أن يكون بين الناس حاكم يفصل بينهم

---

[١] ليتجنب: لان يتجنب، ز؛ لتجتنب، ٧٤
[٢] ممثلات: ممثولات، ز، پ
[٣] ممثلات: ممثل، پ، ٧٤؛ ممثول، هـ

الحوادث فلا يكون لهم محيص عنه ولا[1] عن حكمه ولا مهرب عن قضائه، كما كان النبي صلى الله عليه وآله في أيامه، فأخبر الله عنه بقوله: «فَلَا وَرَبِّكَ لا يُؤْمِنُونَ حَتَّى يُحَكِّمُوكَ فِيمَا شَجَرَ بَيْنَهُمْ ثُمَّ لا يَجِدُوا فِي أَنْفُسِهِمْ حَرَجًا مِمَّا قَضَيْتَ وَيُسَلِّمُوا تَسْلِيمًا» [٤:٦٥] والحاكم الإمام. إذاً الإمامة واجبة.

البرهان الخامس: لما كان الله تعالى عادلاً لا يجور ولا يظلم وكان الله تعالى قد خص الأمة التي كانت في أيام النبي صلوات الله عليه بالفضيلة العظيمة بإيجاده كون الرسول عليه السلام فيما بين ظهرانيهم أمانًا لهم من العذاب، كما أخبر الله[2] تعالى بقوله: «وَمَا كَانَ اللهُ لِيُعَذِّبَهُمْ وَأَنْتَ فِيهِمْ» [٨: ٣٣]، ووسيلة لهم يستغفر لهم[3] عند زلاتهم، كما أخبر تعالى في تنزيله بقوله: «وَلَو أَنَّهُم إِذْ ظَلَمُوا أَنْفُسَهُم جَاؤُوكَ فَاسْتَغْفَرُوا اللهَ وَاسْتَغْفَرَ لَهُمُ الرَسُولُ لَوَجَدُوا اللهَ تَوَّابًا رَحِيمًا» [٤: ٦٤]، وبقوله حكاية عن المنافقين حين كانوا يدعون ليستغفر لهم الرسول صلوات الله عليه: «وَإِذَا قِيلَ لَهُم تَعَالَوا يَسْتَغْفِرْ لَكُم رَسُولُ الله لَوَّوْا رُؤُوسَهُم وَرَأَيْتَهُم يَصُدُّونَ وَهُم مُسْتَكْبِرُونَ» [٦٣: ٥]. ولم يكن أولئك الأمة بهذه الفضيلة من كون الرسول بين ظهرانيهم فاصلاً أحكامهم، معلّمًا لهم معالم دينهم وفرائضهم، باعثًا لهم على طلب الآخرة والجهاد في سبيل الله، مستغفراً لهم عن ذنوبهم، ولا بوجود مثله فيما بينهم، أولى من غيرهم مع كون الرسول رسولاً إلى الكافة ووسيلة للجماعة، وجب من حيث أن الله ليس بظلام للعبيد أن يوجد[4] في الأمة بعد نبيها مَن يقوم مقامه ويسد مسده في كونه أمانًا لها ووسيلة يستغفر الله لها ويحفظ نظامها

---

[1] عنه ولا: -، ٧٤، هـ

[2] الله: -، ٤٨

[3] لهم: لذنوبهم، هـ، ٧٤، پ

[4] يوجد: يكون، ٤٨، ز

ويبعثها على ما فيه صلاحها، مع فرض الله تعالى طلب الوسيلة إليه بقوله: «يَا أَيُّهَا الذينَ آمَنُوا اتَّقُوا اللهَ وَابْتَغُوا إِلَيْهِ الوَسِيلَةَ» [٥: ٣٥]، وامتناع توهم إعدام الله تعالى الأمة الوسيلة مع إيجابه عليها طلبها، والقائم مقام الرسول هو الإمام. إذاً الإمامة واجبة.

البرهان السادس: نقول إن الله تعالى لما جعل محمداً صلوات الله عليه رسولاً إلى الناس كافة، الكائن منهم في زمانه ومن يجيء إلى الكون إلى يوم القيامة بعد وفاته، وأمره بدعائهم إليه بقوله: «أُدعُ إلى سَبِيلِ رَبِّكَ بِالحِكْمَةِ وَالمَوْعِظَةِ الحَسَنَةِ» [١٦: ١٢٥]، وفعل النبي صلوات الله عليه ما أمره ربه به بجهده[١] وطاقته بالقول والفعل أيام حياته، وكان من بقي من الناس الذين لم يدخلوا شرع دينه ممن لزم دعاؤهم بالقول والجهاد أكثر ممن دخلوه واتبعوه فيه، وكان معلومًا أن النبي صلوات الله عليه لا يبقى في العالم أبداً فيتولى الدعوة إلى الله تعالى بنفسه إلى أن يظهر دينه على كل الأديان جميعًا كما وعد تبارك وتعالى، وجب من حيث لزم امتناع بقاء الرسول بين الخلق أجمع إلى يوم القيامة للقيام بما أمره الله تعالى من دعائهم أن يقوم مقام الرسول، لما لم يكن في المقدور أن يبقى طبيعي، مَن يدعو إلى دار السلام بالترغيب والترهيب والقول والجهاد ليكون أمر الله مفعولاً، والذي يقوم مقام الرسول هو الإمام. إذاً الإمامة واجبة.

البرهان السابع: نقول إن الله تعالى لما قال لمحمد النبي صلوات الله عليه: «خُذْ مِن أَمْوَالِهِم صَدَقَةً تُطَهِّرُهُم وَتُزَكِّيهِم بِهَا» [٩: ١٠٣]، وكان محمد صلوات الله عليه رسولاً إلى[٢] من كان في وقته ومن يولد بعد موته، ومأموراً بأخذ ذلك من أموال المسلمين كافة وتطهيرهم، وجب مع استحالة كون الرسول بين ظهراني المسلمين إلى يوم القيامة لأخذ ذلك

---

[١] بجهده: جهده، هـ، ٤٨

[٢] الى: + كل، ز، ٤٨

منهم وتطهيرهم أبداً أن يقوم مقام الرسول مَن يأخذ المأمور به ويطهر الناس ليكون أمر الله قائمًا ، والذي يقوم مقام الرسول هو[١] الإمام. إذاً الإمامة واجبة.

البرهان الثامن: لما كانت الشريعة سبب انسداد أبواب الفتن بإقامة رسومها وانحسام مواد الظلم بإحياء حدودها ، وكانت الشريعة تجمع أعمالاً مستكرهة مثل القتل والصلب والجلد والرجم والنفي وغير ذلك، وكان البشر غير منفك من ارتكاب المعاصي التي بها يستحق أن يفعل به، مثل هذه الأفعال، وفي طبعه أن لا يريد السوء والآلام لنفسه ولا القتل إذا وجب عليه، ولا الصلب ولا غير ذلك، وكان في الإمكان أن لو كان سبيل هذه الأعمال كسبيل غيرها مما كان موكولاً إلى أمانة الناس قضاؤه، مثل الصلاة والزكاة وغيرها ، أن يخون فيها ويخل بها ، وجب من طريق الحكمة أن يكون مثل هذه الأعمال موكولة[٢] إلى مَن يقوم بها وبإقامتها على مستحقها لئلا تتعطل الرسوم والحدود فيعدم الأمن وتنفتح أبواب الشر، ومن يقوم بتلك[٣] هو الإمام. إذاً الإمامة واجبة.

البرهان التاسع: لما أوجب الله تعالى الرجوع فيما لا يعلم به ويختلف فيه إلي الرسول[٤] صلوات الله عليه وحكم بالرد إليه بقوله: «فَإِنْ تَنَازَعْتُم فِي شَيْءٍ فَرُدُّوهُ إلىَ الله وَالرَسُولِ» [٤: ٥٩]، وكان المرجع فيما يراد معرفته مما كان يقع فيه نزاع وخلاف من أمر الدين أيام حياة الرسول صلوات الله عليه إليه، وكان غير ممكن ولا مقدر[٥] بقاء الرسول صلوات الله عليه في العالم ليكون بين ظهراني أمته فيرجعون إليه فيما يقع[٦] فيه خلاف ولا

[١] والذي يقوم مقام الرسول هو: والقائم مقام الرسول، پ، ٧٤، هـ
[٢] موكولة: مؤكلة، ز
[٣] بتلك: +، الاعمال، ٧٤
[٤] الرسول: النبي، ٧٤، هـ
[٥] مقدر: مقدور، ز
[٦] يقع: يكون، ز

يعلمونه من أمر الدين، وجب أن يقوم مقام الرسول صلوات الله عليه مَن يرد إليه ما يُختلف فيه من أمر الدين، فيكون الحكم إليه فيه ليكون أمر الله قائمًا، والذي يقوم مقام الرسول صلوات الله عليه هو الإمام. إذاً الإمامة واجبة.

البرهان العاشر: لما كان القياس تحكيم النفس فيما يراد معرفته مما يقع فيه خلاف وشك والرجوع فيه إليها والاستدلال من جهتها على طلب وجهه، وكان الله تعالى قد منع الأمة من القياس بقوله: «وَمَا اخْتَلَفْتُم فِيهِ مِن شَيْءٍ فَحُكْمُهُ إلى الله» [٤٢: ١٠]، ولم يقل وما اختلفتم فيه من شيء[١] فحكمه إليكم فيطرد القياس، وأكده بدلالته إياهم على من يُردّ إليه بقوله: «فَإِنْ تَنَازَعْتُم فِي شَيْءٍ فَرُدُّوهُ إِلَى اللهِ وَالرَّسُولِ» [٤: ٥٩]، وجب من حيث منعهم من القياس أن يوجد فيهم مَن يفتيهم فيما اختلفوا[٢] فيه بعد النبي صلوات الله عليه إذا رد إليه، ومَن يرد إليه هو الإمام. إذاً الإمامة واجبة.

البرهان الحادي عشر: لما قال الله تعالى: «يَومَ نَدْعُو كُلَّ أنَاسٍ بِإمَامِهِم» [١٧: ٧١]، وكان لو كان لا يكون إمام في كل عصر وزمان[٣] وتخلو الأرض منه مع مجيء الناس إلى الكون أولاً فأولاً لكان[٤] قول الله تعالى كذبًا، وكان غير متوهم في قول الله تعالى الكذب، كان منه الإيجاب بأن لكل زمان إمامًا يدعو الله يوم القيامة أناسه به. إذاً الإمامة واجبة.

البرهان الثاني عشر: لما أوجب الله تعالى على المؤمنين بقوله: «يَا أَيُّهَا الذينَ آمَنُوا أَطِيعُوا اللهَ وَأَطِيعُوا الرَسُولَ وَأولِي الأَمْرِ مِنكُم» [٤: ٥٩]

---

[١] وما...من شيء: -، ز، پ
[٢] فيما اختلفوا: مما يختلفون، پ، ٧٤، هـ
[٣] عصر وزمان: زمان، هـ، ٧٤، پ
[٤] لكان: -، هـ، ٧٤

ثلاث طاعات في آية واحدة موصولة بعضها ببعض، وكانت طاعة أولي الأمر غير طاعة الرسول وطاعة الرسول غير طاعة الله، وكانت لا يقبل أحدها إلا بثانيها ولا ثانيها إلا بثالثها، وكانت المخاطبة في الآية لعامة المؤمنين، من كان في عصر الرسول ومن يكون بعده ولم يكن فيها تخصيص، وكان من الله تعالى مستحيلاً إيجاب طاعة على عبيده لأحد ويقرنها بطاعته وطاعة رسوله ولا يوجد لهم[1] عين ذلك الأحد فيكون ذلك تكليف ما لا يطاق، أو لا يجعله كالرسول المعصوم المتوج بالمكارم القدسانية، وجب من حيث كون المخاطبة في الآية عامة، ليس فيها تخصيص، قوم دون قوم مع استحالة إعدام الله تعالى الأمة من يفرض طاعته عليها أن يكون موجوداً للأمة مَن يؤدي حقَّ طاعتها بالائتمار له في الله وفي دين الله، والمؤتمر له هو الإمام. إذاً الإمامة واجبة.

البرهان الثالث عشر: لما خلق الله تعالى كبرياؤه الأنفس وجعلها حية قادرة على فعل الخير والشر، وأوجب لها الجزاء، ولم يرض بعدله تعالى حتى أعلمها ما قد فرض لها من الجزاء على ألسن رسله إعذاراً وإنذاراً، وكان لو كان لا يكون بعد الرسول إمام بعد إمام يحفظ رسائل الله تعالى وأمره ونهيه، ويلقيها إلى من يجيء إلى الكون من الأمم على صيغتها ما رآه بعدله من الإعلام[2] والإنذار مختصًا به قومَ الرسول وأهل عصره[3] من دون من يولد بعدهم من الأمم، وكان إذا اختص بالإعلام والإنذار قومًا دون قوم، بطل عدل الله تعالى مع الجزاء العام، وجب من تمام عدل الله وثبوته أن يكون بعد الرسول أبداً إمام يقوم بإعذار أهل زمانه وإنذارهم وتبشيرهم وتحذيرهم لئلا يقولوا: «مَا جَاءَنَا مِن بَشِيرٍ وَلا نَذِيرٍ» [٥: ١٩]

---

[1] يوجد لهم: يوجدهم، هـ

[2] الاعلام: الاعذار، ٤٨

[3] عصره: عصرهم، هـ، پ، ٧٤

إذا مضي واحد قام مقامه آخر بأمره ونصّه[١]. إذاً الإمامة واجبة.

البرهان الرابع عشر: لما كان موجوداً من حكمة الباري تعالى كبرياؤه أن كل ما خلقه غير[٢] عالِم ولا قادر، قد وكّل به عالمًا قادراً يحفظه ويرعاه على هيئته[٣]، ولولاه لتعطل، وقرنهما، مثل العالَم الكبير الذي هو الدنيا بأفلاكها ونجومها وأركانها التي خلقها غير عالمة ولا قادرة، فوكّل بها ملائكة مقربين يحفظون نظامها وقرن بينهما، ولهم العلم والقدرة، ولولاهم لتعطلت، ومثل العالَم الصغير الذي هو شخص البشر[٤] بأيديه وأرجله ورؤوسه وأحشائه الذي خلقه الله تعالى غير عالِم ولا قادر، فجعل أمره إلى النفس تسوسه وتحفظ نظامه إلى الوقت المقدر له وقرن بينهما، وهي عالمة قادرة، ولولاها لتعطل كما يتعطل إذا فارقته. وكان ما جاء به سيد الأنبياء وخاتمهم محمد[٥] صلوات الله عليه عن الله تعالى[٦] من الشريعة عالمًا برأسه، وكان هذا العالَم عالَم الوضع بما يجمعه من الصلاة والزكاة والحج وغيرها صورة أعمال، والأعمال أفعال، والأفعال غير عالمة بذاتها، وجب في الحكمة من حيث وجب حفظها وإلا تعطلت أن يجعل أَمرها إلى مَن يحفظها ويرعاها كغيرها من العوالم. ولذلك كانت ولاية الإمام آخر الفرائض فتمّ عالم الشرع به، وأخبر الله تعالي حين فرضها فقال: «الْيَوْمَ أَكْمَلْتُ لَكُم دِينَكُم وَأَتْمَمْتُ عَلَيْكُم نِعْمَتِي[٧]» [٥: ٣]، وقرن النبي صلوات الله عليه الصامت بالناطق فقال: «إني تارك فيكم الثقلين كتاب الله وعترتي»، فأجرى العترة من الكتاب والشريعة مجرى النفس من عالَم

[١] نصه: نعته، ٤٨؛ اذا مضي...نصه -، هـ
[٢] غير: لا، ز
[٣] هيئته: هينة،٤٨، هـ
[٤] شخص البشر: الشخص البشري، ز
[٥] محمد: +، المصطفى، ٤٨
[٦] عن الله تعالى:-، ز
[٧] نعمتي: + ورضيت لكم الاسلام دينا، ٧٤

الشخص والملائكة من عالَم الدنيا. إذاً الإمامة واجبة.

المصباح الثاني من المقالة الثانية

في إثبات عصمة الإمام ووجوبها

البرهان الأول: نقول إن الحاجة إلى الإمام إنما كانت لأن يكون قائمًا مقام الرسول صلوات الله عليه فيما كان يتعلق به من أمر الدين وحفظ نظامه، ولما كانت الحاجة إلى القائم مقام الرسول صلوات الله عليه لذلك، وكان لو جاز أن يكون غير معصوم لا يقع الأمن من أن يسلك بالأمة غير سبيل النبي[1] في بعض أحكامه أو كلها، وكان ذلك مؤديًا إلى الظلم وحمل الناس على شق العصا ومفارقة الجماعة، وجب أن يكون معصومًا فتكون عصمته سبب ائتلاف الجماعة على الطاعة. إذاً الإمام معصوم، فاعرفه.

البرهان الثاني: لما كان أخذ الزكاة والصدقات والخمس إلى القائم مقام الرسول صلوات الله عليه على ما يراه، وكان في الطبع حبّ المال وطلبه، وجب أن يكون معصومًا ليؤمن منه العدول به عن وجهه وإنفاقه في غير ما أمره الله به فيكون أمره[2] حاملاً للناس على الامتناع عن أدائها والعصيان في الله[3] لأجلها. إذاً الإمام معصوم.

البرهان الثالث: لما كان الرد فيما يراد معرفته من أسباب الدين إلى الإمام بعد النبي صلوات الله عليه، وكان ممكنًا لو لم تكن له عصمة وقوة

[1] النبي: الرسول، ٤٨

[2] امره:-، ٤٨، هـ

[3] في الله: لله، ز

على الإصابة أن يخطىء فيما يجيب به عما يسأل عنه فيكون خطأه مؤديًا إلى الضلال، وجب من حيث أنه دليل الهداية أن يكون له عصمة. إذاً الإمام معصوم، فاعرفه.

البرهان الرابع: لما كان في الشريعة وأحكامها غير جائز أن يقيم حداً على غيره من لزمه في نفسه حد، وكان إلى الإمام إقامة الحدود، وجب أن تكون له عصمة تعصمه من ارتكاب ما يلزمه به حد وتحفظه مما يصير به كغيره في استحقاق إقامة الحد عليه، فلا يكون إلى إقامته عليه سبيل من جهة الأمة. إذاً الإمام معصوم.

البرهان الخامس: لما كانت أعمال الشرع متعلقة بالإمام، والإمام لو كان مثل غيره في العصمة لكان لا يؤمن منه أن يصلي بالناس وهو غير طاهر وأن يجاهد قومًا وهو لهم ظالم[1]، وكان إذا[2] كان ذلك لا يؤمن منه فالأمة في صلاتهم وعبادتهم في شك، والشك في الدين والعبادة طريق النار، وجب من حيث مصير زمام الدين إليه أن يكون له عصمة. إذاً الإمام معصوم.

البرهان السادس: لما أوجب الله تعالى طاعة الإمام بقوله: «يَا أَيُّهَا الذينَ آمَنُوا أَطِيعُوا اللهَ وَأَطِيعُوا الرَسُولَ وأولِي الأمْرِ مِنكُم»، ووصلها بطاعته وطاعة رسوله، وكان في الحكمة غير موجود وصل الدرة بالبعرة ولا الشريف بالرذل[3] ولا الطاهر بالنجس، كان من ذلك الإيجاب أن وصل طاعة الإمام بطاعة الرسول المعصوم لم يكون إلا لكونها مثلها، وإذا كان وصل طاعة الإمام بطاعة الرسول المعصوم لم تكن إلا لكونها مثلها، وكان طاعة الرسول صلوات الله عليه وافتراضها له لعصمته، وجب أن تكون طاعة الإمام لم تفترض إلا لعصمته. إذاً الإمام معصوم.

---

[1] ظالم: ظالم لنفسه، ٧٤

[2] وكان اذا: فاذا، ز، ٤٨

[3] بالرذل: بالدني، ز، ٤٨

البرهان السابع: لما كان الرسول صلوات الله عليه مَقَرّ الوحي ومعدن الحكمة والعلم، وكان ما أنزل الله إليه[١] من العلم الذي به الخلاص لازمًا له أداؤه إلى الأمم من حيث كان رسولاً إليهم أجمع إلى يوم القيامة، وكان لا سبيل له في أدائه إلى الأمم مع مفارقته العالم وعدم استطاعة الأمة قبولها دفعة واحدة، مع امتناع وجود من يجيء إلى الكون إلى يوم القيامة جملة، إلا بتعليم كل ما أنزل إليه من ربه من يقوم مقامه في أداء الأمانة فيه، وكان القائم مقام الرسول صلوات الله عليه هو الإمام، وجب أن يكون أمينًا ثقة معصومًا لا يجوز عليه الخيانة فيما يستودع ولا الخطأ فيما يجعل إليه. إذاً الإمام معصوم.

المصباح الثالث من المقالة الثانية

في إثبات بطلان اختيار الأمة إمامها[٢]

البرهان الأول: نقول لما كان إقامة الحدود على الأمة إلى الإمام من دونها وكان إذا كان إقامة الحدود التي هي بعض رسوم الشريعة المبسوطة إلى الإمام من دون الأمة، كانت إقامة الإمام الذي به يتعلق كل أمور الشريعة ومقامه مقام رب العالمين أولى أن لا يكون إلى الأمة، [و]كان من ذلك الإيجاب بأن الاختيار منها باطل. إذاً اختيار الأمة إمامها باطل.

البرهان الثاني: نقول إنه لا يقع صحة العلم بأن المختار للأمر يُختار إلا وهو كاف فيه، وإذا كان من يُختار للإمامة لا يُستصلح لها حق

[١] اليه، ز، ٧٤، پ، هـ؛ عليه، ٤٨
[٢] امامها: اماما، ز

الاستصلاح إلا بعد الإحاطة بجميع ما يحتاج إليه في الإمامة، أولاً من علم الشريعة والكتاب والأحكام، ثم العلم بأن ما عرف مما يحتاج إليه في الإمامة موجود فيمَن يُختار لها وهو كاف فيه، وإذا كان مَن يُختار للإمامة عالمًا بجميع ما يحتاج إليه فيها، والأمة التي تختار أيضًا عالمة بذلك[١] ، فليس المختار بأن يكون إمامًا أولى من غيره إذ الأقدام قد استوت في العلة التي لأجلها يستحق التقدم على الغير، وإذا استوت الأقدام بطل الاختيار من الأمة والتقديم من جهتها. إذاً الاختيار منها باطل.

البرهان الثالث: نقول إن العلل حيث وجدت أعطيت معلولها[٢]، فإن كان علة الحق في الإمامة إجماع[٣] الناس واختيارهم، وجب أن يكون حيث وجد الإجماع[٤] والاختيار منهم كان الحق مقرونًا به، وإذا كان ذلك كذلك وقد وجدنا الناس قاطبةً من اليهود والنصارى والمجوس والصابئة وغيرهم كانوا قد أجمعوا أيام مبعث الرسول[٥] صلوات الله عليه وآله على أن محمداً صلوات الله عليه كاذب وساحر ومجنون وليس بنبي، واختاروا غيره عليه، ولم يكن إجماعهم ولا اختيارهم حجة ولا علة تنقض نبوة النبي[٦] صلوات الله عليه، وإذا لم يكن إجماعهم ولا اختيارهم حجة ولا علة تنقض نبوته صلى الله عليه وآله كان الإجماع[٧] والاختيار من الناس باطلاً. إذاً الاختيار من الأمة باطل، فاعرفه.

البرهان الرابع: نقول لو كان جائزاً للأمة اختيارهم[٨] الإمام لكان جائزاً

---

[١] بذلك: لذلك، ٧٤
[٢] معلولها: ومعناها، ٤٨
[٣] اجماع: اجتماع، ٤٨، هـ
[٤] الاجماع: الاجتماع، ٧٤، ٤٨، هـ
[٥] الرسول: النبي، ٧٤، پ
[٦] نبوة النبي: نبوته، ٤٨
[٧] الاجماع: الاجتماع، ٤٨
[٨] اختيارهم: اختيار، پ

لها اختيار القضاة وتعديل العدول، ولو كان جائزاً لها اختيار القضاة وتعديل العدول لكان جائزاً لها إنكاح اليتامى والحجر عليهم إلى أن يؤنس منهم الرشد، ولما لم يجز للأمة ولا كان جائزاً لها الحجر على اليتامى وإنكاحهم لم يكن لهم اختيار القضاة[١] ولا تعديل العدول، وإذا لم يكن لها اختيار القضاة ولا تعديل العدول لم يكن لها اختيار الإمام. إذاً الاختيار من الأمة باطل.

البرهان الخامس: لما كان في سنة الله تعالى وسنة رسوله[٢] صلى الله عليه التي يجري عليها الحكم إلى يوم القيامة أن لا يصح قيام أحد مقام غيره، لا في وكالة ولا في ولاية ولا في خلافة ولا في نيابة في طلب حق وإمضاء أمر له بقول قائل واختيار مختار غيره، وكان مقام الإمام في عباد الله وحفظهم ورعايتهم وهدايتهم مقام الرسول صلوات الله عليه، كان من ذلك الحكمُ بأن اختيار الإمام من الأمة وإقامتها إياه مقام الرسول صلوات الله عليه وآله أولى أن لا يصح. إذاً الاختيار من الأمة باطل. فاعرفه.

البرهان السادس: لما كان الإمام لا يكون إلا معصومًا، وكانت عصمة الإمام ليست بوسمة على الوجه ولا بحال ظاهرة في الخلقة[٣] فتكون للأمة سببًا إلى معرفته، استحال وبطل أن يكون إلى الأمة اختياره. إذاً الاختيار منها باطل.

البرهان السابع: لما كان الملائكة المقربون المعصومون الذين لا يقع منهم زلة، حين أراد الله أن يجعل في الأرض خليفة له فقال[٤]: «إِنِّي جَاعِلٌ فِي الأَرْضِ خَلِيفَةً» [٢: ٣٠]، اختارت أن تكون الخلافة لهم بقولهم:

[١] اختيار القضاة: الاختيار للقضاة، ٤٨، ز

[٢] رسوله: نبيه، پ

[٣] الخلقة: الخلق، هـ

[٤] آية ٣٠ من سورة البقرة: «واذ قال ربك للملائكة رني جاعل في الارض خليفة قالوا اتجعل فيها من يفسد فيها ويسفك الدماء ونحن نسبح بحمدك ويقدس لك قال اني اعلم ما لا تعلمون»

«أَتَجْعَلُ فِيهَا مَن يُفْسِدُ فِيهَا وَيَسْفِكُ الدِّمَاءَ وَنَحْنُ نُسَبِّحُ بِحَمْدِكَ وَنُقَدِّسُ لَكَ» [٢: ٣٠] ، فمنعهم الله تعالى عن اختيارهم مع عصمتهم وطهارتهم ووبخهم على قولهم ذلك بقوله تعالى: «إِنِّي أَعْلَمُ مَا لا تَعْلَمُونَ» [٢: ٣٠]، كانت الأمة الغير معصومة[١] أولى أن تكون ممنوعة عن اختيارها. إذاً الاختيار منها باطل[٢].

المصباح الرابع من المقالة الثانية

في إثبات كون صحة الإمامة بالنص من الله تعالى واختيار الرسول

البرهان الأول: لما كانت نبوة الأنبياء صلوات الله عليهم التي هي الخلافة عن الله تعالى في أرضه في إمضاء الأحكام بين عبيده لا تصح إلا بنص من الله واختياره إياهم للقيام مقامه في الحكم والأمر والنهي، وكانت النبوة أصلاً للإمامة، كانت الإمامة[٣] التي هي فرع على[٤] النبوة وهي الخلافة عن الرسول والقيام مقامه أولى أن لا تصح إلا باختيار الله واختيار رسوله والنص عليه. إذاً الإمامة لا تصح إلا بالنص والتوقيف.

البرهان الثاني: لما كان حكم ما أنزل الله تعالى وسنة رسوله صلوات

---

[١] الغير معصومة: الغير المعصومة، ٧٤؛ غير معصومة، ز؛ غير المعصومة، هـ، پ، ٤٨

[٢] باطل: + وفي بعض ما أوردناه في هذه البراهين قطع لما ذهب إليه هذا المارق ومن ينتحل نحلته من ضلال الأمة في أن الإمامة تكون بالاختيار دون النص سواء كان الاختيار للأمة كلها أو لواحد غير معصوم، ٤٨، پ

[٣] كانت الامامة: –، ز

[٤] على: من، پ، ز

الله عليه فيما بين الناس أن لا يصح قيام أحد مقام الآخر إلا باختيار منه ونص عليه، وكانت الإمامة هي القيام مقام الرسول، وجب بحكم الله وبحكم رسوله أن لا تصح إلا باختيار الرسول صلوات الله عليه ونصه. إذاً الإمامة لا تصح إلا بالنص والتوقيف.

البرهان الثالث: لما قال الله تعالى: «وَرَبُّكَ يَخْلُقُ مَا يَشَاءُ وَيَخْتَارُ مَا كَانَ لَهُمُ الخِيَرَةُ» [٢٨: ٦٨]، كان من ذلك الإيجاب أن الاختيار إلى الله، وإذا كان الاختيار إلى الله، فاختيار من يحتاج في قيامه إلى استبراء سريرته التي لا يطلع عليها إلا الله أولى أن يكون باختيار الله. إذاً الإمامة لا تصح إلا باختيار الله ونص الرسول عليه السلام.

البرهان الرابع: لما كان الله العالم بسرائر الخلق والشرير منهم والخير، وكان الأصلح للإمامة الأخْير والأفضل، وكانت استطاعة البشر عاجزة عن معرفة السرائر فيختار الأخْير الأفضل، كان من ذلك الحكم بأن الاختيار إلى الله والرسول صلوات الله عليه من دون الغير، وإذا كان الاختيار إلى الله والرسول، فلا تصح الإمامة إلا باختيارهما والاختيار هو النص. إذاً الإمامة لا تصح إلا بالنص والتوقيف.

البرهان الخامس: لما كانت الإمامة ليست بعلامة ظاهرة موجودة في الخلقة بزيادة في عضو أو نقصان من عضو فيكون الموجود فيه تلك العلامة إماماً، مثل طول العنق في الجمل وكون الخرطوم في الفيل، الذي متى وجد ذلك فيه دلت خلقته على نوعه، وكانت معرفة الإمام واجبة في الدين، وكانت المعارف الدينية لا سبيل إليها[١] إلا من جهة الرسول، كانت الإمامة لا تصح إلا باختياره ونصه وإشارته. إذاً الإمامة لا تصح إلا بالنص والتوقيف.

البرهان السادس: لما كان الناس قاطبة أجمعوا وقت مبعث النبي

---

[١] اليها: لها، ز، پ، ٤٨

صلوات الله عليه على أن نبوته كذب وسحر، وكان لو كان بإجماعهم تصح النبوة كانت نبوته باطلة، ولما كانت نبوته باختيار الله لم تبطل، بل علت أعلامها وتوطدت أرجاؤها، فالإمامة أولى أن تبطل باختيار الأمة وأحق أن تثبت باختيار الله. إذاً الإمامة لا تصح إلا باختيار الله واختيار الرسول الذي هو النص والتوقيف.

البرهان السابع: لما كان الله تعالى قد أخبر في كتابه الكريم أنه هو الذي يجعل في الأرض الخليفة بقوله: «إِنّي جَاعِلٌ فِي الأَرْضِ خَلِيفَةً»، ولم يجعل الأمر في ذلك إلى الملائكة المقربين الذين كانوا معصومين ووبخهم على قولهم: «أتجعل فيها من يفسد فيها ويسفك الدماء» بقوله تعالى: «إِنِّي أَعْلَمُ مَا لا تَعْلَمُونَ»، كانت من ذلك أن اختيار الخلفاء إلى الله، وإذا كان الاختيار إليه فلا يصح إلا باختياره ونصه. إذاً الإمامة التي هي الخلافة لا تصح إلا باختيار الله ونص الرسول.

المصباح الخامس من المقالة الثانية

في أن الإمامة بعد النبي صلوات الله عليه لأمير المؤمنين علي بن أبي طالب صلوات الله عليه من دون غيره

البرهان الأول: لما كان الصنائع كثيرة وكانت كلها على تفاوتها واختلافها تنقسم إلى[1] علم وعمل، مثل الطب الذي ينقسم إلى العلم بطبائع الأدوية وعلل الأمراض وإلى العمل الذي هي المعالجة، ومثل

---

[1] الى: على، پ

النجوم التي تنقسم إلى العلم بهيئة الفلك[1] ونجومه وطبائع الكواكب ومسيرها وتأثيراتها وإلى العمل الذي هو التسيير والحكم، ومثل السياسة التي تنقسم إلى العلم بتدبير أمور الممالك وحفظها وكيفية جباية الأموال وجمعها وحفظ نظام الأمور وإلى العمل الذي هو التوقيع والضرب والحبس والقتل والإطلاق والإحسان، وكان العلم والعمل كالآلة وكان من لا آلة له في صنعة من عمل وعلم بها مستحيل[2] صحتها منه، وكان في أوائل العقول أن من كانت آلته في صنعته أتمّ فهو بتلك الصنعة أولى من غيره، مثل الرجل الذي تكون معرفته بالطب وعمله به أكثر من غيره فيكون[3] هو أولى بالطب من غيره وكانت أحكام الإسلام من الصنائع النبوية كغيرها تنقسم إلى العلم بكيفية الفرائض والحلال والحرام والحدود والأحكام والتنزيل والتأويل وإلى العمل الذي هو الطهارة والصلاة والزكاة والصوم والحج[4] والضرب بالسيف وما يجري مجراه، وكان العلم والعمل لعلي بن أبي طالب عليه السلام أكثر مما كان لمن كان بعد النبي صلوات الله عليه من الصحابة، كان من ذلك الحكم بأنه بالحكم أولى وبالإمامة أحرى. إذاً الإمامة لعلي بن أبي طالب عليه السلام.

البرهان الثاني: لما أخبر الله تعالى عن الأحق أن يتبع بقوله: «أَفَمَن يَهْدِي إِلىَ الحَقِّ أَحَقُّ أَنْ يُتَّبَعَ أم مَن لا يَهِدِّي إلاّ أَنْ يُهْدى فَمَالَكُم كَيفَ تَحْكُمُونَ» [١٠: ٣٥] ، وكانت الصحابة بعد نبيها صلوات الله عليه محتاجة إلى هداية علي بن أبي طالب عليه السلام إياهم في فصل الأحكام التي التبست عليهم وجوهها، كان علي بن أبي طالب عليه السلام بقول الله تعالى بالإمامة أحق، وإذا كان أحق فهو الإمام. إذاً

[1] الفلك: الافلاك، ٧٤
[2] مستحيل: مستحالة، ٤٨؛ ستحال، هـ، پ؛ يستحال، ٧٤
[3] فيكون: فكان، پ؛ كان، ٧٤
[4] والحج: + والجهاد، ز

الإمامة لعلي بن أبي طالب عليه السلام.

البرهان الثالث: لما قال الله تعالى: «إِنَّمَا وَلِيُّهُم اللهُ وَرَسُولُهُ وَالذينَ آمَنُوا الذينَ يُقِيمُونَ الصَلاةَ وَيُؤْتُونَ الزكاةَ وَهُم رَاكِعُونَ» [٥: ٥٥]، وكان علي بن أبي طالب عليه السلام المعطي للزكاة في حال ركوعه، وكان الولي في اللغة هو القيم بأمور من هو وليه والموالي لمن يواليه وينصره جميعًا، وبطل أن المراد به الموالاة لاستحالة ورود الآية على ما هي عليه من صيغة الحصر والقطع بأن يكون للأمة ولي غير الله ورسوله وعلي في معنى الموالاة مع قول الله تعالى: «وَالمُؤْمِنُونَ وَالمُؤْمِنَاتُ بَعْضُهُم أولِيَاءُ بَعْضٍ» [٩: ٧١]، ثبت أنه نص من الله على علي عليه السلام بأنه القيم بأمور الأمة. إذاً علي بن أبي طالب عليه السلام المنصوص عليه بالإمامة.

البرهان الرابع: لما قال الله تعالى: «النَبِيُّ أولىَ بِالمُؤْمِنِينَ مِن أَنْفُسِهِم» [٣٣: ٦]، وكان ذلك ولاية ولاها الله إياه من المؤمنين بأن يأمرهم وينهاهم، وأخذ النبي صلوات الله عليه من المؤمنين بغدير خم إقرارهم حين قال: «ألست أولى بكم من أنفسكم» بجوابهم له «بلى» ثلاثًا، ووصل كلامه عقب أخذ هذا[1] الإقرار منهم بقوله صلوات الله عليه: «فمن كنت مولاه فعلي مولاه»، وكان معنى[2] ذلك راجعًا إلى ما أخذ إقرارهم به مما ولاه الله تعالى إياه منهم من الأمر والنهي فيهم وطاعتهم له من دون ما توجبه اللغة من المعاني الأخر التي تتضمن[3] هذه اللفظة التي توجب أن يكون معناها: فمن كنت معتقه أو معتَقه أو ابن عمه أو عاقبه أو جاره، لاستحالة جميع هذه المعاني في قوله مع ما أردفه من قوله: «فعلي مولاه» الذي يوجب أن يكون معناه «فمن كنت» معتقه أو معتقه أو ابن عمه فعلي معتقه أو معتقه أو ابن عمه، كان من ذلك العلم بأن قوله

[1] هذا: -، ز
[2] معنى: + قول، پ
[3] تتضمن: تضمن، پ

«فعلي مولاه» بعد ما تقدم من أخذه إقرارهم بأنه مولاهم مع قوله «فمن كنت مولاه» نص على علي بن أبي طالب عليه السلام بأنه ولي المؤمنين والقائم بأمور دينهم والآمر والناهي فيهم إذ قد أجراه مجرى نفسه فيما كان له من الولاية على المؤمنين، وإنما أردف قوله «فعلي مولاه» من قوله ودعائه «اللهم وال من والاه وعاد من عاداه وانصر من نصره واخذل من خذله»، تأكيداً لأمره، إذ لو لم[1] يكن قد جعل أمر الدين موكولاً إليه ولا كان معصومًا لا يزل ولا يخطىء فيما اعتمد فيه عليه حتى يكون من يخالفه ولا ينصره ويخذله ولا يتبع أمره عاصيًا مستحقًا لما دعى عليه من الخذلان وعداوة الله تعالى له لكان مع جواز التوهم فيه ما يستحق به معاداته ويستوجب لأجله خذلانه من المناكير مثل هذا الدعاء من النبي صلوات الله عليه له محالاً لكونه ظلمًا لمن يخذله ويعاديه لارتكابه ما كان جائزاً التوهم فيه لو فعل، ولكان لا يدعو له بمثل ذلك كما لم يكن أحد من الصحابة يتعلق به من أمر الدين شيء، ولم[2] يكن معصومًا لم يدع له بمثل هذا التغليظ، ولما كان هذا الدعاء بمثل ذلك لا يجب إلا لمن يكون معصومًا موكولاً إليه أمر الدين بعده حتى يستحق من عصاه ما دعا به عليه النبي صلى الله عليه وآله كان الدعاء له وعلى من يخذله حرجًا على الأمة في النكول[3] عن طاعته وتضييقًا عليها للقعود عن التزام إمامته وتأكيداً للنص عليه بالإمامة بعده بقوله «فعلي مولاه». إذاً علي بن أبي طالب عليه السلام المنصوص عليه في الإمامة وهو الإمام.

البرهان الخامس: لما قال الله تعالى: «وَمَا آتَاكُمُ الرَسُولُ فَخُذُوهُ وَمَا نَهَاكُم عَنْهُ فَانْتَهُوا» [٥٩: ٧]، وكان قول النبي صلوات الله عليه بهذه الآية قائمًا مقام قول الله تعالى، وقال النبي صلوات الله عليه: «علي مني

---

[1] اذا لو لم: اذا لم، ٧٤

[2] ولم: كما، ز

[3] النكول: النكوص، ٧٤

كهارون من موسى إلا أنه لا نبي بعدي»، وكان لهارون من موسى عليهما السلام معان تجمعهما منها كونه من أمه وأبيه، ومنها شركته معه في النبوة، ومنها خلافته عنه في قومه عند غيبته، ولم يكن لعلي عليه السلام من هذه المعاني، لا كونه من أم محمد ولا من أبيه، ولا شركته معه في النبوة[١]، كان قول محمد صلوات الله عليه «علي مني كهارون من موسى إلا أنه لا نبي بعدي» بعد بطلان ما بطل منه من المعاني في علي عليه السلام كقوله: علي مني في الخلافة عني[٢] كهارون من موسى، إذ لم يبق من المعاني التي توجب نسب قوله «علي مني كهارون من موسى» إليها غير الخلافة، ولما كان من المعاني لم يبق إلا الخلافة، وكان قول النبي صلوات الله عليه «إلا أنه لا نبي بعدي» عقب قوله «علي مني كهارون من موسى»، كان من ذلك العلم بأن نفي النبوة بعده هو الدلالة على الوقت الذي فيه تكون خلافته التي أوجبها له بقوله «علي مني كهارون من موسى»، إذ لو لم يكن وقت خلافة علي عليه السلام بعده لما عقب قوله «علي مني كهارون من موسى» بنفي النبوة بعده فقال «إلا أنه لا نبي بعدي»، ولترك القول على جملته حتى كان محمولاً على أن خلافته عنه كانت في حياته كما كانت خلافة هارون من[٣] موسى في حياته، فلما عقب قوله بقوله «بعدي» في نفي النبوة، كان قوله ذلك نصًا منه عليه السلام على وقت خلافته وخلافة غيره من الأئمة عليهم أفضل الصلاة والسلام. فلو لم يكن ذلك كذلك وأن الغرض في قوله ذلك النص على وقت الخلافة كما نص له عليها بقوله «علي مني كهارون من موسى» لكان النبي صلوات الله عليه مع الموجود في نص الكتاب بأنه رسول الله صلوات الله عليه وخاتم النبيين مستغنيًا عن تكلف نفي النبوة بعده

---

[١] في النبوة: من نبوة، پ
[٢] عني: -، ز، پ
[٣] من: عن، ٧٤، هـ

ولكان معلوماً أن النبوة بمحمد صلى الله عليه وآله مختومة بنص الآية، وأنه لا يكون نبي[١] بعده إلى يوم القيامة، لا علي ولا غيره. وإذا كان ذلك كذلك كان منه الإيجاب أن نفي النبي[٢] صلوات الله عليه النبوة بعده هو إثبات الخلافة له بعده. إذاً علي بن أبي طالب عليه السلام المنصوص عليه بالإمامة وهو الإمام.

البرهان السادس: لما قال النبي صلوات الله عليه وعلى آله نصاً على الحسن والحسين عليهما السلام بالإمامة: «الحسن والحسين إمامان قاماً أو قعداً وأبوهما خير منهما»، وكان قوله عليه السلام «وأبوهما خير منهما» عقب إشارته بالإمامة إليهما، كان من ذلك العلم بأن المراد بقوله «خير منهما» أن علي بن أبي طالب عليه السلام خير منهما فيما جعله صفة[٣] للحسن والحسين، وهو الإمامة بقوله «إمامان». إذاً علي بن أبي طالب المنصوص عليه بالإمامة وهو الإمام.

البرهان السابع: لما كانت للأشياء كلها صفات، وكان الذي يجمعه منها وما هو من جنسه من الصفات أكثر كان به أشبه وله أمثل وإليه أقرب وبأن يسد مسده بعد عدمه أولى، مثل الفضة التي هي بالذهب أشبه من غيرها مما هو من جنسها[٤] من المعدنيات التي هي الحديد والنحاس والآنك والقلعي والزيبق للمعاني التي جمعتها، وهي في الأخرى ليست كما في الفضة من صفاء الجوهر والبقاء على تصرم الأزمان والصبر على النار واللين والانطراق والعز وكثرة الثمن، وهي بهذه المعاني بأن يسد مسد الذهب بعد عدمه أولى من غيرها، ومثل كل نوع من النبات في مصير بعضها بما جمعه وما هو من جنسه من المعاني والصفات بأن يسد

---

[١] نبي: نبيا، هـ، ز، پ. ٤٨، ٧٤

[٢] النبي: -، پ، ٧٤، هـ

[٣] صفة: صفته، پ

[٤] غيرها...جنسها: غيرهما...جنسهما، هـ، ٤٨

مسده أولى من غيره، كالشعير الذي هو بالحنطة أشبه وإليها أقرب من غيره من الحبوب المغذية، وهو بأن يسد مسد الحنطة بعد عدمها أولى من غيره من الحبوب، ومثل الأدوية التي تجمع بعضها وما هو من جنسها قوى إذا عدم دواء سد مسده دواء آخر مما يقاربه في فعله، وهو بأن يسد مسده أولى من غيره، كالعفص في القبض والعقد[١]، إذا عدم كان البلوط أولى بأن يسد مسده من غيره لما يجمعه وإياه من القوة في القبض، وكذلك قشور الرمان وأقماعه. وكان النبي صلوات الله عليه بإرقاء الله إياه إلى درجة النبوة جامعًا لخصال[٢] ومعان منها الوحي والنص من الله والطهارة والعفة والورع والشجاعة والسخاء والصدق والزهد والعدل والرحمة والإيمان والعلم وغير ذلك، ولم يكن بعد النبي صلى الله عليه وآله مَن كان يجمعه وإياه من هذه الصفات ما يجمعه غير علي بن أبي طالب عليه السلام، كما صورناه بالجداول على نهج الحساب بالعريضة آخر هذا البرهان ليعاين، كان علي بن أبي طالب عليه السلام بوجود هذه الخصال[٣] فيه بأن يسد مسد النبي صلوات الله عليه ويقوم مقامه أولى من غيره من أبناء جنسه من الأصحاب. إذاً علي بن أبي طالب عليه السلام الإمام.

صورة العريضة المعمولة بالخصال الموجودة في النبي وما منها موجود في الأصحاب ليوقف منها على الأحق بأن يقوم مقام النبي صلوات الله عليه منهم بعده، ونعرف هذه العريضة بالمسير على نهج الحساب:

---

[١] العقد: العفص، ز؛ الفعل، ٤٨؛ العقل، ٧٤
[٢] لخصال: للخصال، ٧٤
[٣] الخصال: الخصائل، ٧٤

[What follows here is the text of the table of the Prophet's virtues and characteristics. For the format of the table itself see plates 1 - 4]

محمد المصطفى صلى الله عليه وعلى آله

[١] الأسماء والوحي من الله[١]: كان يوحى إليه من الله تعالى

[٢] النص من الله: كان منصوصًا عليه من الله على ألسن رسله بقوله تعالى[٢] في السفر[٣] الخامس من التوراة بشارة به وقال موسى «إذوناي» الله و«مسينا بو وذوروح مساعير لومو وهوفيع مي هار» من سينا تجلى[٤] وأشرق من بلاد عيص لهم[٥] وظهر من جبل «فورون واوثو مير ففوث قوذش ميمينو اش» تهامة وأتى من ربوات القدس من [في يمينه؟] نار «دوث لومو» شبه لهم [شريعة له؟][٦]

---

[١] الله: + تعالى، ز

[٢] بقوله تعالى: بقول الله تعالى، ز؛ بقول الله، ٧٤

[٣] السفر: السورة، هـ، ٧٤

[٤] تجلى: على، ٧٤

[٥] عيص لهم: عنصرهم (؟)، ٧٤

[٦] قال قاضي النعمان في كتاب اساس التأويل (ص ٣٢١): «وجاء الله من سيناء وأشرق من ساعير واستعلن من جبال فاران وسيأتي من ربوات القدس في يمينه نار هي شريعة له، فقالوا: عنى بمجيئه من سيناء إرساله موسى إذ نزل التوراة عليه في طور سيناء، وإشراقه من ساعير إرساله عيسى منها وكان يسكن بقرية تسمى ناصر وهي من ارض الجليل وكذلك استعلاءه من جبال فاران إرساله محمد وفاران هي مكة باللسان الذي أنزل الله به التوراة، وبذلك نذكر ونعرف أن في جبالها نبأ الله محمد وأنزل كتابه عليه وإتيانه من ربوات القدس ظهور قائم القيامة والنار التي هي في يمينه هي إظهار باطن الشريعة ...» قال ابو حانم الرازي في كتاب اعلام النبوة (ص ١٩٥): «وفي التوراة أيضًا: جاء الله من سيناء وأشرق من ساعير وأضاء من جبال فاران» [تثنيه، ٢/٣٣] فمجيء الله من سيناء هو مجيء موسى لأن الله أعطاه الألواح بطور سيناء، وإشراقه من ساعير هو خروج المسيح لأنه كان من ساعير من أرض الجليل من قرية يقال إنها ناصرة، وإضاءته من جبال فاران هي ظهور محمد من مكة لان فاران هو مكة.»

[٣] الطهارة والعصمة[١]: كان طاهراً مطهراً معصوماً لم يعبد وثناً ولا صنماً ولا سجد إلا الله تعالى خالصاً

[٤] العفة: كان عفيفاً لم يرتكب قط[٢] معصية ولا زلة ولا شرب خمراً ولا تعاطى فساداً

[٥] الورع: كان ورعاً لا يطمع في مال[٣] أحد وكان لكونه أميناً ثقة يسمى الأمين وتودع[٤] عنده الودائع قبل مبعثه

[٦] الشجاعة والقوة[٥]: كان شجاعاً مقداماً لا يروعه كثرة الكفار فقام بالدعاء إلى الله[٦] مع[٧] قلة عدده حتى علت كلمته

[٧] السخاء: كان سخياً لا يدخر لنفسه شيئاً يعطي لوجه الله وأولياء الله تعالى

[٨] الزهد: كان زاهداً لا يرغب في الدنيا وينهي عنها والاغترار بها عاملاً[٨] لوجه الله تعالى

[٩] العدل والرحمة: كان عادلاً رحيماً سماه الله رؤوفاً رحيماً وقال لرجل عاتبه في قسمة مال فئ: إذا لم أعدل فمن يعدل وأنا أمين من في السماء ومن في الأرض[٩]؟

[١٠] السبق إلى الإيمان: كان أسبق السباق إلى الإيمان وأول الأولين[١٠]

---

[١] العصمة: -، پ؛ العفة ، ٤٨

[٢] كان عفيفاً لم يرتكب قط: كان عفيفاً قط لم يركب، ز و ٤٨ و پ

[٣] مال: -، ز

[٤] تودع: يودع، ز و پ

[٥] القوة: -، ز

[٦] الله: + تعالى، ز و پ

[٧] مع: -، ز و ٤٨

[٨] عاملا: عامدا، ٧٤

[٩] ومن في الأرض: -، ز

[١٠] الأولين: = له، ز و پ

منه ظهر الإيمان وبه يقوى ويقتدى[1]

[١١] العالم بكتاب الله: كان عالمًا بما كان وما[2] يكون وبما[3] أنزله الله[4] إليه وافتخر فقال: لو كان آدم ونوح وابراهيم وموسى وعيسى في زماننا لبركوا بين يدي وتعلموا مني

[١٢] العلم بتأويل كتاب الله والشريعة: كان عالمًا بالأمثال والمثلات في جميع ما جاء به

[١٣] العلم بالحكم بما أنزل الله: كان حاكمًا لا محيص عن حكمه ولا اختيار[5] دونه فيه يقول الله تعالى: «فَلا وَرَبِّكَ لا يُؤْمِنُونَ حَتَّى يُحَكِّمُوكَ فِيمَا شَجَرَ بَيْنَهُم ثُمَّ لا يَجِدُوا فِي أَنْفُسِهِم حَرَجًا مِمَّا قَضَيْتَ وَيُسَلِّمُوا تَسْلِيمًا» [٤: ٦٥]

[١٤] العلم بالحلال والحرام: كان عالمًا بما حلل وحرم عن الله تعالى ومنه تعلم

[١٥] المحبة من الله: كان محبوبًا من الله تعالى مصطفى مختاراً وهو حبيب الله تعالى

[١٦] القرب من الله: كان قريبًا من الله تعالى فدنا منه قاب قوسين أو أدنى

فالذي ظهر بطور سيناء كان موسى عليه السلم والذي ظهر من بلاد عيص التي هي الشام ونواحي الروم كان عيسى عليه السلام والذي ظهر من جبال تهامة كان محمد صلوات الله عليه. ثم قال في التوراة جوابًا لدعاء إبراهيم عليه السلم: «وليشموعيل شمعتيخو وهني بيرختي اوتو

---

[1] ويقتدي: وتهتدي، ٤٨ و پ

[2] ما: -، ز و ٤٨

[3] بما: مما، ز

[4] الله: = تعالى، ز

[5] اختيار: الاختيار، ز

وهربيثي ووثو وهفريثي ووثو [بماوذ]»، لإسمعيل سمعت دعاءك وأنا أبارك فيه وأتمم بركتي عليه وأجدد بركاتي عليه بمحمد[١] «بماوذ ماوذ شنيم عوسور نسائم يوليد ونثتى» محمد اثنا عشر سبطًا أجلاء أشرف[٢] يولد ويكون منه[٣] شعب كثير «لغوي كودول»[٤]. نقول[٥] إن الأصل في لغة العبرانية[٦] «ماوذ» من ذال، وإنما ينصرف في وجوه المعاني بزيادات تدل على أنواع التصريف، مثل «اوذي»، وتفسيره أحمد وأشكر و«نوذي» و«توذي» و«يوذي»، أي نحمد وتحمده ويحمده، وتركيب الميم فيه في «ماوذ» لكونه في معنى المفعول، كما يقال في لغة العرب محمد محمود مشكور، وإذا أردنا أن نأمر واحداً بلغة العبرانية[٧] أن يشكر ويحمد غيره قلنا «هوذه»، وليس عن هذا معدل في لغتهم أصلاً. إذاً «ماوذ» محمد وقد بشر الله تعالى به إبراهيم عليه السلام.

وقال ايشاعيا النبي عليه السلام في التوراة: «كيخو اومار اذونوى الا ليخ هاعميد هامصفي اشار يراي يكيد» كذا قال الله: لي امض وأقم ديدبان حتى يخبر بما يرى، «ورواو راخف صامد بورشيم راخف حومور وراخف كومول»، فنظر ورأى راكبين، أحدهما[٨] راكب حمار والآخر[٩]

---

[١] بمحمد: لمحمد، ٤٨

[٢] اشرف: + مولد، ز؛ + مولود، ٧٤

[٣] منه: من، ٤٨؛ -، هـ

[٤] قال قاضي النعمان في كتاب اساس التأويل (ص ٣٢٠-٣٢١): «...ويذكرون آية من التوراة والإنجيل هذا عدا عما صرفوه منهما مما فيه ذكره: قد سُمِعَتْ دعاءك وأجبْته وباركت عليه وأكبرته وعظمته جداً جداً وسيلد ملكًا وأجعلُ له اثنى عشر عظيمًا وَأجعله لأمّة عظيمة [تكوين ٢٠/ ١٧] أي محمد والعظماء الاثنى عشر حدوده وهم النقباء في كل عصر.»

[٥] نقول: يقول، ز، هـ

[٦] العبرانية: العربية، ز، هـ، ٤٨، ٧٤، پ

[٧] العبرانية: العربية، ز، هـ، ٤٨، ٧٤، پ

[٨] احدهما: واحد، پ، ٤٨، ٧٤، هـ

[٩] الآخر: -، ٤٨

راكب جمل[١]، ويصيح «وياعن ويومر نوفلو نوفلو بوبال بسيلي الاهو»، ويقول: الويل الويل لبابل سيكسّر معبودهم، فراكب الحمار كان عيسى عليه السلام وراكب الجمل كان محمد صلوات الله عليه، وذلك بشارة به ونص عليه.[٢]

وقال صاحب الإنجيل: «موذوثى فارقليطو هو ذينو مشادرنو لخون روحو شرورو» يجيء العالِم الذي يرسله الاب إليكم بروح الحق «وا هو نحاكم لخون شرورو كوليه»، وهو يعلّمكم الأشياء كلها.[٣] وقال صاحب كتاب إقليمس المنسوب إلى شمعون الصفا وصاحب كتاب بطرس أنه سيجيء من أولاد إسماعيل نبي أول اسمه ميم وآخره دال، ويفتح البلاد كلها وسيخرب الكنائس بأسرها. فهذا كله نصوص من الله من جهة

[١] احدهما راكب حمار والآخر راكب جمل: واحد راكب حمار واحد راكب جمل، ٧٤ و ٤٨

[٢] قال ابو حاتم الرازي في كتاب اعلام النبوة (ص ١٩٦-١٩٧): «وفي كتاب اشعياء: قال لي الرب أقم نظاراً ليخبر بما يرى فكان الذي رأى صاحب المنظرة قال: قد أقبل راكبان أحدهما على حمار والآخر على جمل؛ فبينا أنا كذلك إذ أقبل أحد الراكبين وهو يقول: هوت هوت بابل ونكست جميع آلهتها النخرة على الأرض [اشعياء ٢١: ٦-٩] فهذا الذي سمعت من الرب إله إسرائيل العزيز قد نبأتكم به يعني براكب الحمار المسيح لأنه دخل أورشليم وهو راكب حماراً؛ ويعني براكب الجمل محمداً لأنه دخل المدينة وهو راكب الجمل، وعلى يديه فتحت بابل وكسرت أصنامها».

[٣] قال ابو حاتم الرازي في كتاب اعلام النبوة (ص ١٩٦): «وفي الانجيل، قال المسيح: اني ذاهب وسياتيكم البارقليط روح الحق الذي لا يتكلم من قبل نفسه ويعلمكم كل شيء وهو يشهد لي كما شهدت له وهو يرسل باسمي. [يوحنا، ١٥: ٢٦]، قوله يرسل باسمي أي يكون صاحب شريعة مثله، ولم يخرج بعده صاحب شريعة مثله إلى محمد وهو شهد له كما شهد محمد له.» وقال قاضي النعمان في كتاب أساس التأويل (ص ٣٢٢): «ومما ذكروا من ذلك أن في الإنجيل قول المسيح للحواريين: «إني ذاهب وسيأتي البارقليط روح القدس الذي لا يتكلم من قبل نفسه إنما هو كما يقال إنه يقول وهو يشهد علي وأنتم تشهدون لي ولأنكم معي من قبل الناس وكل شيء أعده الله لكم يخبركم» وفي حكاية يوحنا عن المسيح أنه قال «البارقليط لا يجيئكم ما لم أذهب أنا فإذا جاء وبخ العالم على الخطيئة ولا يقول من تلقاء نفسه ولكنه يسبح به ويكلمكم ويسوسكم بالحق ويخبركم بالحوادث والغيوب» وفي حكاية أخرى «أن البارقليط روح الحق الذي يرسله أبي يسميه فهو يعلمكم كل شيء وقال: إني سائل أبي أن يبعث إليكم بارقليط آخر يكون معكم إلى الأبد وهو يعلمكم كل شيء» يعني بقوله يكون معكم إلى الأبد أي شريعته تبقى إلى الأبد وفي حكاية أخرى «أن البشر ذاهب والبارقليط من بعده يجيء لكم بالأسرار ويقر لكم كل شيء وهو يشهد لي كما شهدت له فإني جئتكم بالأمثال وهو يجيئكم بالتأويل.»

أوليائه وأنبيائه على النبي صلوات الله عليه.

قال قُسّ بن ساعدة الإيادي لما جاء إلى مكة ووقف على سوق عكاظ على جمل له أورق بشارة بالنبي صلوات الله عليه وبالدين الذي يدعو إليه: «أيها الناس من عاش مات ومن مات فات، وكل ما هو آت آت، ليل داج، وسماء ذات أبراج، ونجوم تزهر، وبحار[1] تذخر، وبنون وبنات، وآباء وأمهات، وذاهب وآت، إن في السماء لعبراً وإن في الأرض لخبراً، ما لي أرى الناس يذهبون ولا يرجعون؟ أرضوا بالمقام فأقاموا أم تركوا فناموا؟ أقسم بالله قُسّ قسمًا ما على الأرض دين هو أكرم على الله من دين قد أظلكم زمانه، وأدرككم أوانه، طوبى لمن أدركه فاتّبعه وويل لمن خالفه، ثم قال شعراً:

فِي الذّاهِبِينَ الأوّلِينَ ... مِنَ القُرُونِ لَنَا بَصَائِرْ
لَمّا رَأَيْتُ مَوَارِداً ... لِلمَوْتِ لَيْسَ لَهَا مَصَادِرْ
وَرَأَيْتُ قَوْمِي نَحْوَهَا ... يَمْضِي[2] الأصَاغِرُ وَالأكَابِرْ
لاَ يَرْجِعُ المَاضِي إليَّ ... وَلاَ مِنَ البَاقِينَ غَابِرْ
أيْقَنْتُ أنِّي لاَ مَحَا ... لَةَ حَيْثُ صَارَ القَوْمُ صَائِرْ

وقد قال الله تعالى كبرياؤه في القرآن: «وَمَا مُحَمَّدٌ إلاّ رَسُولٌ قَدْ خَلَتْ من قَبْله الرُسُلُ» [٣: ١٤٤]، وقال تعالى: «مُحَمَّدٌ رَسُولُ الله وَالذين مَعَهُ أَشداَّءُ عَلَى الكُفَّارِ رُحَمَاءُ بَيْنَهُم» [٤٨: ٢٩]، وقال تعالى: «مَا كَانَ مُحَمَّدٌ أَبَا أحَدٍ من رِجَالِكُم وَلَكِن رَسُولَ الله وَخَاتَمَ النَبِيِّينَ» [٣٣: ٤٠]، وقال تعالى: «اَلنَبِيَّ الأمِيَّ الذي يَجِدُونَهُ مَكْتُوبًا عِندَهُم في التَورَاة وَالإنْجِيلِ» [٧: ١٥٧]، وقال تعالى: «وَمُبَشِّراً بِرَسُولٍ يَأتِي مِن بَعْدِي اسْمُهُ أحْمَدُ» [٦١: ٦].

---

[1] بحار: تجار، ز، ٤٨

[2] يمضي: تمضي، شيخو، ٢١٣

ذكر الصحابة وما كانت مشهورة به من الخصال التي في جدول النبوة محصورة سوى ما حذف تحريًا للإيجاز لضيق عرضة العريضة، ونبتدىء بذكر أبي بكر ليكون الانتهاء إلى إقامة الغرض.

[Text of the tables at the end of *miṣbāḥ* 5, *burhān* 7. For the format of these tables see plates 5 - 14]

أبو بكر: لم يكن له وحي من الله؛ لم يكن عفيفًا لشربه الخمر في الجاهلية وارتكابه الكبائر؛ لم يكن منصوصًا عليه لا من الله ولا من رسوله؛ لم يكن طاهرًا ولا مطهراً قد عبد الأوثان وسجد لها من دون الله؛ لم يكن شجاعًا ولا عرف بالقوة والشجاعة؛ كان ورعًا لا يطمع؛ كان سخيًا منفقًا؛ لم يكن مختاراً من الله ولا[1] من رسوله ولا محبوبًا منهما ولا ممن وصف بذلك؛ لم يكن من الموصوفين بالزهد؛ لم يعدل في حكم ولا رحم ابنة رسول الله حين غصبها مالها؛ كان سابقًا إلى الإسلام؛ لم يكن عالمًا بكتاب الله ولا مذكوراً به؛ لم يكن عالمًا بالحلال[2] والحرام ولا من المذكورين به؛ لم يكن عالمًا بالتأويل؛ لم يكن عارفًا بالحكم واحتاج فيه إلى علي[3]؛ لم يكن قريبًا من الله ولا من رسوله صلى الله عليه .

عمر: تلك سبيله؛تلك سبيله؛تلك سبيله؛تلك سبيله؛تلك سبيله؛ كان له ورع[4] ؛ كان سخيًا منفقًا؛ ___؛ ___؛ ___؛ لم يكن سبق[5] إلى الإسلام[6] كأبي بكر؛ ___؛ كان عالمًا بالحلال والحرام؛ ___؛ ___؛

[1] لا: -، ز
[2] بالحلال: في الحلال، پ
[3] علي: + بن ابي طالب، پ، ٧٤
[4] كان له ورع: لم يكن له ورع، ٧٤
[5] سبق: له يلق، پ
[6] الى الإسلام: -، ز

___

عثمان: تلك سبيله؛ تلك سبيله؛تلك سبيله؛تلك سبيله؛تلك سبيله؛لم يكن ورعًا[١] ؛ كان سخيًا منفقًا؛ ___؛ ___؛ ___؛ كان من السابقين؛ كان من الموصوفين بعلم كتاب الله؛ لم يكن عالمًا[٢] [بالحلال والحرام]؛ ___؛ ___؛ ___

زيد بن حارث[ة]: ___؛ ___؛ ___؛ ___؛ ___؛ ___؛ ___؛ ___؛ ___؛ ___؛ كان من السابقين؛ كان من الموصوفين به بعلم كتاب الله؛ كان من الموصوفين[٣] [بعلم الحلال والحرام]؛ ___؛ ___؛ ___

طلحة: ___؛ ___؛ ___؛ ___؛ كان شجاعًا؛ ___؛ ___؛ ___؛ ___؛ كان من السابقين؛ ___؛ ___؛ ___؛ ___؛ ___

الزبير: ___؛ ___؛ ___؛ ___؛ كان شجاعًا؛ ___؛ ___؛ ___؛ ___؛ كان من السابقين؛ ___؛ ___؛ ___؛ ___؛ ___

سعد[٤] بن عبد الرحمن: ___؛ ___؛ ___؛ ___؛ ___؛ ___؛ ___؛ ___؛ ___؛ ___؛ كان من السابقين؛ ___؛ ___؛ ___؛ ___؛ ___

سلمان: ___؛ ___؛ ___؛ كان عفيفًا[٥]؛ كان طاهراً[٦]؛ كان ورعًا؛ كان سخيًا؛ ___؛ كان محبوبًا من الرسول؛ كان زاهداً من الموصوفين به؛

---

[١] ورعا: له ورع، ٤٨، ٧٤؛ لم تكن له ورع، ز

[٢] لم يكن عالما: -، ز و پ

[٣] كان من الموصوفين: -، هـ و ٤٨

[٤] سعد: سعيد، ز

[٥] كان عفيفا: - هـ، ٤٨ و ز و ٧٤

[٦] كان طاهرا: -، هـ، ٤٨ و ز و ٧٤

كان من السابقين؛ ___؛ كان عالمًا بالحلال والحرام[١]؛ ___؛ ___؛ كان قريبًا من الرسول لقوله: «سلمان منّا أهل البيت»

أبو ذرّ: ___؛ ___؛ ___؛ كان عفيفًا[٢]؛ كان طاهراً[٣]؛ كان ورعًا؛ كان سخيًا؛ ___؛ كان زاهداً ومن المذكورين به؛ ___؛ كان من السابقين؛ ___؛ ___؛ ___؛ ___؛ ___

مِقداد: ___؛ ___؛ ___؛ ___؛ ___؛ ___؛ ___؛ كان ورعًا؛ كان سخيًا؛ كان من الزاهدين المذكورين[٤] [به]؛ كان من السابقين؛ ___؛ ___؛ ___؛ ___؛ ___؛ ___

عمّار: ___؛ ___؛ ___؛ ___؛ ___؛ ___؛ ___؛ كان ورعًا؛ كان سخيًا؛ ___؛ كان من الزاهدين المذكورين [به]؛ كان من السابقين؛ ___؛ ___؛ ___؛ ___؛ ___؛ ___

عبد الله بن مسعود: ___؛ ___؛ ___؛ ___؛ ___؛ ___؛ ___؛ كان ورعًا؛ كان سخيًا منفقًا؛ ___؛

عبد الله بن عبّاس: ___؛ ___؛ ___؛ ___؛ ___؛ ___؛ ___؛ كان ورعًا[٥]؛ كان سخيًا[٦]؛ كان عالمًا بكتاب الله؛ كان عالمًا فقيهًا؛ كان عارفًا بالحكم؛ كان قريبًا من الرسول وهو ابن عمّه[٧]

علي بن أبي طالب صلوات الله عليه وسلم[٨]: كان منصوصًا عليه من الله ومن رسوله على ما أقمنا عليه البراهين في مصباح أمامه؛ كان طاهراً مطهراً لم يعبد وثنًا ولا صنمًا ولا سجد إلا الله خالصًا معروفًا بذلك؛

---

[١] كان عالما بالحلال والحرام: -، ٧٤

[٢] كان عفيفا: -، هـ، ٤٨، ز

[٣] كان طاهرا: -، ز، هـ ٧٤ و ٤٨

[٤] كان من الزاهدين المذكورين: -، ٤٨ و پ

[٥] كان ورعا: - ٧٤، ٤٨ و ز

[٦] كان سخيا: -، ٧٤، ٤٨ و ز

[٧] كان قريبا من الرسول وهو ابن عنه: -، پ و هـ؛ وهو ابن عنه: -، ٧٤ و ٤٨

[٨] وسلم: والسلام، ز

كان عفيفًا لم يرتكب قطّ معصية لا زلة[١] ولا شرب خمراً ولا تعاطى فساداً معروفًا بذلك؛ كان شجاعًا مقدامًا مشهوراً بذلك[٢] لا ينكتم أمره ويضرب به المثل؛ كان ورعًا لا يطمع في مال أحد شديداً في أمر الله، لا يأخذه في الله لومة لائم معروفًا بذلك؛ كان سخيًا ذكره الله تعالى في سورة هل أتى معروفًا بذلك؛ كان زاهداً في الدنيا معروفًا بذلك؛ كان عادلاً رحيمًا وعدله صار علة لاستقضاء من استقضى[٣]، ومعروف بذلك؛ كان من السابقين الأولين وهو ثاني مَن آمن بالله وبالرسول [بعد الأولى] التي هي خديجة عليها السلام؛ كان عالمًا بكتاب الله تعالى وجميع ما أنزل الله، معروفًا بذلك؛ كان عالمًا بالحلال والحرام فقيهًا[٤] معروفًا بذلك؛ كان عارفًا بالحكم ولذلك قال النبي صلى الله عليه وآله «عليّ اقضاكم»؛ كان عالمًا بتأويل كتاب الله تعالى ولذلك قال النبي صلى الله عليه وآله «عليّ صاحب التأويل»؛ كان محبوبًا من الله تعالى بقول النبي يوم أعطاه الراية في فتح خيبر «لأعطينّ الراية رجلاً كرّار غير فرّار يحبه الله ورسوله ويحب الله ورسوله»؛ كان قريبًا من النبي وهو ابن عمّه كان قريبًا من النبي ومَن كان قريبًا من الرسول فهو قريب من الله، وهو [من] أصحاب الكساء يوم المباهلة وابن عمه وخليفته ووصيه عليه السلام.

[١] زلة: + له، ٧٤
[٢] بذلك: -، ز
[٣] استقضى: الاستقضاء، پ
[٤] فقيها: -، ز

[Text of the 2nd, circle table at the end of 5: 7; from center circle to outside; concentric circles (plates 13 and 14)]

[١] عالم القضاء

[٢] الوحي؛ النص؛ الطهارة؛ العفة؛ الورع؛ الشجاعة؛ السخاء؛ الزهد؛ العدل؛ السبق؛ العلم؛ العلم؛ العلم بالتأويل[١]؛العلم بالحكم؛ المحبة؛ القريب[٢]

[٣] محمد: كان منصوص من الله؛ كان طاهراً مطهراً؛ كان عفيفًا[٣]؛ كان ورعًا؛ كان شجاعًا؛ كان سخيًا؛ كان زاهداً؛ كان عادلاً رحيمًا؛ كان أول السابقين؛ كان عالمًا بكتاب الله؛ كان عالمًا بالحلال والحرام؛ كان عالمًا بتأويل كتاب الله؛ كان عالمًا بالحكم؛ كان حبيبًا من الله؛ كان قريبًا من الله

[٤] أبو بكر: خالي؛ خالي؛ خالي؛ كان ورعًا؛ خالي؛ كان مذكوراً[٤]؛ خالي؛ خالي؛ ؛كان من السابقين؛ خالي؛ خالي؛ خالي؛ خالي؛ خالي؛ خالي.

[٥] عمر: خالي؛ خالي؛ خالي؛ ؛كان ورعًا؛ خالي؛ كان سخيًا منفقًا؛ خالي؛ خالي؛ خالي؛ كان عالمًا بالحلال والحرام؛ خالي؛ خالي؛ خالي؛ خالي.

[٦] عثمان: خالي؛ خالي؛ خالي؛ خالي؛ خالي؛ كان سخيًا منفقًا؛ خالي؛ خالي؛ كان من السابقين؛ كان عالمًا بكتاب الله؛ خالي؛ خالي؛ خالي؛ خالي؛ خالي.

---

[١] بالتأويل: -، ز

[٢] القريب: التقريب، هـ

[٣] عفيفا: ـلا يرتكب زلة، ٧٤، هـ

[٤] مذكورا: سخيا، ٧٤

[٧] علي عليه السلام[١] لم يكن يوحي إليه؛ كان منصوصًا عليه من الله ومن رسوله؛ كان طاهراً مطهراً لم يرتكب زلة قط؛ كان عفيفًا لم يتعاطى فساداً قط؛ كان ورعًا لا يطمع في مال أحدٍ؛ كان شجاعًا مقدمًا قدامًا مشهوراً بذلك؛ كان سخيًا ذكره[٢] الله في كتابه وسنة رسوله[٣]؛ كان زاهراً من المعروفين؛ كان عادلاً لا يأخذه في الله لومة لائم؛ كان أول السابقين من[٤] المؤمنين؛ كان عالمًا بكتاب الله ظاهراً وباطنًا؛ كان عالمًا بالحلال والحرام فقيهًا فيه؛ كان عالمًا بتأويل كتاب الله جل ذكره؛ كان عارفًا بالحكم لقول النبي «علي اقضاكم»؛ كان محبوبًا من الله لقول النبي فيه يوم خيبر[٥]؛ كان قريبًا من رسول الله صلى الله عليه وآله.

قد تبين بهذه العريضة أن علي بن أبي طالب عليه أفضل الصلاة والسلام كان جامعًا لجميع ما كان في النبي صلى الله عليه وآله من الخصال إلا الوحي الذي خص الله به نبيه عليه السلام، وأنه الأحق بمقام رسول الله صلى الله عليه وآله بعده وأنه هو الإمام من دون الجماعة التي خلت جداولهم من الخصال، والله ولي المؤمنين وهذه دائرة لِمَن لا يعرف نسق الحساب والعرائض كالكتاب، فيقف منها على الغرض.

---

[١] عليه السلام: صلوات الله عليه وعلى الائمة من ولده، ٧٤

[٢] ذكره: كذا في هـ و هـ٢؛ ذكر، ز و ٤٨

[٣] رسوله: نبيه، ٤٨

[٤] كان اول السابقين من المؤمنين: كان من السابقين واول المؤمنين، ٧٤

[٥] يوم خيبر: يوم غدير خم، هـ

المصباح السادس من المقالة الثانية

في أن الإمامة بعد مجيء النص بها إلى جعفر الصادق عليه أفضل السلام لإسماعيل وذريته عليه السلام دون إخوته

البرهان الأول: لما صح أن الإمامة لا تصح إلا بالنص والتوقيف، وكان النص من النبي صلى الله عليه وآله جاء في علي بن أبي طالب عليه السلام من دون غيره ومن علي جاء في الحسن ولم يستحق أولاده النص بالإمامة بعده مع وجود كون مثل الحسن[1] في العصمة والطهارة وإشارة النبي صلوات الله عليه وآله بالإمامة إليه، وهو الحسين عليه السلام، فجاء النص فيه. ثم لم يستحق أولاد الحسن النص بعد الحسين لكون ذرية الحسين به أولى لقرب الرحم بقول الله تعالى: «وَأُولُوا الأَرْحَامِ بَعْضُهُمْ أولىَ بِبَعْضٍ» [٨: ٧٥]، وكان النص جاء على الولاء في أولاد الحسين إلى جعفر الصادق عليه السلام، وكان جعفر نص على إسماعيل، واختلفت الشيعة فيه بما قالت من موته[2] قبل جعفر، وإشارة جعفر بعد ذلك إلى بعض أولاده وقوله: «ما بدا لله بداءً كما بدا له في إسماعيل». كان لا يخلو الأمر بعد نص جعفر بن محمد على إسماعيل فيما[3] يُدعى من نصه بعد موت إسماعيل على بعض أولاده[4] من وجوه ثلاثة: إما أنه نص على بعض أولاده بعد موت إسماعيل كما يقال ولإسماعيل ولد، أو نص ولم

---

[1] الحسن: الحسين، ٤٨، هـ

[2] من موته: بموته، پ

[3] فيما: مما، ز

[4] اولاده: الاولاد، پ، ٤٨

يكن لإسماعيل ولد، أو لم ينص على أحد بعدما تقدم من نصه على إسماعيل أولاً. فإن كان قد نص ولإسماعيل ولد كان جعفر عليه السلام حاكمًا بغير ما أنزل الله حيث أعطى ميراث إسماعيل مع كون ولد له إخوته من غير علة سالبة لولده، كما سلبت ولد الحسن وأوجبت لولد الحسين، وتوهم مثل ذلك في جعفر غير جائز لصحة إمامته وعصمته. وإذا لم يكن جائزاً كان ما نسب إليه من نصه عليه السلام على بعض أولاده بعد تقدم النص على اسماعيل باطلاً، وإذا كان باطلاً كانت الإمامة لولد إسماعيل ثابتة. وإن كان عليه السلام قد نص ولم يكن لإسماعيل عليه السلام ولد، وكان في علم الله وتقديره أن يكون منقطع النسل، وجب من حيث علم الله وتقديره أن يكون النص لا يجوز فيمن ينقطع نسله مع كون الإمامة محفوظة في العقب أن لا ينص جعفر عليه السلام على إسماعيل، ولما كان وجدناه قد نص عليه، كان منه العلم بأنه غير منقطع النسل والعقب، وإذا كان غير منقطع النسل والعقب، فالإمامة له ولنسله ثابتة. وإن كان عليه السلام لم ينص على أحد بعد نصه على إسماعيل عليه السلام فالإمامة لإسماعيل، فإذا ثبت إمامة إسماعيل ثبت نسله، إذ لا يستحق الإمامة من لا يكون له عقب بكونها محفوظة في العقب، وإذا ثبت نسله فالإمامة لنسله ثابتة. وكان إذا كان لا يخلو من ثلاثة أوجه، وأوجبت الوجوه الثلاثة كون الإمامة لإسماعيل وذريته، فالإمامة ثابتة لإسماعيل وولده. إذاً الإمامة في إسماعيل وذريته عليهم السلام.

البرهان الثاني: نقول إن الإمامة لما كانت في عقب جعفر عليه السلام، وكان الإمام لا ينص على من يجعله إمامًا إلا بعد أن يعلم أنه يصلح لها، وكان أول ما يستصلح للإمام عليه السلام في إمامته أن يكون لا عقيمًا، ثم وجود عقبه ونسله إذ من كان لا عقب له لا يستحق

الإمامة، وكان الإمام جعفر عليه السلام نص على إسماعيل، كان من ذلك الحكمُ بأن لإسماعيل ولداً وعقبًا، وإلا كان لا ينص عليه، وإذا كان له عقب فعقبه أحق بالإمامة من أعمامه. إذاً الإمامة لإسماعيل ولعقبه من دون غيرهم.

البرهان الثالث: لما كان الإمام معصومًا لا تسبق منه زلة، وكان لو لم يكن لإسماعيل ولد ولا عقب ولا ذرية، نص جعفر عليه زلة، وجب من حيث كون عصمة الإمام أن يكون لإسماعيل لما نص عليه عقب وذرية، وإذا كانت له ذرية وعقب، فعقبه بالإمامة أولى من أعمامه. إذاً الإمامة بعد إسماعيل لولده وعقبه من دون غيره.

البرهان الرابع: لما كانت الإمامة لجعفر عليه السلام وكانت محفوظة في عقبه وكان له أولاد أربعة: إسماعيل وعبدالله ومحمد وموسى، فلم يستحقها عبدالله لكونه عقيمًا منقطع النسل، ومصير ذلك من أكبر الشهادات في بطلان إمامته وعلى عدم النص فيه، ولا محمد استحقها لاستعماله ما استعمل مما نافى قول الرسول صلوات الله عليه وخالف أمره من خروجه على من آمنه وآواه وخيانته إياه وتجريده السيف في الحرم المحرم فيه وادعائه فيه الإمامة وانعكاس أمره وخيبة دعوته مع قول النبي صلوات الله عليه: «إن الإمام لا ترد دعوته ورايته إذا دعاها بالحرمين» وتكذيبه نفسه[1] ومصير ذلك كله من أكبر الشهادات ببطلان إمامته وعدم النص فيه، ولا موسى استحقها لما عدم فيه وفي عقبه شرائطها التي هي وجود النص بوجود المنصوص عليه والدعوة القائمة إلى توحيد الله تعالى والعلم بتأويل كتاب الله تعالى وشريعة الرسول صلوات الله عليه بانتهاء الأمر بمن يعتقد إمامته إلى من لا وجود له من نسله من نحو مائتي سنة مع حاجة الأمة إليه لو كان إمامًا، وعدم الخوف الذي هو الشرط في

---

[1] نفسه: + فيه، پ

استتار من يكون إمامًا فيقال: إنه خائف، وانغماد السيف المسلول كان في إهراق دم آل محمد وشيعتهم من جهة بني أمية والطلقاء من آل عباس فيقال: إنه لأجله هارب، ثم بعدم دعوة قائمة له يدعو إلى الله بإمامته مع افتراضها ولزومه إقامتها من حيث لو كان إمامًا ولو بالستر، إذ لا يكون نبيًا ولا إمامًا من لا يكون له دعوة، وعدم علم التأويل لما اختلُف فيه من كتاب الله وتفسيره والحلال والحرام والشريعة عند أصحابه المنتحلين إمامته مع افتراض نشره عليه من حيث لو كان إمامًا ومصير ذلك كله من أكبر الشهادات ببطلان إمامته، ثبتت لإسماعيل عليه السلام من حيث أنها في عقب جعفر مع بطلان مقالات الأخر من الأولاد، وإذا ثبت لإسماعيل الإمامة وكانت لا تثبت إلا لمن له عقب كانت الإمامة بعد إسماعيل لولده محمد عليه السلام. إذاً الإمامة بعد إسماعيل لولده.

البرهان الخامس: لما كان كل شيء أخرجته القدرة إلى الكون يختص بصفات يباين بها غيره، وكان الشيء الذي يختلف فيه لا سبيل إلى معرفته بالحقيقة إلا من جهة[1] الصفات المختص بها نوعه وطلبها فيه، وكان إذا كان لا سبيل إلى معرفته بالحقيقة إلا من جهة الصفات المختص بها نوعه وطلبها فيه، فإذا ثبتت صفاته ووجدت فيه صح وثبت أنه عين الشيء، كالشيء المختلف في كونه أترجًا إذا ردت صفاته في ميزان الاعتبار التي هي الجداول كما أثبتناه آخر البرهان إلى صفات نوع الأترجية، وكانت صفاته قد شغلت جداول صفات نوع الأترجية بتمامها، لم يختلف في صحة كونه أترجًا، وإذا اعتبرت صفاته فوجدت قد شغلت بعض الجداول وخلا منها بعض لم يشك في بطلان كونه أترجًا. وكان أمر الإمام في إمامته مشابهًا في جميع الحالات لذلك من كون الإمام ذا خصال نفسانية[2] وسعادات جسمانية[3] وتعلق صحة إمامته بوجود تلك

---

[1] جهة: جهات، ز، پ
[2] نفسانية: نفسانيات، پ، هـ

الخصال والسعادات، وكنا إذا اعتمدنا في معرفة صحة إمامة محمد وموسى وعبدالله بني جعفر، وزيد بن علي وغيرهم ممن تقدم ميزان الاعتبار بالجداول التي أقمناها على صفات الإمام اختلفت جداولهم بوجود بعض الخصال وعدم بعض إلا جدول إسماعيل، ثبت أن الإمامة لإسماعيل، وإذا ثبت لإسماعيل كان عقبه مع عدم علة مانعة بها أولى. إذاً الإمامة لإسماعيل وعقبه.

جدول صفات نوع الأترج ليتبين به ما ليس بأترج مقدمة لجدول الإمامة.

[Text of the tables at the end of *miṣbāḥ* 6 *burhān* 5. For the format of these tables and an illustration of an *utrūj*, see plates 15 - 20]

مقدمة لجدول الإمامة

الذات؛ كون شكله إلى الطول، مجيب الجهات؛ كون لونه أصفر؛ كون رائحته عطرة؛ كون شحم له، طعم حلو؛ كون لب له، طعم حامض؛ كون النوع حقًا

ذات غير مختلفة في كونها أترجًا؛ شكله إلى الطول مجيب الجهات؛ لونه أصفر؛ رائحته عطرة؛ له شحم وطعمه حلو؛ له لب طعمه حامض؛ [كان] أترجًا[1] حقًا

ذات مختلفة في كونها أترجًا؛ شكله إلى الطول؛ لونه أصفر؛ لا رائحة له عطرة[2]؛ لا شحم له؛ لا لب له؛ ليس بأترج حقًا وهو معمول مُزَوَّر

---

[3] جسمانية: جسمانيات، پ

[1] وهو اترج، ٧٤

[2] عطرة: -، ز

ذات مختلفة في كونها أترجًا؛ شكله مدور؛ لونه أصفر؛ رائحته عطرة؛ شحمه حامض؛ لا لب له؛ ليس بأترج وهو سفرجلة

جداول اعتبار صحة إمامة المتقدمين الذين انقرضوا[1] ليتبيّن[2] به بطلان إمامة من ليس بإمام منهم

الأسماء والكون من ذرية النبوة من نسل الحسين عليه السلام؛ وجود العقب المنصوص عليه من دون غيره لعلة سالبة للعقب شرف الإمامة؛ وجود العلم بما أنزل الله من جهة العقب المنصوص عليه؛ وجود العمل بأحكام الله تعالى من جهة العقب المنصوص عليه؛ وجود الأمر بالمعروف والنهي عن المنكر من جهة العقب المنصوص عليه؛ وجود الدعوة إلى طاعة الله تعالى من جهة العقب المنصوص عليه؛ الكون إمامًا حقًا.

جعفر الصادق عليه السلام كان من ذرية الحسين بن علي عليه السلام؛ عقبه والمنصوص عليه موجود وهو الحاكم بأمر الله أمير المؤمنين سلام الله عليه؛ علمه بأحكام الله قائم من جهة المنصوص عليه من عقبه[3]؛ عمله بأحكام الله قائم من جهة العقب المنصوص عليه؛ أمره[4] بالمعروف والنهي عن المنكر قائم من جهة المنصوص عليه؛ دعوته إلى طاعة الله قائمة من جهة المنصوص عليه من عقبه؛ إمام حقًا.

علي بن محمد صاحب البصرة حسني لم يكن من ولد الحسين؛ ليس

---

[1] انقرضوا: انفرضوا، ز

[2] ليتبين: ليبين، ز و ٤٨

[3] من عقبه: -، ٤٨

[4] امره: وجود امره، ٧٤

بموجود منصوصه[١]؛ ليس بموجود علمه؛ ليس بموجود عمله؛ ليس بموجود أمره بالمعروف ونهيه عن المنكر؛ ليس بموجود دعوته؛ ليس بإمام

المأمون العباسي لم يكون من ذرية الحسين؛ ليس بموجود؛ ليس بموجود؛ ليس بموجود؛ ليس بموجود؛ ليس بموجود؛ ليس بإمام.

زيد بن علي كان من نسل الحسين عليه السلام؛ ليس بموجود؛ ليس بموجود؛ ليس بموجود؛ ليس بموجود؛ ليس بموجود؛ ليس بإمام.

محمد بن جعفر كان من نسل الحسين؛ ليس بموجود؛ ليس بموجود؛ ليس بموجود؛ ليس بموجود؛ ليس بموجود؛ ليس بإمام.

عبد الله بن جعفر كان من نسل الحسين؛ ليس بموجود؛ ليس بموجود؛ ليس بموجود؛ ليس بموجود؛ ليس بموجود؛ ليس بإمام.

موسى بن جعفر كان من نسل الحسين عليه السلام؛ ليس بموجود؛ ليس بموجود؛ ليس بموجود؛ ليس بموجود؛ ليس بموجود؛ ليس بإمام.

إسماعيل بن جعفر من ذرية النبوة ونسل الحسين عليه السلام؛ عقبه المنصوص عليه موجود وهو الحاكم بأمر الله أمير المؤمنين سلام الله عليه؛ علمه بما أنزل الله تعالى موجود من جهة عقبه المنصوص عليه؛ عمله[٢] بأحكام الله موجود قائم[٣] بموجود[٤] المنصوص عليه من عقبه؛ أمره بالمعروف ونهيه عن المنكر قائم من جهة المنصوص عليه من عقبه؛ دعوته إلى طاعة الله تعالى قائمة[٥] من جهة المنصوص عليه من عقبه؛ إمامٌ حقًا.

---

[١] منصوصه: منصوصا، ز

[٢] عمله: علمه، ز

[٣] قائم: وقائم، ٤٨

[٤] بموجود: بالوجود، ٧٤؛ بموجوده، ٤٨

[٥] قائمة: قائم، ٧٤، ز، ٤٨

البرهان السادس: لما كانت الحاجة إلى الإمام إنما كانت لأن يكون حافظًا رسوم الشريعة وعين الكتاب من أن يزاد فيها أو ينقص منها[١]، وداعيًا إلى الإسلام[٢] بالترغيب والترهيب، ووافداً بالمسلمين على ربهم يوم الحساب، ومخرجًا إياهم من اختلاف ما يختلفون بعلمه وتفسيره، وقاضيًا بما[٣] يحدث من الحوادث بينهم بما أنزل الله، ومستغفراً لهم، ومصليًا بهم، ومطهراً لهم بأخذ ما أمر الله بأخذه عنهم على ما يراه، ومقيمًا عليهم الحدود، ومجيبًا عما يردّ إليه مما يراد معرفته من أمر الدين، ومبلغًا إلى الأمة ما قاله الرسول، وساداً مسده في جميع ما كان يتعلق به من طلب مصالح الأمة، وكان لولا هذه الأسباب لا يحتاج إلى إمام[٤]، وكان من لا يكون حافظًا رسوم الشريعة ولا مخرجًا للناس من اختلافهم إذا ردوا إليه ولا قاضيًا ولا قائمًا بجميع ما ذكرناه مقام الرسول بأمره، فليس بإمام. وكان المنتظر الذي تنتظره كل فرقة من الشيعة ممن يقول بإمامة محمد وعبد الله وموسى وغيرهم لا حافظًا للكتاب ولا الشريعة ولا مخرجًا للناس من اختلافاتهم[٥] ولا قاضيًا فيما يحدث بينهم من الحوادث ولا مستغفراً لهم ولا مصليًا بهم ولا داعيًا ولا مطهراً ولا مقيمًا للحدود ولا مجيبًا ولا وافداً ولا مبلغًا ولا ساداً مسد الرسول في جميع ما كان يتعلق به بأمره، ثبت أنه ليس بإمام. وإذا ثبت أنه ليس بإمام، كان منه الإيجاب بأن شرف الإمامة وتاج النص والتوقيف لو كان فيهم لكان لا ينقطع في نسل من له نسل منهم إمارتها، وإذا انقطع فيهم ذلك مع ثبوت كون

---

[١] فيها...منها: فيهما...منهما، ز، پ، هـ
[٢] الاسلام: الله، ٧٤
[٣] بما: فيما، پ
[٤] امام: الامام، پ
[٥] اختلافاتهم: اختلافهم، ز

الإمامة في عقب جعفر عليه السلام ووجود إمارتها في عقب إسماعيل، صح أن الإمامة لإسماعيل ولعقبه. إذاً الإمامة لإسماعيل وذريته من دون غيرهم.

البرهان السابع: لما قال النبي: «كائن في أمتي ما كان في الأمم الخالية حذوَ النعل بالنعل والقذة بالقذة»، وكان الله تعالى قد أخبر بكون فتية آمنوا بربهم وأنه زادهم هدى وربط على قلوبهم، وأنهم لما رأوا قومهم قد اتخذوا أولياء من دون الله آووا إلى الكهف ولبثوا فيه ثلاث مائة سنة وتسع سنين على شدة حالهم التي أعلم الله نبيه صلى الله عليه وآله بها، فقال: «لَوِ اطَّلَعْتَ عَلَيْهِم لَوَلَّيْتَ مِنْهُم فِرَاراً وَلَمُلِئْتَ مِنْهُم رُعْبًا» [١٨: ١٨]، وفرج الله عنهم بعد هذه الحالة الشديدة والمدة الطويلة. وصح كون مثل هذا في ذرية[١] محمد صلى الله عليه التي هي أمته بالحقيقة قذة بقذة بكون الأئمة بعد نبيها صلوات الله وسلامه عليه وعليهم تحت الغضب والظلم والخوف والاستتار محفوظين مكلوئين متقلبين في الآفاق ذات يمين وشمال[٢] مدة ثلاثمائة سنة وتسع سنين إلى وقت خروج المهدي بالله أبي محمد عليه السلام وقيامه بالجهاد بالمغرب. وكان استقرار كون ما أخبر الله تعالى به من حديث أصحاب الكهف عن صحته من أمة محمد صلوات الله عليه في نسل إسماعيل من دون نسل أخيه من أولاد جعفر بظهور المهدي بالله عليه السلام بالمغرب الذي بخروجه مجاهداً في سنة تسع وثلاثمائة من هجرة النبي صلى الله عليه وآله وعلى الأئمة من ولده الطاهرين أزال الله عن الأئمة حجاب الخوف وطلعت الشمس من مغربها ودار رحى الدين على قطبه وعاد الحق إلى أهله وصارت أعلامهم مشهورة وراياتهم في الذب عن حقهم منصورة، وكان المهدي بالله عليه السلام الرابع من ولد إسماعيل وسلالته وصفوته، ثبت أن الإمامة لإسماعيل

---

[١] ذرية: امة، ز

[٢] ذات يمين وشمال: ذات طرف يمين، هـ؛ ذات يمين وذات شمال، پ

عليه السلام وذريته[1]. إذاً الإمامة لإسماعيل وعقبه.

المصباح السابع من المقالة الثانية

في وجوب إمامة الحاكم بأمر الله أمير المؤمنين سلام الله عليه وافتراض طاعته واتباعه على المقالات كلها

البرهان الأول: لما كان[2] المسلمون أجمع في اعتقاد الإمامة فرقتين: فرقة تقول بإمامة أبي بكر وتقديمه، وهم المرجئة على ما ينقسمون إليه من أصحاب الرأي والحديث والحنبلي والداودي والمعتزلي وغيرهم، وكان من قولهم واعتقادهم أن من قام، كائنًا من كان من المسلمين، قريشيًا كان أم حبشيًا، وكان له قوة وسلطان ونجدة فأمر بالمعروف ونهى عن المنكر وأقام الحدود وحفظ الأمة وأحيى السنة، فهو إمام واجب بيعته وطاعته ما لزم النهج القويم، وكان من له السلطان الشامخ والملك الباذخ والبرهان القائم والسيف الشاهر في نصرة الإسلام والأمر بالمعروف والنهي عن المنكر وإقامة الحدود وحفظ الثغور ورعاية الجمهور وإحياء السنة وحفظ الجماعة والاجتهاد في الجهاد وقصم ذوي العناد[3] وبسط العدل والرحمة، فضلاً عن سبب النص والتوقيف وشرف الحسب العميم، الحاكم بأمر الله سلام الله عليه، كان منه الإيجاب بأنه إمام واجب عليهم بيعته لازمة لهم طاعته. وفرقة تقول بإمامة أمير المؤمنين علي بن أبي طالب سلام الله عليه، وهم

[1] وذريته: وعقبه، ز، ٧٤

[2] كان: كانت، ٧٤

[3] العناد: الالحاد، ٧٤؛ وقصم قطع ذوي العناد، هـ

الشيعة على ما ينقسمون إليه من زيدي وإمامي وكيساني وغالٍ وغيرهم، وتتفرق هذه الفرقة فرقتين: فرقة تقول بالنص والتوقيف الجلي وفرقة تقول بالنص الخفي. وكان من قول من يقول بالنص الخفي أن من كان من ذرية النبي صلوات الله عليه، حسنيًا كان أم حسينيًا، فهو من العترة وأهل البيت وأن من شهر سيفه منهم وأمر بالمعروف ونهى عن المنكر وكان عالمًا زاهداً سخيًا شجاعًا ورعًا، لزم بقول النبي صلوات الله عليه: «إني تارك فيكم الثقلين كتاب الله وعترتي أهل بيتي فتمسكوا بهما فإنكم لن تضلوا ما أن تمسكتم بهما»، وبقوله عليه السلام: «من لم يجب داعينا أهل البيت أكبه الله لوجهه[١] في النار» فلزم الأمة اتباعه ووجب عليها طاعته. وكان من كان سيفه شاهراً وأمرُه بالمعروف ونهيه عن المنكر قائمًا وعلمه[٢] مبسوطًا وشجاعته وزهده وسخاؤه معروفًا، وهو من سلالة العترة الطاهرة وذرية النبوة فضلاً عن الموجود فيه من شرف النص والتوقيف الحاكم بأمر الله أمير المؤمنين سلام الله عليه، كان من ذلك الإيجاب بأنه إمام واجبة بيعته عليهم لازمة ومقدرة[٣] طاعته لهم. وكان من قول من يقول بالنص الجلي أن الإمامة لا يستحقها بعد الحسين إلا أولاده على العموم، وأن شرفها لا يُستوجب إلا بالنص على الخصوص، وأن الأرض لا تخلو من إمام قائم لله بحقه، إما ظاهراً مكشوفًا وإما خائفًا مغموراً مستوراً، كما قال أمير المؤمنين علي بن أبي طالب عليه السلام، وأن الإمام له معجز به تصح إمامته ويجب اتباعه وبه يمتاز من غيره، وكان الموجود من نسل الحسين عليه السلام الذي قام لله بحقه في أرضه، ظاهراً حيث يبلغه سيفه بعماله وأوليائه ومستتراً حيث لم يشمله[٤] أمره بخلفائه

---

[١] لوجهه: على وجهه، ز

[٢] وعلمه: وعمله، ٧٤

[٣] ومقدرة: ومقدر، ٤٨؛ -، پ

[٤] يشمله: يشتمله، ٤٨

وأولي ولائه، هداية إلى توحيده، ودعاء بإمامته إلى تجريده، وإنذاراً للخلق بوعده ووعيده، وبسطًا للعدل في عبيده، وأمراً بما أمر به من معروفه، ونهيًا عما نهى عنه عن[1] منكره، وله معجز بل معجزات وإخبار بالكائنات قبل كونها، وإظهار للعلوم المكنونة والحكم الموضوعة في جميع ما جاء به النبي صلوات الله عليه من الكتاب[2] والشريعة، وخصوصًا في الحروف البسيطة التي في أوائل السور من القرآن التي ضاق بالأمم قاطبة الطريق[3] إلى الخوض فيها وابتغاء تأويلها كما خاضوا في تفسير غيرها، فأصبحوا بآرائهم عاجزين فضلاً عن علوم اللميات في غيرها التي حرسها الله به وبأمثاله من الأئمة عليهم السلام عن أن يمسها إلا المطهرون فقال: «إِنَّهُ لَقُرْآنٌ كَرِيمٌ، فِي كِتَابٍ مَكْنُونٍ لا يَمَسُّهُ إلاّ الْمُطَهَّرُونَ» [٥٦: ٧٧-٧٩]. وقال: «فِي صُحُفٍ مُكَرَّمَةٍ مَرْفُوعَةٍ مُطَهَّرَةٍ بِأَيْدِي سَفَرَةٍ كِرَامٍ بَرَرَةٍ» [٨٠: ١٣-١٦]، فامتاز بذلك عن غيره كما امتاز في غير ذلك الحاكم بأمر الله أمير المؤمنين سلام الله عليه لا غيره، كان منه الإيجاب بأنه هو الذي لم تخل الأرض منه في زماننا بوجود الشرط من القيام لله بحقه ظاهراً ومستتراً، والإعجاز بعلمه وإخباره عن الغيب إذ الإمام من يقوم لله بحقه ظاهراً [حيث] أمكنه أم خفيًا، لا من يضيع حق الله فلا يقوم به لا ظاهراً ولا خفيًا، وإذا كان الذي لا تخلو الأرض منه بوجوده ووجود ما هو متعلق بالإمامة مما هو ثمرة النص والتوقيف من الأمر بالمعروف والنهي عن المنكر والإعجاز[4] الحاكم بأمر الله أمير المؤمنين سلام الله عليه لا غيره فاتباعه بقولهم واجب عليهم وطاعته لازمة لهم. وكان إذا كان المسلمون فرقتين وأوجبت كل فرقة إمامته بمقالاتهم فيها، فإمامته ثابتة. إذاً الحاكم بأمر

---

[1] عن: من، ز
[2] من الكتاب: بالكتاب، پ
[3] الطريق: كل الطريق، هـ
[4] والاعجاز: + بعلمه واخباره عن الغيب، ٧٤

الله أمير المؤمنين سلام الله عليه إمام مفترض الطاعة.

البرهان الثاني: لما جعل محمد صلوات الله عليه حجة على بطلان ما عليه الكفار من العكوف على الأصنام حين[١] دعاهم إلى الإسلام ودعوه إلى عبادة الأوثان عدم دعوة الأوثان في الدنيا والآخرة فقال: «مَا لِي أَدْعُوكُم إِلىَ النَجَاة وَتَدْعُونَني إِلىَ النَار تَدْعُونَني لأَكْفُرَ بالله وَأَشْرِكَ بِه مَا لَيْسَ لِي بِه عِلْمٌ وَأَنَا أَدْعُوكُم إِلىَ العَزِيزِ الغَفَّار لا جَرَمَ أَنَّمَا تَدْعُونَني إِلَيْه لَيْسَ لَهُ دَعْوَةٌ فِي الدُنْيَا وَلا فِي الآخِرَةِ وَأَنَّ مَرَدَّنَا إِلىَ الله وَأَنَّ الْمُسْرِفِينَ هُم أَصْحَابُ النَار» [٤٠: ٤١-٤٣] ، كان قيام الدعوة للأنبياء والأئمة عليهم السلام القائمين[٢] مقامهم ظاهراً أم خفيًا أكبر حجة لله وأوضح محجة[٣] إلى الله، وإذا كان قيام الدعوة وكونها أكبر حجة وكانت دعوة الحاكم بأمر الله أمير المؤمنين سلام الله عليه قائمة لا يخلو بلد ولا بقعة من بلدان الإسلام إلا ودعاته فيها يدعون إلى طاعة الله بإمامته وإلي توحيد الله بواسطته ظاهراً حيث أمكن وباطنًا حيث أعجز، كان من ذلك الإيجاب أنه[٤] إمام مفترض الطاعة. إذاً الحاكم بأمر الله أمير المؤمنين سلام الله عليه إمام مفترض الطاعة.

البرهان الثالث: لما كانت الإمامة لا تصح إلا بالنص والتوقيف، وكان النص من النبي جاء في علي، ومن علي جاء في الحسن، ومنه[٥] في الحسين، ومنه في علي، ومنه في محمد، ومنه في جعفر عليهم السلام، يقوم خلف مقام سلف، وكان النص منتهيًا إلى الحاكم بأمر الله أمير المؤمنين سلام الله عليه وتحياته والنص فيه موجود، كان الحاكم بأمر الله أمير المؤمنين إمامًا مفترض الطاعة.

---

[١] حين: حتى، ز
[٢] القائمين: -، ٤٨
[٣] محجة: حجته، پ
[٤] أنه: بانه، ٧٤
[٥] منه: من الحسن جاء في، ٧٤

البرهان الرابع: لما كانت العلة التي لأجلها وجب وجود الإمام وجوب حفظ الشريعة والكتاب من أن يزاد فيهما أو[١] ينقص منهما بعد ما كان ممكنًا الزيادة فيهما والنقصان منهما[٢]، والدعوة إليهما وإلى الإسلام بالترغيب والترهيب، وحاجة الأمة إلى من يصلي بهم، ويعلّمهم معالم دينهم، ويخرجهم مما يختلفون فيه، ويقضي فيما بينهم بما أنزل الله، ويستغفر لهم، ويطهرهم، ويقيم عليهم الحدود، ويجيب عما يرد إليه، ويبلغهم ما قاله الرسول صلى الله عليه وآله، ويأخذ منهم حقوق الله على ما يراه، ويسد مسد النبي صلوات الله عليه فيما بين ظهرانيهم بأمره عليه السلام، وكان من كان حافظًا للكتاب والشريعة على رسومها ويدعو إلى الإسلام وإليهما ويذب[٣] بالترغيب والترهيب عنهما ويصلي بالناس ويعلمهم معالم دينهم ويخرجهم مما يختلفون فيه إذا رجعوا فيه إليه ويقضي بما أنزل الله ويستغفر الله لمن يستغفره ويطهرهم ويقيم عليهم الحدود ويجيب عما يرد إليه من المسائل ويبلغهم ما قاله الرسول صلوات الله عليه على صيغته ويأخذ منهم حقوق الله تعالى وينفقها في وجهها ويسد مسد النبي صلى الله عليه وآله فيما بين الأمة بأمره بنص القائم مقامه فهو إمام، وكان الحاكم بأمر الله أمير المؤمنين قائمًا بجميع ذلك ساداً مسد النبي صلى الله عليه وآله بنص من تقدمه موجوداً فيه هذه الأفعال والخصال، كان إمامًا واجب الطاعة. إذاً الحاكم بأمر الله أمير المؤمنين سلام الله عليه إمام مفترض الطاعة.

البرهان الخامس: لما كان وجود الإمام واجبًا لا بد منه في عبادة الله تعالى، وكان الله تعالى لا يخلي أرضه في كل زمان من إمام قائم لله

---

[١] او: + ان، هـ
[٢] منهما: فيهما، ٨٤
[٣] ويذب: + ويرغب، ٤٨

بحقه وبالهداية إلى توحيده حجة منه على عباده، ووافداً بهم إلى[1] ربهم «يَوْمَ نَدْعُو كُلَّ أُنَاسٍ بِإِمَامِهِم» [١٧: ٧١]، وكان من يجرّ شرف الإمامة إلى حوزته ويدعيه في زماننا الحاكم بأمر الله أمير المؤمنين سلام الله عليه، وأحمد بن إسحاق من آل عباس المقيم ببغداد، والهاروني الحسيني الزيدي المقيم بهوسم في نواحي جيلان، وعمر النزواني المقيم في جبال عمان، والأموي المقيم بالأندلس وما وراء القيروان، والمسمون أنفسهم السادة[2] بالأحساء من أولاد الجنابي. وكانت هذه الخصال المانعة من استحقاق الإمامة قد شغلت الجداول التي أقمناها آخر البرهان باسمائهم إلا جداول الحاكم بأمر الله أمير المؤمنين التي خلت منها، كان منه الحكم بأن الحاكم بأمر الله أمير المؤمنين سلام الله عليه مع بطلان استحقاق الغير الإمامة وامتناع خلو الأرض من الإمام إمام مفترض الطاعة. إذاً الحاكم بأمر الله أمير المؤمنين سلام الله عليه إمام واجب الطاعة على الجماعة.

جداول الخصال المانعة من استحقاق الإمامة على مثال العريضة ليعرف منها بطلان إمامة من يدعيها ووجوبها للمحق منهم الصادق.

[Text of the table at the end of *miṣbāḥ* 7, *burhān* 5. For the format of this table see plates 21 - 26]

الأسماء: الكون من غير نسل الحسين عليه السلام يمنع الإمامة؛ الكون في النفس والجسد غير طاهر يمنع الإمامة؛ الرعونة[3] التي هي الحكم في كل شيء بجهالة واستعمال الخيرات في الوجوه[4] المذمومة تمنع

---

[1] الى: على، هـ، ٧٤

[2] السادة: + المقيمون، پ، ٤٨

[3] الرعونة: الدعوة، ز، ٧٤ و ٤٨

[4] الوجوه: وجوه، ز

الإمامة؛ الخلو من العلوم الدينية التي هي المعرفة بالحلال والحرام والتنزيل والتأويل يمنع الإمامة؛ الاستهانة بأحكام الله والأمر بالمعروف والنهي عن المنكر وإقامة الدعوة إلى الله يمنع الإمامة؛ الخلو من شرف النصّ والتوقيف[١] مقام الرسول عليه السلام وعلى آله يمنع الإمامة.

أحمد بن إسحاق المقيم ببغداد: كان من غير نسل الحسين عليه أفضل السلام؛ غير طاهر في النفس بأكله السحت وإثمانه[٢] الخمر التي تباع له في ضياعه ببغداد وسوادها والجهل المتمكن فيه لقلة العلم[٣]؛ موجود فيه بإدعائه ما ليس يعلمه[٤] من الإمامة واستعماله[٥] من الخيرات في غير وجوه محامد الدين؛ خال من العلوم المتعلقة بتوحيد الله الدينية ومعوّله[٦] على رؤساء المرجئة مثل أبي بكر الباقلاني[٧] وغيره؛ مستهين بأحكام الله لا يأمر بالمعروف ولا ينهى عن المنكر في داره وحواشيه[٨] فضلاً عن غيرهم من المسلمين؛ خال من نصّ القائم مقام الرسول وهو منصوب الأمير السعيد بهاء الدولة رحمة الله عليه[٩].

الهاروني الحسني[١٠] المقيم بهوسم: كان من غير نسل الحسين عليه أفضل السلام؛ غير طاهر في الجسد بالبرص المتمكن منه ولا في النفس

---

[١] والتوقيف: والتولية من جهة القائم، ٤٨، ٧٤

[٢] اثمانه: اثمان، پ

[٣] فيه لقلة العلم: قلد بالعلم، ٤٨؛ المقلد بالحلم، ٧٤؛ والجهل منه بقلة العلم، ز

[٤] يعلمه: الحكم، پ

[٥] يعلمه من الامامة واستعماله: بعمله من الاقامة والاستعمالة، ٤٨، ٧٤

[٦] الدينية ومعوله: منع الرغبة ومشغوله، ٤٨؛ مع الرغبة، ٧٤

[٧] الباقلاني: البغدادي، پ؛ البلاد، ز؛ البلادياني، ٧٤

[٨] وحواشيه: ويواسيه، ٤٨، ٧٤؛ وحو، ز

[٩] رحمة الله عليه: رحمه، ٧٤

[١٠] الحسني: الحسيني، ز

بجهله توحيد الله تعالى جل جلاله؛ موجود فيه[١] حكمه[٢] في كل شيء بجهالة[٣] وجوابه عما يسأل عنه بما لا[٤] يعلم من مذهبه ولا مذهب غيره؛ خالٍ من العلوم المتعلقة بتوحيد الله ومعوّله على أقاويل الحشوية وغيرهم[٥]؛ موجود فيه الاستهانة بأحكام الله، يخلو[٦] بلدان المسلمين من دعوته إلى الله تعالى؛ خالٍ من شرف النصّ والتوقيف[٧] وهو كغيره ممن لم يرث[٨] الإمامة.

عمر النزواني المقيم بجبال عمان[٩]: كان من غير نسل الحسين عليه السلام؛ غير طاهر في الجسد بالبرص المتمكن منه في أكثر يده[١٠] وفي النفس بالجهل؛ موجود فيه بادعائه ما ليس يعلمه[١١]؛ خالٍ من العلوم الدينية؛ موجود فيه الاستهانة بأحكام الله لا يأمر بالمعروف ولا ينهى عن المنكر؛ خالٍ من النص والتوقيف.

الأموي المقيم بالأندلس: كان من غير نسل الحسين عليه السلام؛ غير طاهر بكونه من شجرة[١٢] الزقوم الذين هم بنو أمية[١٣]؛ موجود فيه بادعائه ما ليس من شانه؛ خالٍ من العلوم؛ موجود فيه الاستهانة

---

[١] فيه: – ز و پ

[٢] حكمه: بحكم، ٤٨؛ بحكمه، ٧٤

[٣] بجهالة: بجهله، ٧٤

[٤] عنه بما لا: منه ما لا، پ

[٥] خال من العلوم...وغيرهم: الخلو من العلوم الدينية التي هي المعرفة بالحلال والحرام والتنزيل والتأويل يمنع الامامة، ٧٤

[٦] الله يخلو: الله في الخلق، ٤٨؛ الله بل يخلو، پ

[٧] التوقيف: التوفيق، ز

[٨] يرث: يورث، پ

[٩] عمان: عمارة، ٤٨، ز، ٧٤؛ عثمان(؟)، پ

[١٠] يده: يديه، ٤٨، ٧٤

[١١] يعلمه: بعله، ٤٨

[١٢] شجرة: شجر، ز

[١٣] غير طاهر بكون...بنو امية: غير طاهر لشربه الخمر، ٧٤

بأحكام ما[1] يجريه في رعيته بغير سيرة النبي صلوات الله عليه؛ خالٍ من النص والتوقيف.

المسمون أنفسهم السادة المقيمون بالأحساء[2]: كائنون من غير نسل الحسين عليه السلام؛ غير طاهرين لشربهم الخمر؛ موجود فيهم بإنفاق مالهم في غير محامد[3] الدين؛ موجود فيهم الاستهانة بأحكام الله تعالى[4] ذكره باستحلالهم المحرمات؛ خالون من العلوم الدينية؛ خالون من النص والتوقيف.

الحاكم بأمر الله أمير المؤمنين سلام الله عليه: كان من نسل الحسين عليه السلام؛ طاهراً[5] في الجسد والنفس[6]؛ منفق ماله في محامد[7] الدين وصلاحه؛ عالم بالحلال والحرام والقضايا والأحكام؛ آمر بالمعروف وناهٍ عن المنكر؛ منصوص عليه من آبائه الطاهرين من ذرية الرسول صلى الله عليه وآله.

البرهان السادس: لما كان سمة ما يقال ولا تقوم عليه الآثار والدلالات أن لا يكون صدقًا، وكان سمة ما يقال وتقوم عليه الآثار والدلالات أن يكون صدقًا، وكان ما يقوله الحاكم بأمر الله أمير المؤمنين سلام الله عليه من كونه علويًا حسينيًا إمامًا منصوصًا عليه عالمًا عادلاً ورعًا آمراً بالمعروف وناهيًا عن المنكر شجاعًا زاهداً جامعًا للأخلاق الفاضلة مختاراً

---

[1] ما: -، ٤٨

[2] المقيمون بالاحساء: المعمور بالاحسان، ٤٨؛ بالاحسان، ٧٤

[3] محامد: مجاهد٧٤؛ بجاهد امر، ٤٨

[4] تعالى: -، ٤٨

[5] طاهرا: طاهر، پ، ٧٤

[6] طاهر في الجسد والنفس: طاهر بعقبه، ٤٨، ٧٤

[7] محامد: مجالس، ٧٤

من جهة الله قائمة[١] عليه الآثار والدلالات بمجيء الشهادة بصحة قوله من جهة العلويين الحسنيين والحسينيين بالحرمين عامًا وممن هو في غير ممالكه من جهة العلويين الحسنيين والحسينيين الممتنع شهادتهم من اطراد قول طاعن فيها بأنها لرغبة أو لرهبة الذين ليست شهادتهم في القبول بأقل من شهادة غيرهم بالعكس عناداً والتزامهم بيعته وإمامته خاصًا، وقيام آثار عدله الذي يجمع الخاص والعام واستفاض ذكره في الآفاق، وآثار ورعه الذي لا ينكر بتورعه عن أخذ أموال الناس عنوة وتعففه عن الغصب على ما ليس له رحمة[٢] حتى أنه[٣] مات من مات من الغرباء وغيرهم الذين لا يحضرهم وارث وتركوا ما تركوا لا يهز[٤] قناة ورعه طمع في مال ولا يحمله على ارتكاب زلة شره في ظلم نساء ورجال فأمر بإيداعه دار الوديعة التي أوجبت سياسته[٥] نصبها بحسن عدله لحفظ أموال المسلمين وبطلب الوارث وإيصال الحقوق إليهم، وآثار أمره بالمعروف الذي لا ينكر كيفية سيرته فيه بانتصابه ليله ونهاره لتقوية كلمة الحق وإغاثة المظلوم وعمارة المساجد وهدم الكنائس وحفظ جماعة الصلاة وإقامة رسوم الشريعة وتأييدها والحدود وبسط العدل في الرعية والجري فيها بالعفو والإحسان حتى أن الأمم الذين شملهم ظل أمره في مهد الأمن يتقلبون لا يمسهم سوء ولا هم يحزنون، وآثار نهيه عن المنكر[٦] الذي شاع[٧] في الآفاق خبره من حسمه مواد الفسق[٨] والفجور التي كانوا يرخصون فيها المدعون للإمامة من آل أمية وآل عباس الظاهرة كانت بتلك الأمصار، وآثار جهاده

[١] قائمة: قائما، ٤٨، ز
[٢] رجمة:-، هـ، ٧٤
[٣] انه: اذا (؟)
[٤] يهز: + حركة، ه
[٥] سياسته: سياسة، پ
[٦] المنكر: المنكر عن، ه
[٧] شاع: شاع ظاهر، ه
[٨] الفسق: الفسوق، ٤٨

في سبيل الله وحفظه للثغور[1] وتأليفه للجمهور وإيهانه كلمة الباطل وما يكون عائداً بالغميزة على الشريعة التي جاء بها جده محمد صلى الله عليه وآله، وآثار علمه بالكتاب والشريعة والأمور الدينية وتأويلاته الشافية عما عجز الخلق والأمم المتقدمون فيه من أصحاب التفاسير عنه، منها المنتشرة من جهة أمنائه وأوليائه في الجزائر وبيانه عن الرموز بما يطمئن إليه النفوس وتزول به الشكوك، وآثار زهده الذي[2] ذاع في الأمصار خبره ركوبًا للحمار ولبسًا للخشن وأكلاً للجريش مع عظيم ما خوله الله، وآثار شجاعته التي لا تخفى وانتشر في العالم ذكرها فلا تطوى بركوبه وحده فذاً[3] مع عظيم ما حباه الله من الملك، وعلم الصغير والكبير من عساكره ورجاله بأن ركوبه ليس إلا لقتلهم على عصيانهم وسابق زلاتهم في أوقات يعجز غيره في مثلها[4] مع الأمر العظيم عن الركوب إلا برجال وقوة، ولا يردعه عن ذلك وجل ولا يقعد به توهم ما لعله يكون من أعدائه إذا كان وحده ولا فشل وتوسطه وحده من غير عدة ولا عدة عالمًا من الناس من عساكره ورجاله الذين كانوا قد بويعوا غير دفعة على قتله وفرق فيهم أموال جمة على قبضه يعجز عن لقائه جيش، فكيف رجل وحده، فلم يعرجه عنه جبن ولا تداخله منهم خور حتى قذف في قلوبهم الرعب وتفرقوا عباديد، كل ذلك إظهاراً أن الله مؤيده وحافظه، وآثار سخائه الذي لا ينصرم[5] يوم ولا أسبوع ولا شهر إلا عن تفرقه بدر دنانير في معونة[6] أولي الحاجات ورفد ذوي الطلبات. كان من ذلك الحكم بأنه من قبيل ما يكون صدقًا وإذا كان صدقًا فهو صادق،

[1] للثغور: في الثغور، پ
[2] الذي: + ظاهر، ه
[3] فذا: وهذه فلا، ه
[4] مثلها: مثله، هـ، ٤٨
[5] ينصرم: يتصوم، ٧٤؛ ينصر، ه
[6] معونة: معرفة، هـ

والصادق بقول الله «كُونُوا مَعَ الصَّادِقِينَ» [٩: ١١٩] واجب الكون في[١] جملته واتباعه. إذاً الحاكم بأمر الله أمير المؤمنين سلام الله عليه إمام صادق واجب اتباعه وطاعته.

البرهان السابع: لما كان كل شيء لا ينفك من[٢] حدّ يكون به منفصلاً عما سواه، وكان ما له حدّ منفصلاً مما لا يتّحد بحدّه غير داخل في حيزه ولا كائن من جملته، وكنا إذا أقررنا حدّ الإمامة فكان الإمام من يكون من ذرية النبوة ولا يكون عقيمًا، ويكون عالمًا بالكتاب والشريعة والأحكام والسنة ظاهراً وباطنًا وعاملاً بها ومنصوصًا عليه من جهة القائم مقام الرسول، وآمراً بالمعروف وناهيًا عن المنكر، وداعيًا إلى الله تعالى بإمامته، يكون كل من كان داعيًا إلى الله تعالى آمراً بالمعروف وناهيًا عن المنكر منصوصًا عليه من جهة الرسول ورعًا عالمًا وهو من ذرية النبوة لا عقيمًا إمام، إذ لا يكون إمامًا من لا يكون من الذرية الطاهرة لحفظ الله تعالى الإمامة في الذرية المختارة، ولا إمامًا مع كونه من الذرية من لا يكون له عقب يحفظ به الإمامة لكونها محفوظة في العقب، ولا مع كونه من الذرية ووجود العقب من لا علم له لحاجة الأمة إلى العلم، ولا مع كون[٣] الذرية والعقب والعلم من لا يكون ورعًا عاملًا لعموم الفساد بعدم الورع، ولا مع كون[٤] الذرية والعقب والعلم والعمل الذي هو الورع من لا يكون منصوصًا عليه لكون مقامه مقام الرسول صلى الله عليه وآله، ولا يكون منصوصًا عليه من لا يأمر بالمعروف ولا ينهى عن المنكر ولا يدعو إلى طاعة الله بإمامته لكون النص علة للأمر والنهي والدعاء إلى الله وكون الأمر والنهي والدعاء إلى الله تعالى ثمرة النص، وكان الحاكم بأمر

---

[١] في: من، ز
[٢] من: عن، پ
[٣] كون: كونه من، ٤٨، ز، ٧٤
[٤] كون: كونه من، ٤٨، ز، ٧٤

الله أمير المؤمنين سلام الله عليه متحداً[١] بهذا الحد لا كغيره كما بينا في الجداول ليعاين آخر البرهان، كان منه أنه إمام مفترض الطاعة. إذاً الحاكم بأمر الله أمير المؤمنين سلام الله عليه الإمام مفترض الطاعة.

جدول لحدّ الإمامة ليبين به من اتّحد بحدّها ومن لم يتّحد بحدّها ويتحقق أن الإمامة لمن منهم حقًا

[Text of the table at the end of *miṣbāḥ* 7, *burhān* 7. For the format of this table see plates 27 - 30]

الأسماء: والكون من ذرية النبوة ونسل الحسين عليه السلام؛ والكون لا عقيمًا والعلم بكتاب الله تعالى وشريعة الرسول ظاهراً تأويلاً؛ العمل بما جاء به النبي من الأحكام والفرائض والسنن والورع[٢] والشجاعة وجميع الأخلاق الفاضلة؛ وجود النص من القائم مقام الرسول صلى الله عليه وآله؛ الأمر بالمعروف والنهي عن المنكر وظهور الأثر فيه؛ الدعوة إلى الله وإلى توحيده بإقامته.

أحمد بن إسحاق[٣]: ليس بعقيم؛ معوّله[٤] على الباقلاني وغيره من رؤساء المرجئة[٥]؛ ليس موصوف بذلك؛ منصوب الأمير السعيد بهاء الدولة بن عضد الدولة[٦]؛ لا يأمر بمعروف ولا ينهى عن منكر؛ لا دعوة له.

الهاروني الحسيني: غير[٧] عقيم؛ لا يوجد عنده علم كتاب الله وشريعة

---

[١] متحدا: متصل، هـ

[٢] والورع: من الورع، ٤٨، ٧٤

[٣] اسحاق: + العباسي، پ

[٤] معوله: ليس هو عالم بكتاب الله معوله، پ

[٥] المرجئة: الحسين، ٧٤

[٦] الدولة: -، ز

[٧] غير: ليس، ٧٤

الرسول صلى الله عليه؛ ليس بمذكور[1] بهذه الخصال؛ ليس بمنصوب ولا هو أيضًا المنصوب عليه؛ لا دعوة له، لا يأمر بالمعروف ولا ينهى عن منكر؛ ولا ظهور شخصه لأحدٍ.

عمر النزواني: غير عقيم؛ ___؛ ___؛ ___؛ ___؛ لا ظهور شخصه لأحد لا في صلاة ولا في غيرها.

المنتظر من نسل موسى في اعتقاد الاثنى عشرية: أصحابه مقرّون بأنه لا عقب له إلى الآن وهو منتظر؛ ___؛ ___؛ ليس بمنصوص ولا هو أيضًا من المنصوص عليه؛ ___؛ لا دعوة له لا يأمر ولا ينهى بل بالضد.

الحاكم بأمر الله أمير المؤمنين سلام الله عليه على ذكره من ذرية الحسين: كان من ذرية النبوة ومن نسل الحسين عليه السلام؛ كان لا عقيمًا لوجود نسله وعالمًا بكتاب الله وشريعة الرسول صلى الله عليه ظاهراً وباطنًا[2]؛ عاملًا[3] بما جاء به النبي جامعًا للخصال على ما بيّناه فيما تقدم[4]؛ منصوص عليه من جهة آبائه الطاهرين إلى علي بن أبي طالب صلوات الله عليه إلى محمد المصطفى صلى الله عليه وآله؛ قائم الأمر بالمعروف والنهي عن المنكر معروف أثره[5] فيها فلا منكر؛ قائم الدعوة إلى الله تعالى وإلى توحيده بإقامة الدعاة في بلاد الإسلام كلها.

قد تبيّن بذلك أن المتّحد بحدّ الإمامة هو الحاكم بأمر الله أمير المؤمنين سلام الله عليه لا غيره من المدعين وطاعته لازمة للأمة كلها.

---

[1] بمذكور: مذكور، ز، پ و ٧٤
[2] باطنا: تاويلا، ٤٨
[3] عاملا: عالما، ٧٤
[4] تقدم: يصنع، ٤٨
[5] أثره: أمرة، ز

وإذ قد أتينا على ما وعدنا به في أول الكتاب بحسب توفيق الله وحسن نظر وليه في أرضه عليه السلام فنقول: إننا إنما اختصرنا من البراهين التي يجمعها كل مصباح على العدة الموردة فيه ولم نطول بزيادة فيها وبمعارضة المعارض عليها في كل باب والجواب عنها لاستيعاب[1] ذلك كله غير هذا الكتاب مما يتلوه، ثم حذاراً من وقوع ملالة تضيق الصدر فتكلّ النفس بها عن الاستيعاب فتبطل الفائدة، وإلا فنعم الله أكثر من أن تحصى، ثم لكون الكتاب مقدمة لما يجيء في كتابنا المعروف براحة العقل من العلوم التي تليق بالمندرج في المعارف الدينية.

وبعد فقد ختمت كتابي بالحمد لله رب العالمين وبالصلاة على خير الأنبياء وخاتمهم محمد المصطفى وعلى نور الأوصياء وسيدهم علي المرتضى، وعلى عمدة[2] الدين الأئمة الهادين[3] أنوار الدجى، وبالسلام والتحيات عليهم وعلى الإمام أبي علي المنصور الحاكم بأمر الله أمير المؤمنين وعلى المنتظرين إلى يوم الدين. (وخص الله تعالى مولانا وسيدنا الإمام المستنصر بالله معد أبي تميم أمير المؤمنين إمام زماننا بأفضل الصلاة والتسليم وحسبنا الله ونعم الوكيل.)

[1] لاستيعاب: لاستقصينا، ه
[2] عمدة: اعمدة، ز
[3] الهادين: الطاهرين، ٧٤

١ - الأعلام

٢ - الجمعات والفرق

٣ - الأماكن

٤ - الكتب

فهرس الجداول والألواح

Plate 18: Table III (ms. Ar. 130)
Plate 19: Table IVa (ms. Ar. 130)
Plate 20: Table IVb (ms Ar. 130)

جدول ٥ : جداول الخصال المانعة من استحقاق الإمامة ليعرف منها بطلان إمامة من يدعيها ووجوبها للمحق منهم الصادق

[آخر البرهان الخامس من المصباح السابع من المقالة الثانية]

Plate 21: Table Va (ms. Ar. 1226)
Plate 22: Table Vb (ms. Ar. 1226)
Plate 23: Table Vc (ms. Ar. 1226)
Plate 24: Table Vd (ms. Ar. 1226)
Plate 25: Table Va–b (ms Ar. 130)
Plate 26: Table Vb–d (ms. Ar. 130)

جدول ٦ : جدول لحدّ الإمامة ليبين به من اتحد بحدّها ومن لم يتّحد بحدّها ويتحقق أن الإمامة لمن منهم حقًا

[آخر البرهان السابع من المصباح السابع من المقالة الثانية]

Plate 27: Table VIa (ms. Ar. 1226)
Plate 28: Table VIb (ms. Ar. 1226)
Plate 29: Table VIc (ms. Ar. 1226)
Plate 30: Table VIa–c (ms. Ar. 130)

الألواح

المصابيح في إثبات الإمامة

مولانا محمد المصطفى صلى الله عليه وعلى آله

الزهد	السخاء	الشجاعة	الورع	العفة	الطهارة والعصمة	النص من الله	الأسماء والوحي من الله تعالى
كان زاهدا لا يرغب في الدنيا وينهى عنها والاعتبار بها عاملا لوجه الله تعالى	كان سخيا لا يدخر لنفسه شيئا يعطي لوجه الله تع أقليا الله تع	كان شجاعا مقداما لا يروعه كثرة الكفار فقام بالدعاء الى الله تعالى قلة عدده حتى علت كلمته	كان ورعا قط لا يطمع في احد وكان للوثاقة ثقته يسمى الامين ويودع عنده الودائع قبل مبعثه	كان عفيفا قط لم يركب معصية ولا زلة ولا شرب خمرا ولا تعاطى فسادا	كان طاهرا مطهرا معصوما لم يعبد وثنا ولا صنما ولا سجد الا الله تعالى	كان منصوصا عليه من الله على ألسن رسله بقول الله تع في السفر الخامس من التورية بشارة به قال موسى اذ نادى الله [illegible]	كان يوحى اليه من الله تعالى

Plate 1: Table Ia (ms. Ar. 1226)

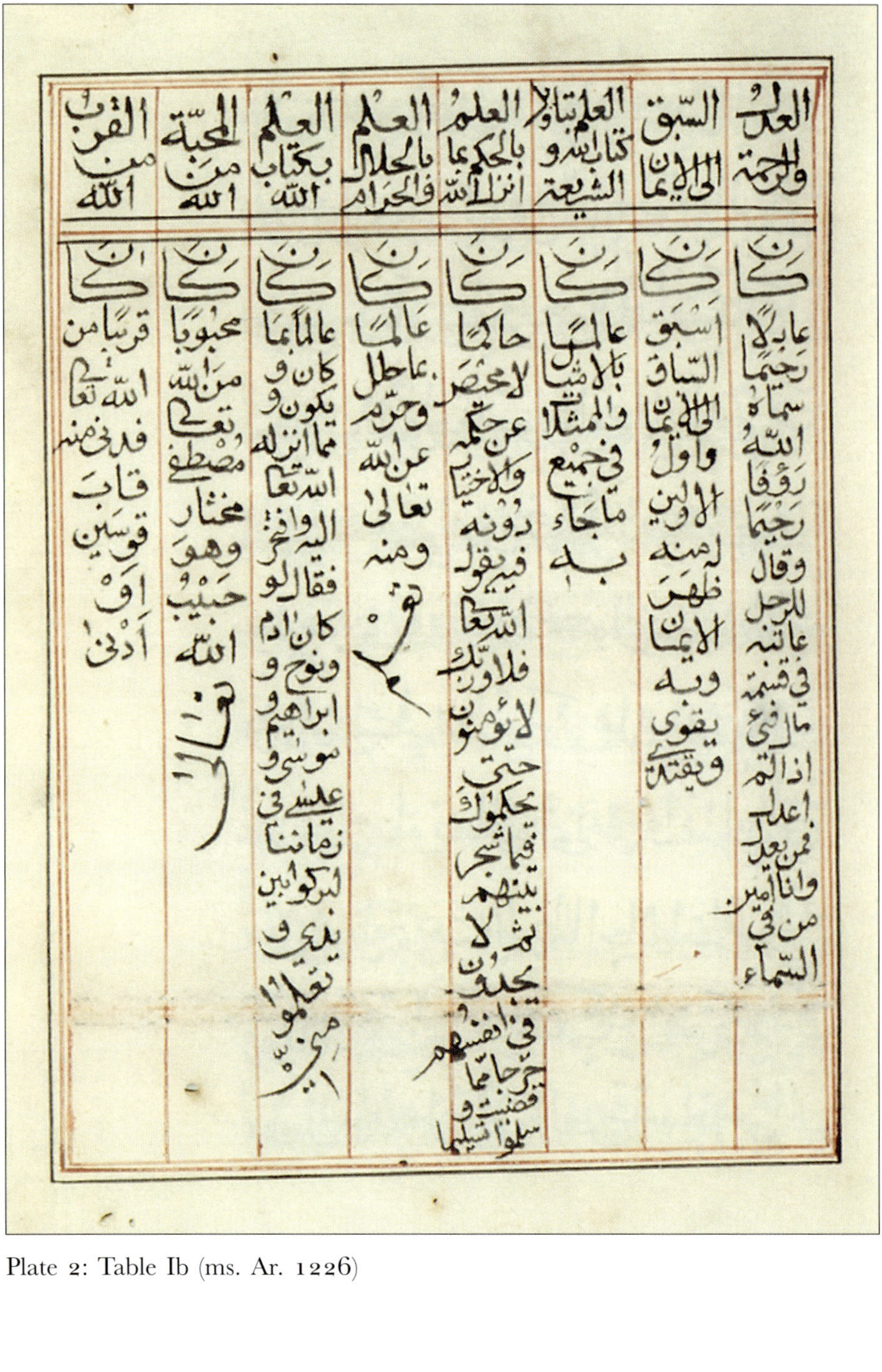

العدل والرحمة	السبق الى الايمان	العلم بتاويل كتاب الله والشريعة	العلم بالحكم بما انزل الله	العلم بالحلال والحرام	العلم بكتاب الله	المحبة من الله	القرب من الله
كان عادلا رحيما سماه الله رؤوفا رحيما وقال للرجل عاتبه في قسمة مال فيء اذا لم اعدل فمن يعدل وانا امين من في السماء	كان اسبق السباق الى الايمان واول الاولين لانه ظهر الايمان وبه يقوى ويقتدى	كان عالما بالاشباه والامثال في جميع ما جاء به	كان حاكما لا مختصر عن حكمه والاختيار دونه فيه يقول الله تعالى فلا وربك لا يؤمنون حتى يحكموك فيما شجر بينهم ثم لا يجدون في انفسهم حرجا مما قضيت ويسلموا تسليما	كان عالما عاطل وحرم عن الله تعالى ومنه تم	كان عالما بما كان ويكون ومما انزله الله تعالى اليه وافتخر فقال لو كان ادم ونوح وابراهيم وموسى وعيسى في زماننا لتركوا بين يدي وتعلموا مني	كان محبوبا من الله تعالى مصطفى مختار وهو حبيب الله تعالى	كان قريبا من الله تعالى فدنى منه قاب قوسين او ادنى

Plate 2: Table Ib (ms. Ar. 1226)

Plate 3: Table Ia (ms. Ar. 130)

Plate 4: Table Ib (ms. Ar. 130)

ابو بكر لم يكن له وحي من الله	لم يكن عفيفا لشرب الخمر في الجاهلية وارتكاب الكبائر	لم يكن منصوصا عليه الا من الله ولا من رسوله	لم يكن طاهرا ولا مطهرا قد عبد الاوثان وسجد لها من	لم يكن شجاعا ولا عرف بالقوة والشجاعة	كان ورعا لا يطمع	كان سخيا منفقا
عمر تلك سبيله	تلك سبيله	تلك سبيله	تلك سبيله	تلك سبيله	كان له ورع	كان سخيا منفقا
عثمان تلك سبيله	تلك سبيله	تلك سبيله	تلك سبيله	تلك سبيله	لم تكن له ورع	كان سخيا منفقا
زيد بن حارث						
طلحة				كان شجاعا		
الزبير				كان شجاعا		
سعيد بن عبد الرحمن						
سلمان					كان ورعا	كان سخيا
ابو ذر					كان ورعا	كان سخيا

Plate 5: Table IIa (ms. Ar. 1226)

Plate 6: Table IIb (ms. Ar. 1226)

Plate 7: Table IIc (ms. Ar. 1226)

مقداد	كان نقيبا من النبي						
عمار	كان من السابقين						
عبد الله بن مسعود	كان من السابقين						
عبد الله بن عباس	كان من السابقين	كان عالما بتفسير	كان عالما فقيها		كان عالما بالحكم		كان قريبا من الرسول وهو ابن عمه
علي ابن ابي طالب عليه الصلوة والسلام	كان عادلا رحيما وعدله صار ... [illegible] معروف بذلك	كان من السابقين الاولين هو ثاني من آمن بالله وبالرسول النبي هو خليفته عليه السلام	كان عالما بكتاب الله تعالى وجميع ما انزل الله تعالى معروفا بذلك	كان عالما بالحلال والحرام معروفا بذلك كان عارفا بالحكم والقضاء قال النبي صلعم اقضاكم علي	كان عالما للتأويل وكتاب الله وكذلك قال النبي صلعم علي صاحب التأويل	كان محبوبا من الله تعالى يقول النبي يوم اعطاه الراية ... [illegible]	كان قريبا من النبي ومن كان قريبا من الرسول فهو قريب من الله وهو اصحاب الكساء يوم المباهلة وابن عمه وخليفته ووصيه عليه السلام

Plate 8: Table IId (ms. Ar. 1226)

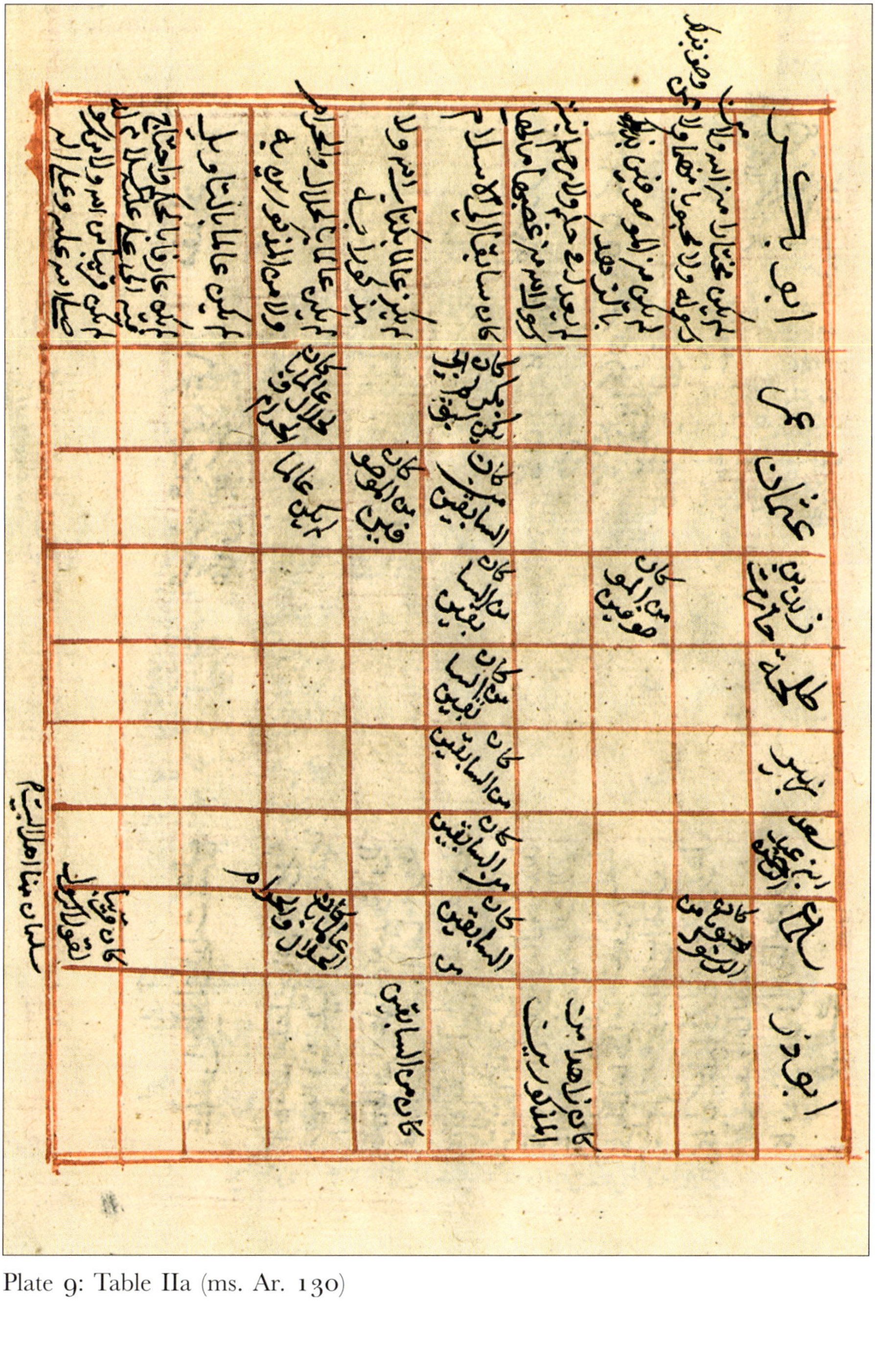

Plate 9: Table IIa (ms. Ar. 130)

وارتكاب الكبائر

ابو بكر لم يكن له من [illegible]	[illegible] لم يكن معصوما [illegible] الرسول	[illegible] الجاهلية	لم يكن قط عبد الأوثان و[illegible] من دون [illegible] مطلقا	لم يكن شجاعا ولا عرف بالقوة والشجاعة	كان ورعا لا يطمع	كان سخيا منفقا	لم يكن عالما [illegible]
عمر تلك سبيله	تلك سبيله	تلك سبيله	تلك سبيله	تلك سبيله	كان له ورع	كان سخيا منفقا	تلك سبيله
عثمان تلك سبيله	تلك سبيله	تلك سبيله	تلك سبيله	تلك سبيله	لم يكن له ورع	كان سخيا	تلك سبيله
زيد حارثة							
طلحة				كان شجاعا			
الزبير				كان شجاعا			
سعد بن عبد الرحمن							
سلمان					كان ورعا	كان سخيا	
ابو ذر					كان ورعا	كان سخيا	

Plate 10: Table IIb (ms. Ar. 130)

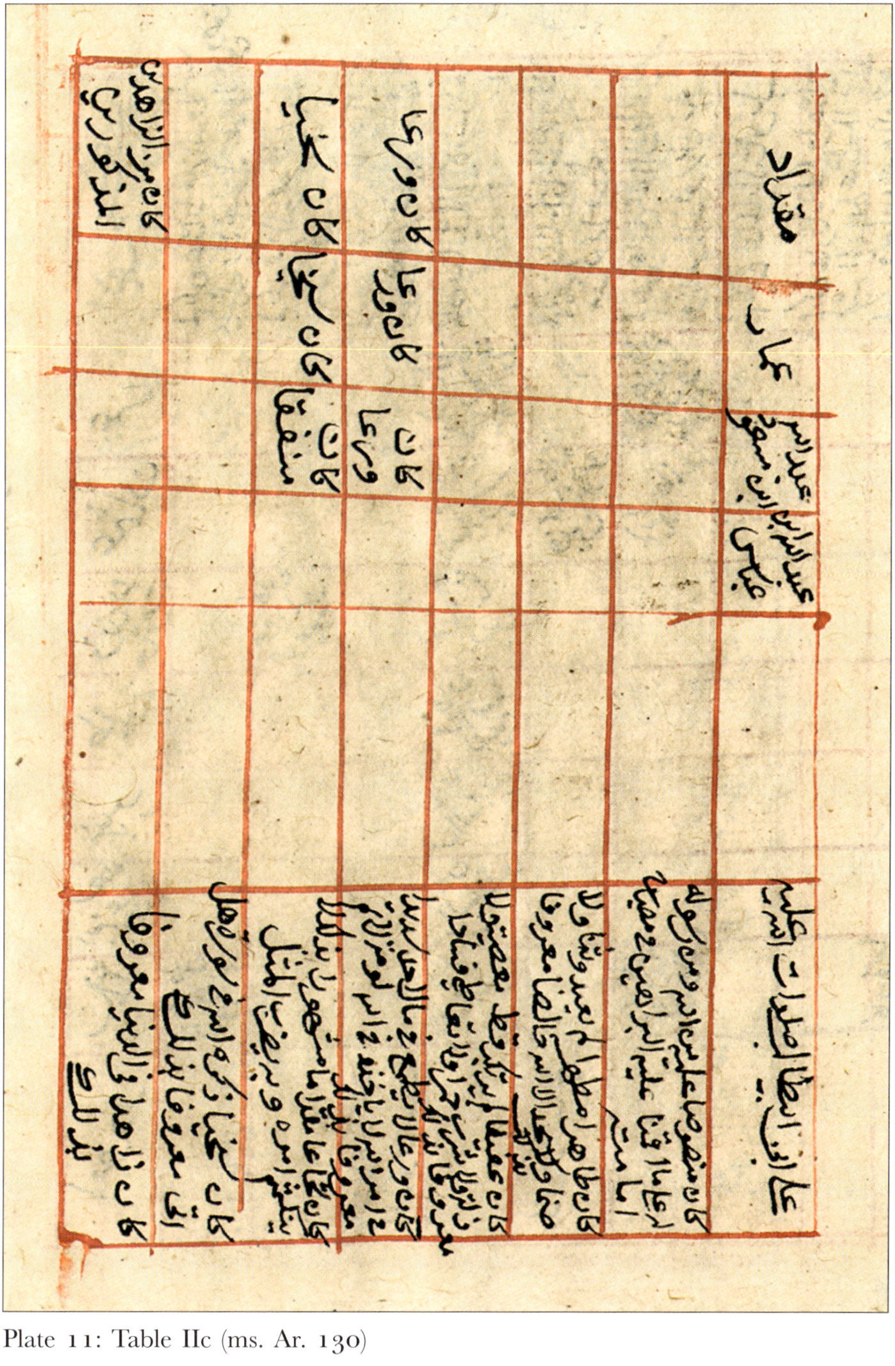

Plate 11: Table IIc (ms. Ar. 130)

مقداد كان من السابقين	عمار كان من السابقين	سعد بن عبد الله كان من السابقين	ابن عباس عبد الله				
كان عادلا في حكمه وعادلا صار عليه الاستقضاء من النبي ... ذلك	كان من السابقين الاولين وهو ثاني من امن بالله وبالرسول التي هي خديجة عليها السلام	كان عالما بكتاب الله تع ذكره وجميع ما انزل الله جل ذكره معروفا بذلك	كان عالما بالحلال والحرام فقيها كان عالما بالحلال والحرام معروفا بذلك	كان عالما بتاويل كتاب الله تع ولذلك قال النبي صلى الله عليه واله علي صاحب التاويل	كان عارفا بالحكم ولذلك قال النبي صلى الله عليه واله علي اقضاكم	كان محبوبا من الله بقول النبي يوم اعطائه الراية في فتح خيبر لاعطين الراية رجلا كرارا غير فرار يحبه الله ورسوله ويحب الله ورسوله	كان قريبا من الرسول وهو ابن عمه كان قريبا من النبي وهو كان قريبا من الرسول فهو قريب من الله وهو من اصحاب الكساء يوم المباهلة وابن عمه وخليفته ووصيه

قد تبين بهذه العريضة ان علي ابن ابي طالب عليه افضل الصلوة والسلام
كان جامعا لجميع ما كان في النبي صلى الله عليه واله من الخصال الا الوحي الذي خصه الله
به نبيه عليه السلام وانه الاحق بمقام رسول الله صلى الله عليه واله وبعده انه هو
الامام من دون الجماعة التي خلت جداولهم من الخصال والله ولي المومنين

Plate 12: Table IId (ms. Ar. 130)

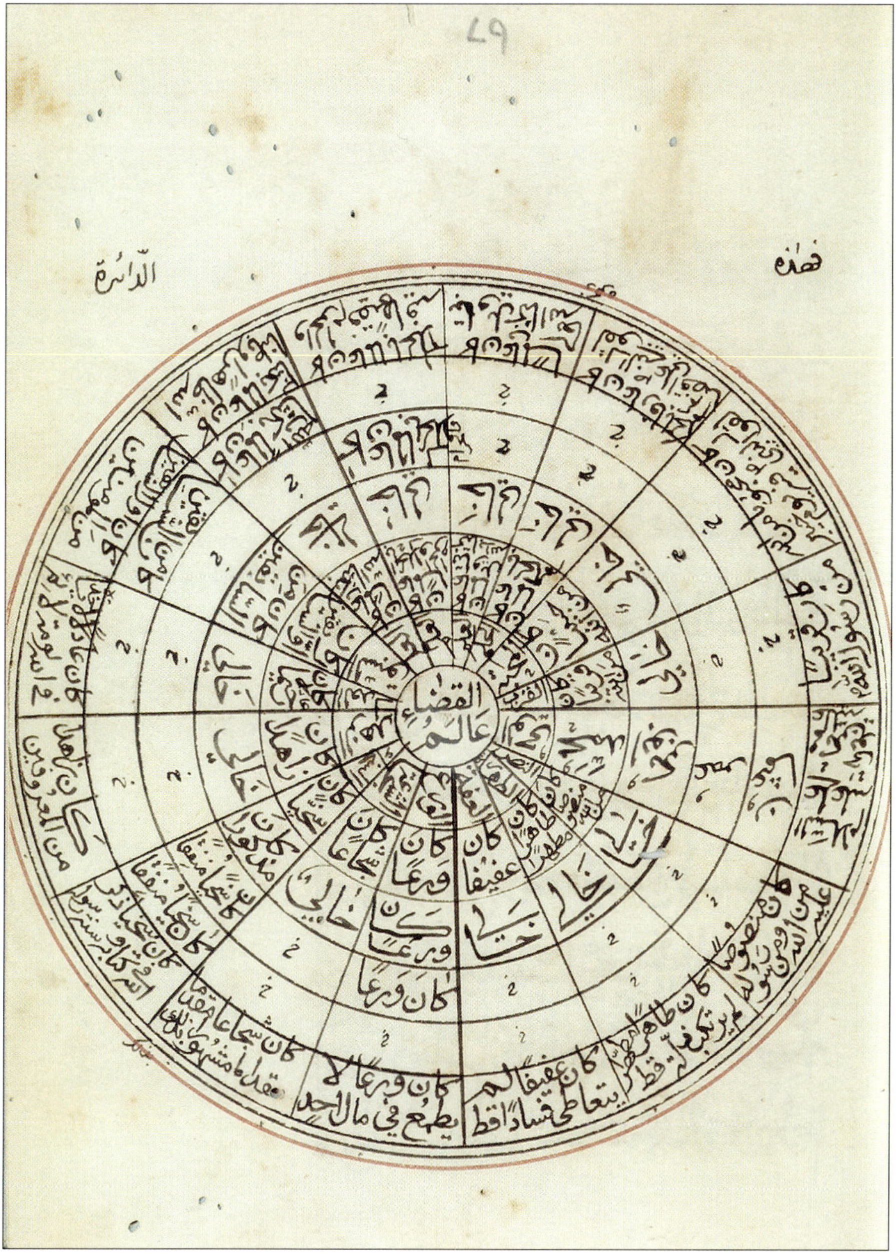

Plate 13: Circular Table (ms. Ar. 1226)

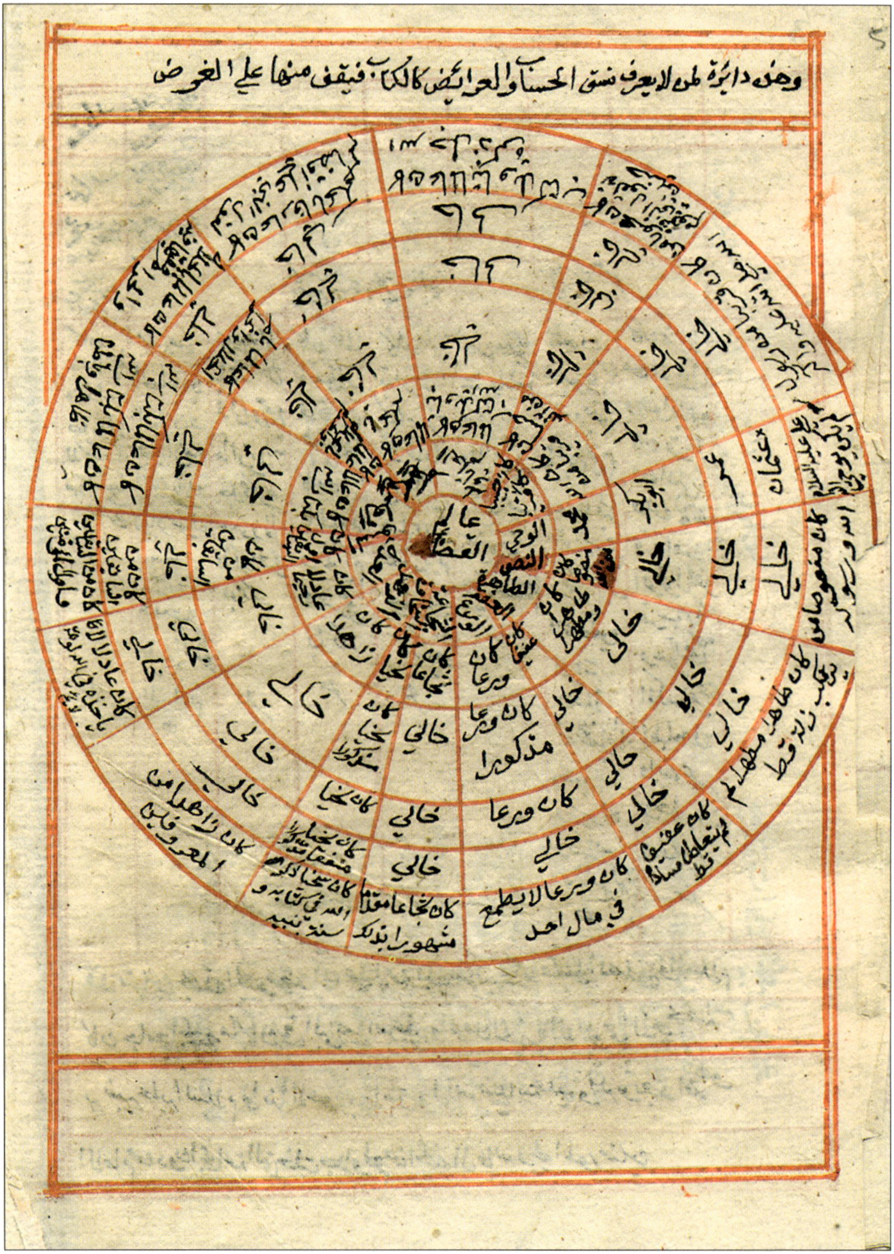

Plate 14: Circular Table (ms. Ar. 130)

Plate 15: citron etrog (*utrūj*)

مقدمة لجدول الامامة

كون شكله الى الطول مجيب الجهات	كون لونه اصفر	يكون رائحة عطرة	كون شحم له طعم حلو	كون لب طعم حامض	كون النوع حقا	كون النوع حقا
ذات غير مختلفة في كونها اترجا	تشكله الى الطول مجيب الجهات	لونه اصفر	رائحته عطرة	له شحم و طعمه حلو	له لب و طعمه حامض	اترج حقا
ذات مختلفة في كونها اترجا	شكله الى الطول	لونه اصفر	لا رائحة له	لا شحم له	لا لب له	ليس باترج و في معمول هو حقا
ذات مختلفة في كونها اترجا	شكله مدور	لونه اصفر	رائحته عطرة	شحمه حامض	لا لب له	ليس باترج و هو سفرجله

جداول اعتبار صحة امامة المتقدمين الذين افترضوا البين ببطلان امامة من ليس بامامهم

الاسماء والكون من ذرية النبوة من نسل الحسين عليه السلام	وجود العقب المنصوص عليه من دون غيره لعلة سالبة للعقب شرف الامامة	وجود العلم باسرار الشرع من جهة العقب المنصوص عليه	وجود العمل باحكام الله تعالى من جهة العقب المنصوص عليه	وجود الامر بالمعروف والنهي عن المنكر من جهة العقب المنصوص عليه	وجود الدعوة الى طاعة الله تعالى من جهة العقب المنصوص عليه	الامام حقا
جعفر الصادق عليه السلام كان من ذرية الحسين بن علي عليه السلام	عقبه والمنصوص عليه موجود وهو الحاكم بامر الله امير المؤمنين سلام الله عليه	علمه باحكام الله تعالى قائم من جهة العقب المنصوص عليه من عقبه	علمه باحكام الله قائم من جهة العقب المنصوص عليه	امره بالمعروف والنهي عن المنكر قائم من جهة المنصوص عليه	دعوته الى طاعة الله تعالى قائمة من جهة المنصوص عليه من عقبه	امام حقا

Plate 16: Table III and IVa (ms. Ar. 1226)

علي بن محمد صاحب البصرة حسني لم يكن من ولد الحسين	ليس بموجود منصوصًا	ليس بموجود علمه	ليس بموجود عمله	ليس بموجود امره بالمعروف ونهيه عن المنكر	ليس بموجود دعوته	ليس بامام
المامون العباسي لم يكن من ذرية الحسين عليه السلام	ليس بموجود	ليس بموجود	ليس بموجود	ليس بموجود	ليس بموجود	ليس بامام
زيد بن علي كان من نسل الحسين عليه السلام	ليس بموجود	ليس بموجود	ليس بموجود	ليس بموجود	ليس بموجود	ليس بامام
محمد بن جعفر كان من نسل الحسين عليه السلام	ليس بموجود	ليس بموجود	ليس بموجود	ليس بموجود	ليس بموجود	ليس بامام
عبد الله بن جعفر كان من نسل الحسين ع م	ليس بموجود	ليس بموجود	ليس بموجود	ليس بموجود	ليس بموجود	ليس بامام
موسى بن جعفر كان من نسل الحسين ع م	ليس بموجود	ليس بموجود	ليس بموجود	ليس بموجود	ليس بموجود	ليس بامام
محمد بن اسمعيل بن جعفر من ذرية الحسين [illegible]	[illegible] عقب المنصوص عليه موجود وهو [illegible]	[illegible] عقب على المنصوص علمًا [illegible] موجود	علمًا بأحكام الله موجود [illegible] المنصوص عليه من عقبه	امره بالمعروف ونهيه عن المنكر [illegible] المنصوص عليه من عقبه	دعوته [illegible] المنصوص عليه من عقبه	امامًا حقا

Plate 17: Table IVb (ms. Ar. 1226)

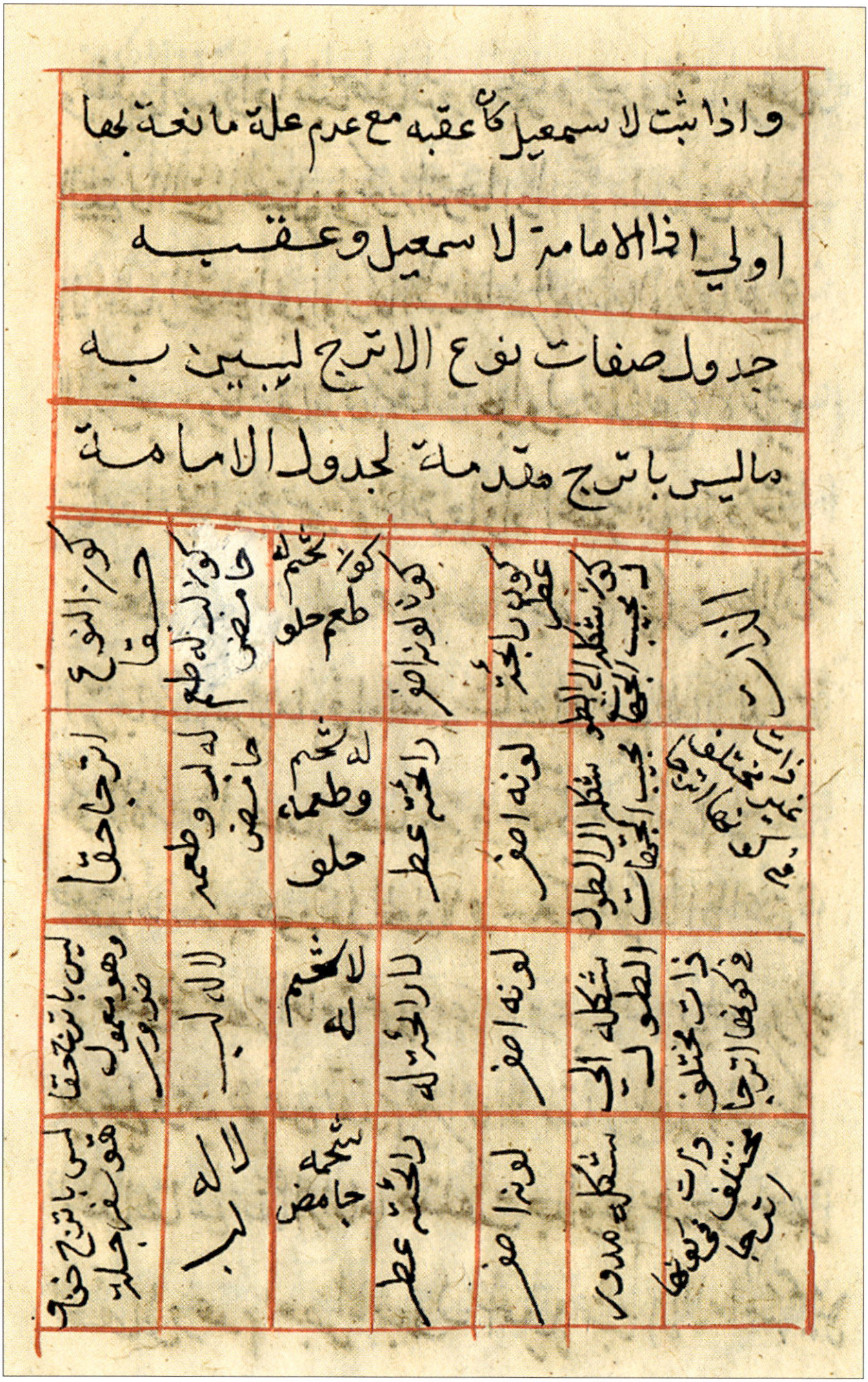
واذا ثبت لاسمعيل كان عقبه مع عدم علة مانعة لهما
اولي انه الامامة لاسمعيل وعقبه
جدول صفات نوع الاترج ليبين به
ماليس باترج مقدمة لجدول الامامة

Plate 18: Table III (ms. Ar. 130)

جدول اعتبار صحة امامة المتقدمين

الذين انقرضوا اليقين به بطلان امامة من ليس بامام منهم

الاسماء والكون من ذرية النبوة من نسل الحسين عليه السلام	وجود العقب المنصوص عليه من دون غيره لعله سالبة للعقب شرف الامامة	وجود العلم باحكام الله من جهة العقب المنصوص عليه	وجود العمل باحكام الله من جهة العقب المنصوص عليه	وجود الامر بالمعروف والنهي عن المنكر من جهة العقب المنصوص عليه	وجود الدعوة الظاهرة عن الله من جهة العقب المنصوص عليه	الكون اماما حقا
جعفر الصادق عليه السلام كان من ذرية الحسين بن علي عليه السلام	عقبه المنصوص عليه موجود وصول الحكم بامر الله امير المومنين سلام الله عليهم	علمه باحكام الله قائم من جهة المنصوص عليه	عمله باحكام الله من جهة المنصوص عليه	امره بالمعروف والنهي عن المنكر قائم من جهة المنصوص عليه	دعوته الظاهرة عن الله قائمة من جهة المنصوص عليه	امام حق

Plate 19: Table IVa (ms. Ar. 130)

[illegible]	ليس بموجود منصوص	ليس بموجود علمه	ليس بموجود عمله	[illegible]	ليس بموجود دعوته	ليس بامام
[illegible]	ليس بموجود	ليس بموجود	ليس بموجود	ليس بموجود	ليس بموجود	ليس بامام
زيد بن علي كان من نسل الحسين	ليس بموجود	ليس بموجود	ليس بموجود	ليس بموجود	ليس بموجود	ليس بامام
محمد بن جعفر كان من نسل الحسين	ليس بموجود	ليس بموجود	ليس بموجود	ليس بموجود	ليس بموجود	ليس بامام
عبد الله ابن جعفر كان من نسل الحسين	ليس بموجود	ليس بموجود	ليس بموجود	ليس بموجود	ليس بموجود	ليس بامام
موسى ابن جعفر كان من نسل الحسين	ليس بموجود	ليس بموجود	ليس بموجود	ليس بموجود	ليس بموجود	ليس بامام
اسمعيل ابن جعفر من ذرية النبوة و نسل الحسين عليه السلام	عقبه المنصوص عليه موجود [illegible] عقبه المنصوص عليه	علمه [illegible] موجود من جهة عقبه المنصوص عليه	عمله [illegible] بوجوده المنصوص عليه من عقبه	[illegible]	[illegible]	امام حق

Plate 20: Table IVb (ms. Ar. 130)

Plate 21: Table Va (ms. Ar. 1226)

Plate 22: Table Vb (ms. Ar. 1226)

Plate 23: Table Vc (ms. Ar. 1226)